Urban Sustainability and River Restoration

Urban Sustainability and River Restoration

Green and Blue Infrastructure

Katia Perini
Paola Sabbion

WILEY Blackwell

Registered Office
John Wiley & Sons Ltd, The Atrium, Southern Gate, Chichester, West Sussex, PO19 8SQ, United Kingdom.

Editorial Offices
9600 Garsington Road, Oxford, OX4 2DQ, United Kingdom.
The Atrium, Southern Gate, Chichester, West Sussex, PO19 8SQ, United Kingdom.

For details of our global editorial offices, for customer services and for information about how to apply for permission to reuse the copyright material in this book please see our website at www.wiley.com/wiley-blackwell.

Library of Congress Cataloging-in-Publication data applied for

ISBN: 9781119244967

A catalogue record for this book is available from the British Library.

Cover image: The Concrete Park Plant - Katia Perini

Set in 10/12pt Sabon by SPi Global, Pondicherry, India
Printed and bound in Malaysia by Vivar Printing Sdn Bhd

10 9 8 7 6 5 4 3 2 1

Contents

Preface

Green and blue infrastructure (GBI) can play a crucial role to reduce environmental issues in cities. GBI thus contributes to the enhancement of human health, residents' quality of life and sustainable development. This topic is usually considered within the boundaries of single disciplines. In this book, instead, it is investigated with a holistic attitude to integrate several disciplinary contributions and design and management approaches. This is the result of the collaboration between two authors with different expertise and backgrounds, concerning environmental sustainability, urban ecology, urban landscape and urban design. This approach provides an analytical outline, which can be useful for urban planners, architects and engineers, nonprofit and community associations, legislators and policy makers alike.

Policies and regulations regarding environmental sustainability represent a key focus of the book, along with technical implementation aspects. The first part of this book presents an overview of the main ecological and environmental problems affecting urban areas due to a combination of anthropic activities and climate change effects. It outlines the related mitigation and adaptation strategies based on GBI implementation and river restoration. The second part analyses the techniques to integrate these mitigation and adaptation strategies in the urban context. The third part of the book defines top-down and bottom-up policies, developed in the United States and in Europe.

Rivers and streams are critical to almost any GBI system and can provide important recreational spaces in cities and access to the water. The discussion of complex technical and political processes focused on the improvement of urban sustainability explains the importance of river renaturation and GBI not only for the future of cities, but also for the capacity to generate broad renovation initiatives, community involvement and a new policy agenda.

This book includes the analysis of six river restoration case studies developed in Europe and in the United States, which depict the successful integration of GBI in urban contexts, highlighting the positive outcomes of different approaches. Renovation processes, in fact, can be based on community initiatives and joint efforts of local community organizations and public bodies (e.g., Bronx River in NYC and LA River in Los Angeles). Conversely, top-down policies can also create praiseworthy renovation projects devising completely new urban landscapes (e.g., Madrid Rìo in Spain and Paillon River in France). These case studies, moreover, are of particular interest as they show the success of policies and governance at different scales – federal, national, administrative and local – to restore neglected places and trigger brownfield regeneration (e.g., Thames River in England and Emscher River in Germany).

About the Authors

Katia Perini is adjunct professor and postdoctoral researcher at the Department of Science for Architecture, Polytechnic School of the University of Genoa (Italy). She is part of the Ecosystemic Research Group (http://www.ecosystemics.eu/), which coordinates field studies and academic research on sustainable architecture, urban design, and low-impact building materials. Perini graduated with honours at the Faculty of Architecture of Genoa in March 2008. In 2012, she defended with success her PhD dissertation, "The Integration of Vegetation in Architecture: Innovative Methods and Tools", at the University of Genoa. Perini collaborated with the Delft University of Technology as guest researcher. In 2013, Katia Perini was selected as a Fulbright grantee and completed a research project at the Urban Design Lab of Columbia University, regarding the sustainability of urban areas, focusing on New York City as case study. In 2016, Perini conducted a two-month research period, with a research project entitled: "Climate landscape: A new approach to urban design and landscape architecture" at the Technische Universität München (TUM), Chair of Building Technology and Climate Responsive Design as visiting scholar thanks to a DAAD personal award. Katia Perini research interests include all the effects of vegetation (green infrastructure and green envelopes) in the field of environmental and economic sustainability in (of) urban areas and building/urban design.

Paola Sabbion is landscape architect and adjunct professor at the Department of Science for Architecture at the Polytechnic School of the University of Genoa (Italy). In 2009, she graduated with honours in Landscape Architecture at the Faculty of Architecture of Genoa with a degree thesis on the recovery of degraded landscapes. Paola was the winner of a Research Fellowship and has been working from 2010 to 2012 at the Municipality of Genoa's Urban Planning Office, with the advisory of Richard Burdett (London School of Economics). She has taught several international workshops of the Master's Degree Course in Landscape Architecture at the University of Genoa. These workshops include the Lusatian Lake District Workshop, held in Großräschen (Germany), in collaboration with Internationale Bauausstellung (IBA) and the Workshop Mies van der Rohe: Mediterranean Cities, in collaboration with the University of Genoa and the Universitat Politècnica de Catalunya (UPC) of Barcelona. In April 2015, Sabbion successfully defended at the University of Genoa her PhD dissertation, "Landscape as Experience", focused on the relationship between landscape design and ecology. She is also currently working as a volunteer researcher for several nonprofit organisations in the city of Genoa, contributing with her expertise to cultural enhancement and landscape re-evaluation projects. Paola Sabbion research interests include contemporary and historical landscape architecture theories and methods.

Acknowledgements

The analysis of the Bronx River case study and of U.S. and NYC top-down and bottom-up policies was made possible by a Fulbright Schuman Program grant, which funded Katia Perini's research as Visiting Scholar at the Graduate School of Architecture, Planning and Preservation (GSAPP) of the Columbia University, under the direction of Richard Plunz, Director of the Urban Design Lab.

Dipartimento Architettura e Design, DAD (Architecture and Design Department), Polytechnic School of the University of Genoa (Italy) is acknowledged for the support provided.

We would also like to thank all the experts for their availability and their valuable contribution to our research and for the photos provided, including Thomas Angotti, William Preston Bowling, Matt Brown, Paulina Budryte, Lida Cataldi, FoLAR - Friends of Los Angeles River, Victor Keegan, Jørgen K. H. Knudsen, Robin Kriesberg, Antonina Manzo, Jeroen Musch, Colin Pattenden, Gian Luca Porcile, Artie Rollins, Emanuele Sommariva, Fabrizio Spiniello, West 8, and Case Wyse.

We would like to acknowledge all the members of the Ecosystemics Research Group (http://www.ecosystemics.eu/), in particular, Adriano Magliocco, for their interest and collaboration on the research fields of the book.

Finally, we would like to thank Raffaella Ruffo for her excellent corrections on the English texts and editing.

Drawing and graphics by Fabio Valido (fabio.valido@gmail.com)

Foreword

In recent years it has been widely acknowledged that given our present trajectories for global urbanization, cities hold a key to addressing global ecological dilemmas. In 2014, the United Nations projected that by 2050, well within the lifetimes of most readers of this book, urban growth will increase from 3.9 billion urbanites to 6.4 billion; from 54% to 64% of the global total population (World Urbanization Prospects, 2014). Perhaps for the first time in human history, cities in this period engage the Anthropocene, in geologic time the first period when human activity dominates the global ecosystem. Urbanization is a large component of this shift, such that within this same period, those who directly and indirectly manage our urban futures will be crucial players in addressing global ecological issues, be they scientist, engineer, designer, politician, community stakeholder; all will find this book to be an extremely useful resource.

Urban futures are climate futures, and water lies at the nexus of either deliverance or destruction. Innovation in urban infrastructure is front and center within this paradigm, and the uses and abuses of water-related considerations lie at its very essence. Involved are complicated algorithms. As the authors point out, "undamaged" water ecosystems are among our most diverse and complex infrastructure such that their preservation, reproduction or reinvention can be a daunting proposition. Cities and water are part and parcel of integral Anthropocentric systems everywhere in the world; comprising interrelated oceans, rivers, pipes and all of the interstices between and beyond. As such, water-based green and blue infrastructure (GBI) is at the cutting edge of innovation in urban infrastructure techniques and outcomes. This book systematically clarifies options.

The authors point to water and vegetation as critically symbiotic agents in the next generation of infrastructure paradigms, such that an evolution from "hard" to "soft" engineering approaches is essential. And the authors demonstrate that the co-benefits of "soft" proliferate beyond the normative boundaries of water and vegetation; for example to the energy savings related to heat island reductions, to improved health and well-being related to storm water retention or air quality strategies, to economic advantage related to a host of urban resilience connections, including social-ecological systems and associated livelihoods.

All such considerations interrelate both cause and effect, engaging strategies that are immediate as well as long-term.

Green blue infrastructure is synonymous with vegetated systems that must be diverse and multi-scalar, from riparian corridor to green bioswale to green wall. Critical to note is the importance of managing anthropic activities, to avoid their negative impacts, and the greatest immediate opportunities may simply lie in conversion from un-vegetated systems such as parking lots and roadways to vegetated ones. Much of this activity engages multi-scalar interventions, with a very crucial component having to do with individual micro-scale options such that it is probably safe to say that all innovation in infrastructure has an undeniable social component. Hard infrastructure is also social infrastructure. Next-generation distributed systems are highly dependent on "bottom-up" community stakeholders to guarantee success in mitigation. In this regard, the authors succeed to define ecosystem services as engaging more than natural ecology aspects of urban development, to include economic development. Each goes hand-in-hand with informatics and especially new social media, which is essential for maintenance.

For obvious reasons, no urban infrastructure consideration can be devoid of public policy and community enablement. And herein lie the deepest challenges. The authors have chosen six state-of-the-art urban river case-studies in the United States and Europe. All have successfully engaged the challenges of national and local politics, and all illustrate the importance of knowledge gained through critical in-depth comparative analysis of concepts, implementation and prospects for long-term sustainability. In New York City, the Bronx River restoration is one of the oldest, having originated in the 1970s. It remains one of the city's most comprehensive socioecological enterprises. It is still evolving as a community-based initiative, incorporating a diverse range of public support. More recently on the West Coast, much is to be learned from the attempt to restore the Los Angeles River's ecological functions, through reducing its impervious canalization and systemizing and integrating its larger watershed; as in the Bronx with the considerable involvement of local citizen advocates.

The most transformative of the case studies is the reorganization of the Madrid River channel in Spain, formerly a dysfunctional mélange of water, industry and roads, with no public access. This large public investment has created an entirely new configuration that incorporates a national motorway, river day-lighting and other ecosystem restoration, and an elaborate public park including diverse public education venues within the landscape. Apart from its ecological virtues, the project has recalibrated the public space fabric of the entire city and region, including the many neighborhoods along its path. Similarly for both the Paillon River in France and the Thames in England, consideration of "urban" context of each has recognized the importance of regional strategies, engaging "eco-territories" and "green grid" concepts. And for the Emsher River in Germany, like the Bronx River in New York, the fruits of long-term restoration give ample evidence of the effectiveness of such efforts.

The authors provide a significant contribution to growing global understanding of preservation and reinvention of our crucial urban ecologies, and of the global commonalities in all such strategies. Infrastructural innovation is globalizing, along with urbanization. This compendium of strategies is of value not just in

Europe and North America. Cities in diverse world geographic regions and economies are more and more sharing needs and solutions. There can be critical learning on all sides. Successful water infrastructure management in the Bronx and Madrid, as well as Accra or Nairobi, necessitates shared concepts and strategies. This book provides an overview of approaches and applications for water-based infrastructure that will prove invaluable for the future of cities everywhere.

Richard Plunz

Part A
Definition of the Issue

Chapter 1
Green and Blue Infrastructure in Cities
Katia Perini

1.1   Definitions

Over 50% of the global population currently lives in urban areas. Cities are particularly exposed to climate change and environmental problems due to the impact of anthropic activities. In urban environments, additionally, the negative effects of climate change are amplified by settlement features (impervious surface, buildings, transport infrastructure, socio-economic activities). Flooding, heat and drought, in particular, are hazards which are increasingly characterising the urban areas (see Chapters 2 and 3). More than 40% of urban land is currently covered by impervious surfaces as roads, buildings and parking lots (Benedict and McMahon, 2012). Climate change and anthropogenic pressures, such as land-use conversion, have altered the functions of ecological systems and have consequently modified the flow of ecosystem services in terms of their scale, timing and location (Nelson *et al.*, 2013; see Chapter 5). This trend is going to increase as the urban world population is expected to rise to over 67% by 2050 (UN DESA, 2012).

Urban resilience can be defined as the ability of an urban system to adapt (maintain or rapidly return to previous functions) when facing a disturbance (Pickett *et al.* (eds.), 2013; Lhomme *et al.*, 2013; Meerow *et al.*, 2016). According to academic and policy interests, it is crucial to improve urban resilience to cope especially with climate imbalances and related issues. Implementing a traditional grey approach, alongside green and blue design strategies, can enhance urban resilience, especially in a long-term time frame. Traditional grey infrastructure, as concrete buildings, underground drainpipes, and pumping stations, can be effective but mono-functional and non-adaptive tools. On the contrary, green infrastructure (GI) integrates natural processes and is more flexible and adaptive (Voskamp and

Urban Sustainability and River Restoration: Green and Blue Infrastructure, First Edition.
Katia Perini and Paola Sabbion.
© 2017 John Wiley & Sons Ltd. Published 2017 by John Wiley & Sons Ltd.

Van de Ven, 2015). GI can, thus, have a crucial role to cope with climate change in cities (Elmqvist *et al.*, 2015).

The term *green infrastructure* (GI) was coined in Florida, in 1994, and appears for the first time in a report to the governor on land conservation strategies, which stresses that natural systems are important infrastructure components (Firehock, 2010). Infrastructure is commonly defined as facilities and services necessary for a society, community, and/or economy to function. These facilities and services can be *hard* (e.g., transportation and utilities) or *soft* (e.g., institutional systems such as education, health care and governance). GI is considered *soft* and is important for building capacity, improved health, job opportunities, and community cohesion (Rouse, 2013). It includes natural, semi-natural, and artificial networks of multifunctional ecological systems related to urban areas (Sandstrom, 2002; Tzoulas *et al.*, 2007). It features waterways, wetlands, woodlands, wildlife habitats, greenways, parks, and other natural areas, which contribute to the health and quality of life for communities and people (Benedict & McMahon, 2001; Benedict *et al.*, 2006; European Commission, 2010).

GI, in fact, can be defined as an "interconnected network of green space that conserves natural ecosystem values and functions and provides associated benefits to human populations" (Benedict & McMahon, 2001) or as "a strategically planned and managed network of wilderness, parks, greenways, conservation easements, and working lands with conservation value that supports native species, [and] maintains natural ecological processes". Furthermore, GI is designated as "a successfully tested tool for providing ecological, economic and social benefits through natural solutions" (Benedict & McMahon, 2012).

The 2013 European Commission Communication, *Green Infrastructure (GI) – Enhancing Europe's Natural Capital*, states that GI is strategically designed and managed to provide ecosystem services on a wide scale. It comprises green spaces (or blue spaces in the case of aquatic ecosystems) and other physical terrestrial elements such as coastal and marine features. GI can also be found both in rural and urban settings (European Commission, 2013). In addition, GI is "an effective response to a variety of environmental challenges that is cost-effective, sustainable, and provides multiple desirable environmental outcomes" (EPA Administrator Lisa Jackson, Testimony before the U.S. House of Representatives, Committee on Transportation and Infrastructure, Subcommittee on Water Resources and Environment, March 19, 2009, in New York City Department of Environmental Protection (2010).

Rouse notes that different definitions are related to the scale under observation. At the city and regional scale, GI can be outlined as a multifunctional open space network. At the local and site scale, it can be described as a stormwater management approach that mimics natural hydrologic processes (Rouse, 2013). Benedict and McMahon's investigations specify that it is possible to devise GI at all scales: "the individual parcel, the local community, the state or even the multi-state region" (Benedict and McMahon, 2012). At the parcel scale, green infrastructure can be outlined when home and business design revolves around green space. At the community level, green infrastructure can be planned as a system of greenways connecting public parks. At the state or regional level, green infrastructure can be enacted protecting the linkages already existing between natural resources, as forests and prairies, which are the natural habitat of specific animal species.

The multiscalarity of GI has a great strategic importance. At the landscape scale, as stated by Rouse, GI is most effective in providing services and benefits when it is part of a physically connected system (Rouse, 2013). Planners and designers should, hence, establish physical and functional connections across scales to link sites and neighbourhoods to cities and regions (e.g., connections among natural reserves or regional parks). The growth of ecological engineering acknowledges the importance of merging ecology and design with green infrastructure, replacing conventional engineering structures with green features that can perform ecosystem service functions, such as waste management or energy efficiency retention (Mitsch and Jørgensen, 2003; Margolis and Robinson, 2007).

In official documents (i.e., European directives) GI is a recurrent term, but the definition *green and blue infrastructure* (GBI) is increasingly used to designate all strategies targeted to increase urban resilience to climate change, improving the coping, adaptive and mitigation capacities within cities. Urban settlements, according to this definition, should be able to face weather extremes through water function management and the negative effects of anthropic activities (see Chapters 3 and 4). GBI uses ecosystem functions to deliver multiple benefits. It can enhance the water balance regime, decreasing stormwater runoff peak discharge. It can also reduce soil erosion, providing stormwater runoff cleansing to raise water quality, guaranteeing seasonal water storage and recharging the urban groundwater aquifer (Voskamp and Van de Ven, 2015).

1.2   Economic and environmental benefits

GBI can contribute to curb the negative effects of climate-related hazards, including storm surges, extreme precipitation, and floods (EEA, 2012; UNISDR, 2015). At the city scale, therefore, GBI is important to improve environmental conditions. Planning, developing, and maintaining GBI can integrate urban development, nature conservation, and public health promotion (Schrijnen, 2000; Tzoulas *et al.*, 2007; Van der Ryn, 1996; Walmsley, 2006). GBI plays an important role against intense storms as it enhances the resilience of communities to coastal flood and river flood risks (EEA, 2015). The U.S. Environmental Protection Agency emphasises the role of green and blue infrastructure in stormwater management: "Green infrastructure involves the use of landscape features to store, infiltrate, and evaporate stormwater. This reduces the amount of water draining into sewers and helps to lower the discharge of pollutants into water bodies in that area. Examples of green infrastructure include rain gardens, swales, constructed wetlands, and permeable pavements" (EPA, 2011). Current studies indicate the great contribution provided by GBI in terms of urban ecosystem services (European Commission, 2013).

Several techniques are included in the GBI approach. It is useful to group GBI in vegetated and non-vegetated systems to provide an overview (see Chapters 6 and 7). Combining green and blue measures with the use of vegetation can enhance urban resilience, supporting synergistic interactions at different spatial scales and establishing hydrologic connectivity in the catchment to control water resources and flood risk (Voskamp and Van de Ven, 2015). Moreover, GBI should be integrated in river restoration (see Chapter 8), especially in urbanised areas to maximise the efficiency of ecological and hydrologic connectivity, as demonstrated by the case studies presented in this investigation (see Chapters 9–13). In fact, the analysis of case studies allows describing how river restoration projects reduce ecological and environmental issues and the related social, economic and environmental effects.

Multifunctionality is among the most interesting outcomes of GBI. Environmental co-benefits comprise biodiversity conservation and climate change adaptation; social benefits include water drainage and creation of green spaces (EEA, 2015). Nature-based solutions can provide greater sustainable, cost-effective, multi-purpose and flexible alternatives than traditional grey infrastructure (European Commission, 2015). GBI also provides economic benefits creating job and business opportunities in fields such as landscape management, recreational activities, and tourism. It can stimulate retail sales and commercial vitality as well as other economic activities in local business districts due to the value of ecosystem services (Wolf, 1998; Rouse, 2013). GBI can help to preserve or increase property values (Economy League of Greater Philadelphia, in Southeastern Pennsylvania, 2010; Neelay, 1998); attract visitors, residents, and business to a community (Campos, 2009); and reduce energy, healthcare, and costs (Economy League of Greater Philadelphia, in Southeastern Pennsylvania, 2010; Heisler, 1986; Simpson and McPhearson, 1996).

The benefits of GBI are not easy to quantify due to its multifunctional nature, as different functions may require a range of different forms of measurement (European Commission, 2012). GBI monetary values can be communicated to stakeholders and communities, and can be easily incorporated into the policy decision-making process, although its benefits may be more variable than costs (Vandermeulen *et al.*, 2011; Naumann *et al.*, 2011). Among the most recognised economic benefits can also be mentioned stormwater reduction in the sewer system (Craudereuff *et al.*, 2012). According to Artie Rollins (Assistant Commissioner for Citywide Services, NYC), NYC Departments invest on GI as a cost-effective measure to reduce stormwater runoff, as the building costs of a sewage treatment plant to process water are significantly higher (Rollins, 2013). Benefits of GBI, moreover, are important at the community level. Public bodies play a crucial role to promote this type of urban design features. They actively support the integration of GBI as a sustainable strategy to meet water quality standards, but the involvement of communities can also make a remarkable difference (Angotti, 2008). Urban planning participative processes, above all, could ensure the support of local communities. GBI integration requires "a process of vertical and horizontal reciprocity between scales/agencies [...] to provide the political platform for stakeholder interactivity, leading in the long-term to a consensus on the structure of policy making and GI delivery" (Mell, 2014). A lack of communication can delay the development of consensus (Mell, 2014). An in-depth analysis of top-down (Chapter 10) and bottom-up policies (Chapter 11) provides an explanation of these processes and relative case studies.

The evaluation of different contexts – political, geographical, sociological, environmental – strategies, and actors involved depicts a framework of projects and initiatives targeting the reduction of ecological and environmental issues in urban areas. The analysis of the case studies described is based on several approaches with regard to local/national policies, local community involvement, and private partnership, and includes interviews, on-site surveys, scientific literature reviews, newspaper research. This allows assessing outcomes, positive aspects, and future challenges.

References

Angotti, T. (2008). *New York for sale community planning confronts global real estate.* Cambridge, Mass.: MIT Press.

Benedict, M. A. and McMahon, E. T. (2001). *Green infrastructure: smart conservation for the 21st century.* [Online]. Available at: http://www.sprawlwatch.org/greeninfrastructure.pdf

Benedict, M. A. and McMahon, E. T. (2012). *Green Infrastructure: Linking Landscapes and Communities.* The Conservation Found, Island Press.

Benedict, M. A., McMahon, E. T. and Conservation Fund. (2006). *Green infrastructure: linking landscapes and communities.* Washington, DC: Island Press.

Campos. (2009). *The Great Allegheny Passage Economic Impact Study (2007–2008). For The Progress Fund's Trail Town Program Laurel Highlands Visitors Bureau and Allegheny Trail Alliance August 7.* [Online]. Available at: http://www.atatrail.org/docs/GAPeconomicImpactStudy200809.pdf

Crauderueff, R., Margolis, S., and Tanikawa, S. (2012). *Greening Vacant Lots: Planning and Implementation Strategies. A report prepared for The Nature Conservancy as part of the NatLab collaboration.* [Online]. Available at: http://docs.nrdc.org/water/files/wat_13022701a.pdf

Economy League of Greater Philadelphia, in Southeastern Pennsylvania. (2010). *Return on Environment. The Economic Value of Protected Open Space.* [Online]. Available at: http://economyleague.org/files/Protected_Open_Space_SEPA_2-11.pdf

EEA. (2012). *Annual report 2011and Environmental statement, 2012.*

EEA. (2015). *SOER 2015, The European environment. State and outlook, 2015.*

Elmqvist, T., Setälä, H., Handel, S., van der Ploeg, S., Aronson, J., Blignaut, J., Gómez-Baggethun, E., Nowak, D., Kronenberg, J., and de Groot, R. (2015). Benefits of restoring ecosystem services in urban areas. *Current Opinion in Environmental Sustainability*, 14, p. 101–108. [Online]. Available at: doi:10.1016/j.cosust.2015.05.001

EPA. (2011). *Land Revitalization Fact Sheet Green Infrastructure.* [Online]. Available at: http://www.epa.gov/landrevitalization/download/fs_green_infrastructure.pdf

European Commission. (2010). *Green infrastructure.* [Online]. Available at: http://ec.europa.eu/environment/nature/info/pubs/docs/greeninfrastructure.pdf

European Commission. (2012). *The Multifunctionality of Green Infrastructure. Science for Environment Policy. In-depth Reports, European Commission's Directorate-General Environment.*

European Commission. (2013). *Green Infrastructure (GI) — Enhancing Europe's Natural Capital. Communication from the Commission to the European Parliament, the Council, the European Economic and Social Committee and the Committee of the Regions.* [Online]. Available at: http://eur-lex.europa.eu/LexUriServ/LexUriServ.do?uri=COM:2013:0249:FIN:EN:PDF

European Commission. (2015). *Nature-Based Solutions | Environment - Research & Innovation.* [Online]. Available at: https://ec.europa.eu/research/environment/index.cfm?pg=nbs [Accessed: 10 December 2015].

European Environmental Agency. (2015). *Exploring nature-based solutions. The role of green infrastructure in mitigating the impacts of weather- and climate change-related natural hazards.* [Online]. Available at: file://localhost/Users/katiaperini/Library/

Part A

Application%20Support/Zotero/Profiles/rwxgy8et.default/zotero/storage/DSES69X4/exploring-nature-based-solutions-2014.html

Firehock, K. (2010). *A Short History of the Term Green Infrastructure and Selected Literature.* [Online]. Available at: http://www.gicinc.org/PDFs/GI%20History.pdf

Heisler, G. (1986). Energy savings with trees. *Journal of Arboricolture,* 12(5), p. 13–25.

Lhomme, S., Serre, D., Diab, Y., and Laganier, R. (2013). *Urban technical networks resilience assessment.* In: 2013, p. 109–117. *Scopus.*

Margolis, L. and Robinson, A. (2007). *Living Systems.* Basel - Boston - Berlin: Birkhäuser Architecture.

Meerow, S., Newell, J. P., and Stults, M. (2016). Defining urban resilience: A review. *Landscape and Urban Planning,* 147, p. 38–49. [Online]. Available at: doi:10.1016/j.landurbplan.2015.11.011

Mell, I. C. (2014). Aligning fragmented planning structures through a green infrastructure approach to urban development in the UK and USA. *Urban Forestry & Urban Greening,* 13 (4), p. 612–620. [Online]. Available at: doi:10.1016/j.ufug.2014.07.007

Mitsch, W. J. and Jørgensen, S. E. (2003). Ecological engineering: A field whose time has come. *Ecological Engineering,* 20 (5), p.363–377. [Online]. Available at: doi:10.1016/j.ecoleng.2003.05.001 [Accessed 4 November 2015].

Naumann, S., Davis, M., Kaphengst, T., Pieterse, M., and Rayment, M. (2011). *Design, implementation and cost elements of Green Infrastructure projects. Final report Brussels, European Commission.*

Neelay. (1998). Valutation of landscape trees, shrubs, and other plants. In: *7th ed. Council of Tree and Landscape Appraisers,* 1998, International Society of Arboriculture.

Nelson, E. J., Kareiva, P., Ruckelshaus, M., Arkema, K., Geller, G., Girvetz, E., Goodrich, D., Matzek, V., Pinsky, M., Reid, W., Saunders, M., Semmens, D., and Tallis, H. (2013). Climate change's impact on key ecosystem services and the human well-being they support in the US. *Frontiers in Ecology and the Environment,* 11(9), p. 483–893. [Online]. Available at: doi:10.1890/120312 [Accessed 4 November 2015].

New York City Department of Environmental Protection. (2010). *NYC Green Infrastructure Plan.* [Online]. Available at: http://www.nyc.gov/html/dep/pdf/green_infrastructure/gi_annual_report_2012.pdf

Pickett, S. T. A., Cadenasso, M. L., and McGrath, B. (eds.). (2013). *Resilience in Ecology and Urban Design,* Future City. Dordrecht: Springer Netherlands. [Online]. Available at: http://link.springer.com/10.1007/978-94-007-5341-9 [Accessed 4 January 2016].

Rollins, A. (2013). *Personal communication in: Katia Perini, 2014. Urban areas and green infrastructure. Research report, published by Urban Design Lab Columbia University ISNB 978-09822174-5-0.* [Online]. Available at: http://urbandesignlab.columbia.edu/files/2015/04/3_Urban_Areas_Green_Infrastructure.pdf

Rouse, D. C. (2013). *Green infrastructure: a landscape approach.* Chicago, IL: American Planning Association.

Van der Ryn, S. (1996). *Ecological design.* Washington, D.C.: Island Press.

Sandstrom, U. G. (2002). Green Infrastructure Planning in Urban Sweden. *Planning Practice and Research,* 17(4), p. 373–385. [Online]. Available at: doi:10.1080/02697450216356 [Accessed 13 February 2014].

Schrijnen, P. M. (2000). Infrastructure networks and red–green patterns in city regions. *Landscape and Urban Planning,* 48 (3–4), p. 191–204. [Online]. Available at: doi:10.1016/S0169-2046(00)00042-6 [Accessed 13 February 2014].

Simpson, J. R. and McPhearson, E. G. (1996). Potential of tree shade for reducing Residential energy use in California. *Journal of Arboriculture,* 22(1), p. 10–18.

Tzoulas, K., Korpela, K., Venn, S., Yli-Pelkonen, V., Kaźmierczak, A., Niemela, J., and James, P. (2007). Promoting ecosystem and human health in urban areas using Green Infrastructure: A literature review. *Landscape and Urban Planning,* 81 (3), p. 167–178.

[Online]. Available at: doi:10.1016/j.landurbplan.2007.02.001 [Accessed 22 January 2014].

UN DESA. (2012). *World urbanization prospects: the 2011 revision.* New York.

UNISDR. (2015). *Making Development Sustainable: The Future of Disaster Risk Management. Global Assessment Report on Disaster Risk Reduction. Geneva, Switzerland: United Nations Office for Disaster Risk Reduction (UNISDR).* Publication. [Online]. Available at: http://www.eea.europa.eu/publications/exploring-nature-based-solutions-2014 [Accessed 6 November 2015].

Vandermeulen, V., Verspecht, A., Vermeire, B., Van Huylenbroeck, G. and Gellynck, X. (2011). The use of economic valuation to create public support for green infrastructure investments in urban areas. *Landscape and Urban Planning*, 103 (2), p. 198–206. [Online]. Available at: doi:10.1016/j.landurbplan.2011.07.010.

Voskamp, I. M. and Van de Ven, F. H. M. (2015). Planning support system for climate adaptation: Composing effective sets of blue-green measures to reduce urban vulnerability to extreme weather events. *Building and Environment*, 83, p. 159–167. [Online]. Available at: doi:10.1016/j.buildenv.2014.07.018.

Walmsley, A. (2006). Greenways: multiplying and diversifying in the 21st century. *Landscape and Urban Planning*, 76 (1–4), p. 252–290. [Online]. Available at: doi:10.1016/j.landurbplan.2004.09.036 [Accessed 13 February 2014].

Wolf, K. L. (1998). *Trees in Business Districts: positive effects on consumer behavior. Fact sheet no.5.* University of Washington, College of Forest Resources, Center for Urban Agriculture. [Online]. Available at: http://www.naturewithin.info/CityBiz/Biz3Ps-FS5.pdf

Part A

Chapter 2
Climate Change: Mitigation and Adaptation Strategies
Katia Perini

2.1   Climate change and sustainable development

The term *climate change* refers to changes to the Earth's climate, mostly induced by the production of greenhouse gases such as carbon dioxide (TEEB, 2011). According to the Intergovernmental Panel on Climate Change (IPCC), over the last three decades, the Earth's surface has become increasingly warmer (Pachauri *et al.*, 2014). Anthropogenic greenhouse gas (GHG) emissions have recently created the highest atmospheric concentrations of carbon dioxide ever registered in history and are likely to be the main factor causing global warming (Field *et al.*, 2014). Total anthropogenic GHG emissions have, in fact, continued to increase from 1970 to 2010 (and especially between 2000 and 2010), despite a growing number of climate change mitigation policies (Pachauri *et al.*, 2014).

The Brundtland Commission (the 1987 World Commission on Environment and Development) described sustainable development as "[meeting] the needs of the present without compromising the ability of future generations to meet their own needs" (Waheed *et al.*, 2009). It can also be defined as a dynamic pattern of social, economic, technological and environmental indicators that prompts countries to move toward a better life (Meyar-Naimi and Vaez-Zadeh, 2012). Limiting the effects of climate change is mandatory to achieve sustainable development as the past and future contributions of countries to the accumulation of GHGs in the atmosphere are different and the risks are unevenly distributed. Generally, climate change strongly affects both human and natural systems. It has a bigger impact on disadvantaged people in all countries, due to the environmental degradation and lack of resources that have negative direct consequences on their survival, subsistence and economic conditions. Each country, though, has different capacities and resources to address mitigation and adaptation strategies

Urban Sustainability and River Restoration: Green and Blue Infrastructure, First Edition.
Katia Perini and Paola Sabbion.
© 2017 John Wiley & Sons Ltd. Published 2017 by John Wiley & Sons Ltd.

and there are widespread variations between natural and urban environments (Pachauri *et al.*, 2014).

In the United States, the Environmental Justice Movement (EJM) was created in the 1980s to fight against the disproportionate effects that environmental issues are causing on disadvantaged people (Sze, 2007). Environmental justice brings a progressive approach to sustainability by underlining the role of social justice in environmental and land-use planning. As a result, the most recent community plans devised in the United States have arisen from this movement's struggles (Angotti, 2008), (see Chapter 10). The Bronx River and the LA River case studies (described in Chapters 9.1, 9.2, 13.1 and 13.2) specifically offer a viable example of the successful impact of community-based environmental projects, such as the restoration of an urban river waterfront in low-income neighbourhoods concerned with many social and environmental issues. According to the European case studies analysed, as the Paillon River (Nice, France) and the Madrid Rio (Spain; see Chapters 9.3, 9.4, 13.3, 13.4), top-down approaches can be effective as well. These are projects mainly developed by federal, state and city governments. In this field, the fundamental different historical constitutional approaches in the United States and in Europe drive policies and guidelines (see Chapters 10–11).

2.2   Impacts and risks in (of) urban areas

Climate change poses risks for human and natural systems (Field *et al.*, 2014) and urban areas are highly vulnerable to climate change effects, especially with regard to flooding and heat waves (Commission of the European Communities, 2005; Field *et al.*, 2014). However, the impact of climate change can be even more intense and broader on natural systems than urban areas due to its influence on hydrological systems. It affects, in particular, water resources in terms of quantity and quality, and many terrestrial, freshwater and marine species, which have shifted their geographic ranges, seasonal activities, migration patterns, abundances and interactions in response to ongoing climate change (Pachauri *et al.*, 2014). Climate change, therefore, alters the functions of ecological systems hence impinging on the provision of ecosystem services and the well-being of people that rely on these services (Nelson *et al.*, 2013). As described in Chapter 5, terrestrial ecosystems provide a number of vital services for people and societies, such as biodiversity, food, fibre, water resources, carbon sequestration, and recreation. In the future, the capacity of ecosystems to guarantee these services will be determined by changes in socio-economic characteristics, land use, biodiversity, atmospheric composition and climate (Metzger *et al.*, 2006).

As the Earth's surface temperature is projected to rise over the twenty-first century under all assessed emission scenarios, heat waves will probably occur more often and last longer, and extreme precipitation events will become more intense and frequent in many regions. At the same time, the ocean water will become increasingly warmer and more acid, and the global mean sea level will rise (Edenhofer *et al.*, 2014). Climate change related risks will clearly escalate for both natural and human systems (Pachauri *et al.*, 2014).

Environmental problems and ecological imbalances related to climate change, especially with regard to biodiversity loss and environmental pollution,

Part A

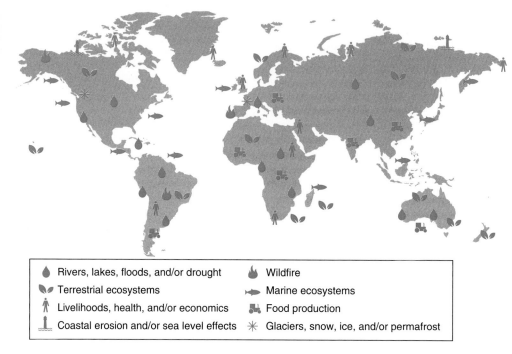

Rivers, lakes, floods, and/or drought   Wildfire

Terrestrial ecosystems   Marine ecosystems

Livelihoods, health, and/or economics   Food production

Coastal erosion and/or sea level effects   Glaciers, snow, ice, and/or permafrost

Figure 2.1   Climate Change Impacts (based on IPCC Report, Field *et al.*, 2014).

demonstrate the need to reduce material and energy flows and curb environmental impacts (Luederitz *et al.*, 2013; Rockström *et al.*, 2009; Seto *et al.*, 2012; Weisz and Steinberger, 2010). After all, "The gamble for ecological survival has always been reliant on technology and design – and when technological limits are obvious, the design adaptation has to be made" (Plunz, 2008). Urban and building design, especially integrating green and blue infrastructures (GBI), as rain gardens or green roofs (see Chapter 6), can be an effective tool to adapt to climate change, reducing at the same time greenhouse gas emissions and furthering the establishment of resilient cities.

2.3   Mitigation and adaptation strategies

Mitigation, that is, a human intervention to reduce the sources or enhancement of greenhouse gases, together with adaptation to climate change, contributes to the objective expressed in Article 2 of the United Nations Framework Convention on Climate Change (UNFCCC; Edenhofer *et al.*, 2014). The ultimate objective of this Convention is to achieve stabilisation of greenhouse gas concentrations in the atmosphere at a level that would prevent dangerous anthropogenic interference with the climate system within the adequate time frame to allow ecosystems to adapt naturally to climate change, ensuring that food production is not threatened and enabling sustainable economic development.

Adaptation is defined by IPCC as "the process of adjustment to actual or expected climate and its effects. In human systems, adaptation seeks to moderate or avoid harm or exploit beneficial opportunities. In some natural systems, human intervention may facilitate adjustment to expected climate and its effects" (Field *et al.*, 2014). Reducing vulnerability and exposure to present climate variability is the first step toward adaptation to future climate change. This can be achieved by integrating such strategy into planning, policy design, and decision making (Pachauri *et al.*, 2014).

In this field, European policies have so far gained important results by means of directives which should be adopted by the Member States (with either more or less positive results (Giachetta, 2013). Green and blue infrastructure is viewed as a matter of priority to meet the EU 2020 targets pertaining to European-wide strategies (COM (2013) 249 final; Commission of the European Communities, 2013). As described in Chapters 10 and 11, a different approach is devised in the United States and in Europe; the latter in fact is characterised by a more perspective normative framework and a top-down oriented approach. In the United States, several associations, organisations and public bodies work to improve environmental conditions in dense urban areas through the integration of green and blue infrastructure. The U.S. Environmental Protection Agency (U.S. EPA) provides cities with local municipal grants, along with technical support in order to implement GBI (EPA, 2011).

According to the 2014 Fifth Assessment Report by the Intergovernmental Panel on Climate Change, "Adaptation and mitigation are complementary strategies for reducing and managing the risks of climate change. Substantial reduction of emissions over the next few decades can lessen climate risks in the twenty-first century and beyond, increasing prospects for effective adaptation, lowering the costs and challenges of mitigation in the longer term and contributing to climate-resilient pathways for sustainable development" (Pachauri *et al.*, 2014). Therefore, mitigation and adaptation plans to moderate greenhouse gas emissions and limit climate change risks should be considered as twin issues (Hamin and Gurran, 2009).

Climate change mitigation is required to avoid *dangerous* and irreversible effects on the climate system and also conserve or enhance natural capital (Rogner *et al.*, 2007). The built environment and the transportation sector can generate greenhouse gas emissions; mitigation strategies seek to reduce current and future emissions (Hamin and Gurran, 2009). The impact of land use change on emissions, sequestration, and albedo also plays an important role in radiative forcing and in the carbon cycle (Fisher *et al.*, 2007). Therefore, converting land use to expand green infrastructure can be an opportunity to mitigate climate change.

As shown in Figure 2.2, vegetated green and blue infrastructure capture CO_2, contributing to climate change mitigation. Vegetation substantially captures carbon dioxide through photosynthesis (Fowler, 2002), sequestering carbon dioxide from the air and storing it as biomass (Getter *et al.*, 2009). Urban vegetation curbs the Urban Heat Island phenomenon as it cools air temperature and reduces greenhouse gas emissions driven by air conditioning (Perini and Magliocco, 2014). Another indirect benefit of green and blue infrastructure is the reduction of transportation needs and related emissions, which can be obtained by promoting greenways. Microclimate regulation (UHI mitigation, see Chapter 3) is also crucial to address ecosystem health in cities. According to the European Environmental

Part A

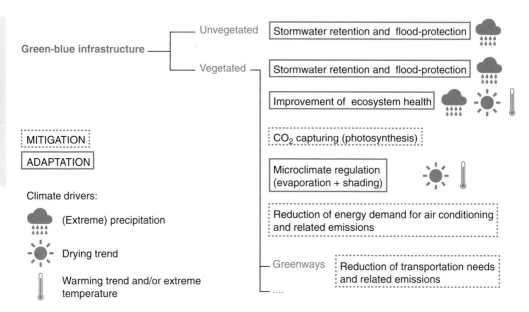

Figure 2.2   Climate-Related Green Infrastructure Mitigation and Adaptation Strategies (based on IPCC Report, Field *et al.*, 2014).

Agency (2015), ecosystems such as urban green areas, play an important role when providing benefits to conventional infrastructure solutions. Green spaces function as stormwater retention areas and mitigate the load on conventional sewage systems. The latter is among the most important benefits of green and blue infrastructure in both vegetated and unvegetated systems (see Chapters 6-7).

Since many aspects of climate change and associated impacts will endure for centuries, even if anthropogenic greenhouse gas emissions are mitigated, adaptation strategies are very important. For this reason, resilience to climate change is gaining momentum, especially in urban areas, as a means of reducing adverse climate change impacts (Abdrabo and Hassaan, 2015). Adaptation strategies can contribute to the present and future well-being of populations and the health of ecosystems (Pachauri *et al.*, 2014; TEEB, 2011).

The success of mitigation and adaptation strategies depends on coordinated policies and cooperation initiatives across international, regional, national and sub-national scales, as single adaptation and mitigation options addressing climate change are not sufficient. Integrated responses linking adaptation and mitigation with other societal objectives can prove to be the most effective responses and can entail technology development, diffusion and transfer and climate change funding (Pachauri *et al.*, 2014).

References

Abdrabo, M. A. and Hassaan, M. A. (2015). An integrated framework for urban resilience to climate change – Case study: Sea level rise impacts on the Nile Delta coastal urban areas. *Urban Climate*, 14, Part 4, p. 554–565. [Online]. Available at: doi:10.1016/j.uclim.2015.09.005 [Accessed 10 December 2015].

Angotti, T. (2008). *New York for sale community planning confronts global real estate*. Cambridge, Mass.: MIT Press.

Commission of the European Communities. (2005). *EUR-Lex - 52005DC0718 - EN*. [Online]. Available at: http://eur-lex.europa.eu/LexUriServ/LexUriServ.do?uri=COM: 2005:0718:FIN:EN:HTML [Accessed 23 January 2014].

Commission of the European Communities. (2013). *Communication From The Commission to the European Parliament, the Council, the European Economic and Social Committee and the Committee of the Regions. Green Infrastructure (GI) — Enhancing Europe's Natural Capital*. [Online]. Available at: http://ec.europa.eu/environment/nature/ecosystems/ docs/green_infrastructures/1_EN_ACT_part1_v5.pdf

Edenhofer, O., Pichs-Madruga, R., Sokona, Y., Farahani, E., Kadner, S., Seyboth, K., Adler, A., Baum, I., Brunner, S., Eickemeier, P. and others. (2014). Climate change 2014: mitigation of climate change. *Contribution of Working Group III to the Fifth Assessment Report of the Intergovernmental Panel on Climate Change*, p. 511–597 [Accessed 9 December 2015].

EPA. (2011). *Land Revitalization Fact Sheet Green Infrastructure*. [Online]. Available at: http://www.epa.gov/landrevitalization/download/fs_green_infrastructure.pdf

European Environmental Agency. (2015). *Exploring nature-based solutions. The role of green infrastructure in mitigating the impacts of weather- and climate change-related natural hazards*. [Online]. Available at: file://localhost/Users/katiaperini/Library/ Application%20Support/Zotero/Profiles/rwxgy8et.default/zotero/storage/DSES69X4/ exploring-nature-based-solutions-2014.html

Field, C. B., Barros, V. R., Mastrandrea, M. D., Mach, K. J., Abdrabo, M.-K., Adger, N., Anokhin, Y. A., Anisimov, O. A., Arent, D. J., Barnett, J. and others. (2014). Climate Change 2014: Summary for policymakers. *Climate change 2014: impacts, adaptation, and vulnerability. Part a: global and sectoral aspects. Contribution of working group II to the fifth assessment report of the intergovernmental panel on climate change*, p. 1–32. [Accessed 4 November 2015].

Fisher, B. S., Nakicenovic, N., Alfsen, K., Morlot Corfee, J., de la Chesnaye, F., Hourcade, J.-C., Jiang, K., Kainuma, M., La Rovere, E., Matysek, A., Rana, A., Riahi, K., Richels, R., Rose, S., van Vuuren, D., and Warren, R. (2007). *Issues related to mitigation in the long term context, In Climate Change 2007: Mitigation. Contribution of Working Group III to the Fourth Assessment Report of the Inter-governmental Panel on Climate Change [B. Metz, O.R. Davidson, P.R. Bosch, R. Dave, L.A. Meyer (eds)]*. Cambridge University Press, Cambridge, United Kingdom and New York, NY, USA.

Fowler, D. (2002). Pollutants depostition and uptake by vegetation. In: Bell, J. N. B. and Treshow, M. (eds.), *Air Pollution and Plant Life*, John Wiley & Sons.

Getter, K. L., Rowe, D. B., Robertson, G. P., Cregg, B. M., and Andresen, J. A. (2009). Carbon Sequestration Potential of Extensive Green Roofs. *Environmental Science & Technology*, 43 (19), p. 7564–7570. [Online]. Available at: doi:10.1021/es901539x [Accessed 13 February 2014].

Giachetta, A. (2013). Diffusion of Sustainable Construction Practices. A Case of International Cooperation. *Open Journal of Energy Efficiency*, 02 (01), p. 46–52. [Online]. Available at: doi:10.4236/ojee.2013.21008 [Accessed 22 January 2014].

Hamin, E. M. and Gurran, N. (2009). Urban form and climate change: Balancing adaptation and mitigation in the U.S. and Australia. *Habitat International*, 33 (3), p. 238–245. [Online]. Available at: doi:10.1016/j.habitatint.2008.10.005 [Accessed 22 January 2014].

Luederitz, C., Lang, D. J., and Von Wehrden, H. (2013). A systematic review of guiding principles for sustainable urban neighborhood development. *Landscape and Urban Planning*, 118, p. 40–52. [Online]. Available at: doi:10.1016/j.landurbplan.2013.06.002 [Accessed 23 January 2014].

Metzger, M. J., Rounsevell, M. D. A., Acosta-Michlik, L., Leemans, R., and Schröter, D. (2006). The vulnerability of ecosystem services to land use change. *Agriculture,*

Part A

Ecosystems & Environment, 114 (1), p. 69–85. [Online]. Available at: doi:10.1016/j.agee.2005.11.025 [Accessed 22 January 2014].

Meyar-Naimi, H. and Vaez-Zadeh, S. (2012). Sustainable development based energy policy making frameworks, a critical review. *Energy Policy*, 43, p. 351–361. [Online]. Available at: doi:10.1016/j.enpol.2012.01.012 [Accessed 23 January 2014].

Nelson, E. J., Kareiva, P., Ruckelshaus, M., Arkema, K., Geller, G., Girvetz, E., Goodrich, D., Matzek, V., Pinsky, M., Reid, W., Saunders, M., Semmens, D., and Tallis, H. (2013). Climate change's impact on key ecosystem services and the human well-being they support in the US. *Frontiers in Ecology and the Environment*, 11 (9), p. 483–893. [Online]. Available at: doi:10.1890/120312 [Accessed 4 November 2015].

Pachauri, R. K., Allen, M. R., Barros, V. R., Broome, J., Cramer, W., Christ, R., Church, J. A., Clarke, L., Dahe, Q., Dasgupta, P. and others. (2014). *Climate Change 2014: Synthesis Report. Contribution of Working Groups I, II and III to the Fifth Assessment Report of the Intergovernmental Panel on Climate Change*. [Online]. Available at: http://epic.awi.de/37530/ [Accessed 9 December 2015].

Perini, K. and Magliocco, A. (2014). Effects of vegetation, urban density, building height, and atmospheric conditions on local temperatures and thermal comfort. *Urban Forestry & Urban Greening*. [Online]. Available at: doi:10.1016/j.ufug.2014.03.003 [Accessed 10 April 2014].

Plunz, R. (2008). The design equation. In: Sutto, M. P. and Plunz, R. (eds.), *Urban climate change crossroads*, New York: Urban Design Lab of the Earth Institute, Columbia University.

Rockström, J., Steffen, W., Noone, K., Persson, Å., Chapin, F. S., Lambin, E. F., Lenton, T. M., Scheffer, M., Folke, C., Schellnhuber, H. J., Nykvist, B., de Wit, C. A., Hughes, T., van der Leeuw, S., Rodhe, H., Sörlin, S., Snyder, P. K., Costanza, R., Svedin, U., Falkenmark, M., Karlberg, L., Corell, R. W., Fabry, V. J., Hansen, J., Walker, B., Liverman, D., Richardson, K., Crutzen, P., and Foley, J. A. (2009). A safe operating space for humanity. *Nature*, 461 (7263), p. 472–475. [Online]. Available at: doi:10.1038/461472a [Accessed 28 January 2014].

Rogner, H.-H., Zhou, D., Bradley, R., Crabbé, P., Edenhofer, O., Hare, B., Kuijpers, L., and Yamaguchi, M. (2007). *Introduction. In Climate Change 2007: Mitigation. Contribution of Working Group III to the Fourth Assessment Report of the Intergovernmental Panel on Climate Change [B. Metz, O.R. Davidson, P.R. Bosch, R. Dave, L.A. Meyer (eds)]*. Cambridge University Press, Cambridge, United Kingdom and New York, NY, USA.

Seto, K. C., Güneralp, B., and Hutyra, L. R. (2012). Global forecasts of urban expansion to 2030 and direct impacts on biodiversity and carbon pools. *Proceedings of the National Academy of Sciences*, 109 (40), p. 16083–16088. [Online]. Available at: doi:10.1073/pnas.1211658109 [Accessed 28 January 2014].

Sze, J. (2007). *Noxious New York: the racial politics of urban health and environmental justice*. Cambridge, Mass.: MIT Press.

TEEB. (2011). *TEEB Manual for cities: ecosystem services in urban management*. UNEP and the European Union (Ed) Ecosystem Services in Urban Management. [Online]. Available at: http://www.teebweb.org/wp-content/uploads/Study%20and%20Reports/Additional%20Reports/Manual%20for%20Cities/TEEB%20Manual%20for%20Cities_English.pdf

Waheed, B., Khan, F., and Veitch, B. (2009). Linkage-Based Frameworks for Sustainability Assessment: Making a Case for Driving Force-Pressure-State-Exposure-Effect-Action (DPSEEA) Frameworks. *Sustainability*, 1 (3), p. 441–463. [Online]. Available at: doi:10.3390/su1030441 [Accessed 23 January 2014].

Weisz, H. and Steinberger, J. K. (2010). Reducing energy and material flows in cities. *Current Opinion in Environmental Sustainability*, 2 (3), p. 185–192. [Online]. Available at: doi:10.1016/j.cosust.2010.05.010 [Accessed: 28 January 2014].

Chapter 3
Environmental and Ecological Imbalances in Dense Urban Areas

Katia Perini

3.1 Sustainable urban design

Urban areas are responsible for 70% of global carbon emissions and for nearly 70% of global energy consumption; this trend is increasing as land converted to urban areas is expected to triple by 2030 (Luederitz *et al.*, 2013; International Energy Agency, 2008; Seto *et al.*, 2012; United Nations, 2012). As explained in Chapter 2, environmental problems within cities have significant consequences on human health, citizens' quality of life and urban economic performance, especially due to the high vulnerability of urban areas to climate change and related flooding and heat waves (Commission of the European Communities, 2005). While human lifestyles, consumerism, and unsustainable material production lead to multiple-scale alterations in urban systems, they also generate negative effects in residents' daily life (Grimm *et al.*, 2008).

Hamin and Gurran (2009) agree that a denser urban environment could reduce the emissions connected to transportation needs and building energy use when compared with suburban and rural lifestyles. Cities could therefore promote sustainable climate change adaptation and mitigation practices (Ewing *et al.*, 2008; Owen, 2010). Higher density might indeed minimise transport demand. In addition, compact development connects population to existing settlements, concentrating human-related activities and helping to protect underdeveloped and sensitive lands and maintaining viable habitats in other areas (Farr, 2008). Urban design should seek to minimise the use of land, energy and materials, and prevent environmental damage (Schubert, 2005). Since more than 40% of total urban land is covered by impervious surfaces as roads, parking, and buildings, green infrastructure at city scale is crucial to improve environmental conditions (Benedict *et al.*, 2006).

Urban Sustainability and River Restoration: Green and Blue Infrastructure, First Edition.
Katia Perini and Paola Sabbion.

Figure 3.1   Chicago: An Example of a Dense Urban Area.

When green and blue infrastructure is proactively planned, developed, and maintained, it can guide urban development by providing a framework for economic growth and nature conservation (Tzoulas *et al.*, 2007). Sustainable urban design can therefore decrease the negative effects of anthropic activities on the environment, and mitigate environmental issues on human health and quality of life. Strategies and actions should limit the impact of anthropic activities inside cities and, at the same time, lessen the impact of cities on a global scale. As described in Chapter 2, when considering current environmental and ecological issues, green and blue infrastructure plays a key role as it reduces environmental and ecological imbalances in urban areas and it can adequately respond to contemporary needs, as highlighted in the twentieth century by the Garden City Movement and the natural-urban planning methods.

Since the end of the nineteenth century, nature has been valued as a key element in sustainable urban design. In 1898, Ebenezer Howard published *Garden Cities of Tomorrow*, featuring towns with the same advantages of cities – as self-contained, employment-generating human communities – while also being surrounded by concentric rings of gardens and country landscape serving as a green belt to protect the establishment from outside encroachment (Howard, 1898). Patrick Geddes also recognised the importance of green belts and open spaces as forms of urban rehabilitation and stated that, when the higher functions of urban development are concentrated in metropolitan centres, a regional approach can overcome problems arising from the polarisation of functions (Geddes, 1973). The Scottish landscape architect Ian McHarg (1969) developed innovative methods based on ecological urban planning and building design to promote the restoration of environmental quality by better integrating their natural systems.

3.2   Imbalances in cities

The major sources of air pollution in urban areas are transportation, industry and heating/air conditioning (Legambiente, 2012; Colvile *et al.*, 2001). High levels of pollution in the atmosphere and the excessive concentration of asphalt and concrete in urban areas cause the Urban Heat Island (UHI) phenomenon resulting in the dramatic 2–5 degrees Celsius temperature differences between cities and their surrounding suburban and rural areas (Taha, 1997). This phenomenon intensified in recent years damaging citizens' health, especially during summer, due to consistently high night temperatures (Rozbicki and Golaszewski, 2003; Tereshchenko and Filonov, 2001). Huge quantities of solar radiations are stored and later radiated in urban areas due to massive amounts of construction materials, the so-called *canyon effect* related to tall buildings and the use of air conditioning, contributing to the Urban Heat Island effect along with the anthropogenic heat generated by power plants and automobiles (Rizwan *et al.*, 2008; Santamouris *et al.*, 2001).

A study conducted in the city of Florence (Italy) shows the impact of green areas on air temperatures inside the city; and draws the conclusion that temperature distribution is connected to the distance from the city centre, the mean number of buildings per square metre, and their height. Higher air temperatures were found in the city centre. Lower temperatures were recorded within green areas located in the city centre (parks or gardens) compared to the ones recorded in the street (1.5–2 °C; Petralli *et al.*, 2006). This happens because greened surfaces have different albedo values compared to artificial hard surfaces (20–30% among vegetation and 5% on asphalt) and a high concentration of water (Taha, 1997).

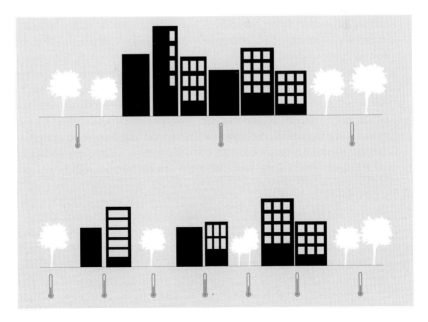

Figure 3.2   Urban Heat Island Phenomenon.

High levels of air pollutants in dense urban areas are also responsible for serious damage to human health. The United Nations Environment Programme (UNEP) links urban air pollution to up to 1 million premature deaths and 1 million pre-native deaths each year. According to a study conducted by Hoek *et al.* (2000), daily mortality is significantly associated with the concentration of all air pollutants and especially ozone, particulate air pollution, and the gaseous pollutants sulphur dioxide (SO_2) and nitrogen dioxide (NO_2). Dust particles smaller than 2.5 mm in diameter are mainly harmful in dense urban areas because they can be inhaled into the lower respiratory tract and thus pose serious health issues (Powe and Willis, 2004).

Pollution in urban areas highly affects water quality as well. As described in Chapter 4, the effects of rainfall on vegetated land and on hard surfaces in built-up areas are very different, thus, stormwater management is among the most important issues that needs to be addressed in urban areas. Most precipitation falls on vegetation and is absorbed in the soil and eventually joins the water table; or is transpired back into the atmosphere. Water cannot be absorbed by hard surfaces such as asphalt and concrete, however, and it runs into rivers through drainage systems (Dunnett and Kingsbury, 2008). About 75% of rainfall on towns and cities is lost directly due to surface runoff compared with an estimated 5% loss in forested areas (Scholz-Barth, 2001). High rainfall in urban areas is also rapidly reflected in river level peaks resulting in flooding (Dunnett and Kingsbury, 2008). Collected rainwater amounts and quality are crucially important (Czemiel Berndtsson, 2010). Polluted stormwater runoff from urban landscapes affects the quality of urban waters, which according to the U.S. Environmental Protection Agency (EPA), are polluted with industrial discharges, mobile sources (i.e., automobiles), residential and commercial wastewater, and litter. Since urban populations often share centralised water sources, this pollution creates public and environmental health hazards, such as reduced drinking water quality and unsafe swimming water (EPA, 2016).

Growing urbanisation has often proved to have dramatic impacts also on natural landscapes (Grimm *et al.*, 2008). In many cases, fragmentation and pollution have caused discontinuities in the ecosystems and biodiversity loss. Soil erosion is also becoming a global environmental problem, which hinders the sustainable development of the environment and its resources. Studies indicate that the occurrence and intensity of soil erosion are mainly caused by human activities, especially land abandonment, deforestation, and afforestation changes (Borrelli *et al.*, 2014; Wang *et al.*, 2016). Soil erosion causes land degradation, flooding, river siltation, nutrients loss, and water pollution (Rickson, 2014).

3.3   Benefits connected to vegetation

Vegetation in urban areas can provide a wide range of benefits. Green areas play an important role for human psychological well-being inside dense cities (Bellomo, 2003). *Biophilia* is the name given to the human love of nature based on the intrinsic interdependence between humans and other living systems (Farr, 2008). According to Wilson (1984), who defines the term *biophilia* as "the urge to affiliate with other forms of life", human beings are instinctively bonded to other living systems. Inadequate quantity of vegetation and green areas within the urban environment translate into poor quality of life as well as the mentioned urban pollution and environmental problems. The concept of *biophilic urbanism* has been championed by Tim Beatley and Peter Newman for several decades as a way to create more liveable cities (Beatley, 2009). Green areas offer recreational amenities and improve residents' quality of life.

Natural environments also have a restorative function. Ulrich (1984) found that hospital patients who could see trees and nature from their windows recovered more quickly than those who had a restricted view of trees caused by the presence of buildings (Chiesura, 2004; Dunnett and Kingsbury, 2008). Vegetation, moreover, improves environmental conditions in cities by acting on both causes and effects; air quality is enhanced by different types of vegetation (Ottelé *et al.*, 2010; Yin *et al.*, 2011); and potential energy demand for air conditioning lowers as a result of urban heat island mitigation (Perini and Magliocco, 2014).

Mitigation strategies, such as urban forestry, living (green) roofs, and light coloured surfaces, could be implemented at the community level to curb a wider UHI phenomenon having regional scale impact on energy demand, air quality and public health (Rosenzweig *et al.*, 2006). Greened paved surfaces intercept solar radiation and can decrease the warming of hard surfaces, thus reducing the UHI phenomenon by 2–4 degrees Celsius. Susca *et al.* (2011) monitored UHI effects in four areas in New York City, finding a 2 degrees Celsius average temperature difference between the most and the least vegetated areas. Although UHI can be mitigated with large amounts of surfaces with higher albedo, such as vegetated or simply white painted surfaces, larger green areas as urban parks may be more effective (Petralli *et al.*, 2006). Ultimately, a combined strategy that maximises the amount of vegetation offers more potential cooling than any individual programme (Rosenzweig *et al.*, 2006).

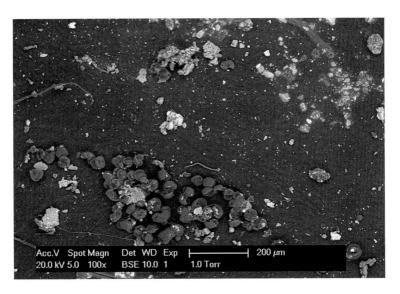

Figure 3.3   Particulate Matter Electron Microphotograph on the Upper Side of a Leaf of *Hedera helix* (taken at the Delft University of Technology).

Vegetation improves air quality mainly because it absorbs fine dust particles and actively consumes gaseous pollutants such as CO_2, NO_2 and SO_2. Plants use carbon dioxide for the photosynthesis process, creating oxygen and biomass; converting nitrogen and sulphur dioxides into nitrates and sulphates in their tissue. Fine dust particles (PM), especially the smaller size fractions ($<10\,\mu m$), mainly adhere to the outer parts of plants (Ottelé et al., 2010, Fig. 3.3). Therefore, vegetation is a perfect anchor for airborne particles at different heights. A study conducted in China demonstrated that vegetation in parks can remove large amounts of airborne pollutants: a reduction of fine dust (2–35%), SO_2 (2–27%) and NO_2 (1–21%) was found at ground level (Yin et al., 2011). However, several factors feature in dense cities. In urban canyons, trees may reduce the air flow, which plays a fundamental role in decreasing automobile pollutants (Vos et al., 2013). Other studies reveal more optimistic results. Brantley et al. (2014) show black carbon (BC) emissions field measurements, demonstrating that wind direction influences pollutants concentration nearby vegetation (with a BC reduction in a range of 7.8–22%). Baik et al. (2012) evaluate air quality improvement stemming from green roofs by means of a CFD model (computational fluid dynamics). Results for a simple building configuration with a street canyon aspect ratio of one, show that the cool air produced thanks to roof greening flows into it, giving rise to strengthened street canyon flow, which enhances pollutant dispersion near the road and lowers pollutant concentration. Design strategies can thus improve air quality in cities, considering the building morphology, vegetation shape and local conditions.

References

Baik, J.-J., Kwak, K.-H., Park, S.-B. and Ryu, Y.-H. (2012). Effects of building roof greening on air quality in street canyons. *Atmospheric Environment*, 61, p. 48–55. [Online]. Available at: doi:10.1016/j.atmosenv.2012.06.076 [Accessed: 11 August 2014].

Beatley, T. (2009). 'Biophilic Urbanism: Inviting Nature Back to Our Communities and Into Our Lives.' *William & Mary Environmental Law and Policy Review* 34 (1), 209–238.

Bellomo, A. (2003). *Pareti verdi : linee guida alla progettazione/Antonella Bellomo*. Napoli: Esselibri.

Benedict, M. A., McMahon, E. T., and Conservation Fund. (2006). *Green infrastructure: linking landscapes and communities*. Washington, DC: Island Press.

Borrelli, P., Ballabio, C., Panagos, P., and Montanarella, L. (2014). Wind erosion susceptibility of European soils. *Geoderma*, 232–234, p. 471–478. [Online]. Available at: doi:10.1016/j.geoderma.2014.06.008.

Brantley, H. L., Hagler, G. S. W., J. Deshmukh, P., and Baldauf, R. W. (2014). Field assessment of the effects of roadside vegetation on near-road black carbon and particulate matter. *Science of The Total Environment*, 468–469, p. 120–129. [Online]. Available at: doi:10.1016/j.scitotenv.2013.08.001 [Accessed 11 August 2014].

Chiesura, A. (2004). The role of urban parks for the sustainable city. *Landscape and Urban Planning*, 68 (1), p.129–138. [Online]. Available at: doi:10.1016/j.landurbplan.2003.08.003 [Accessed 17 February 2014].

Colvile, R. N., Hutchinson, E. J., Mindell, J. S., and Warren, R. F. (2001). The transport sector as a source of air pollution. *Atmospheric Environment*, 35 (9), p. 1537–1565. [Online]. Available at: doi:10.1016/S1352-2310(00)00551-3 [Accessed 30 January 2014].

Commission of the European Communities. (2005). *EUR-Lex - 52005DC0718 - EN.* [Online]. Available at: http://eur-lex.europa.eu/LexUriServ/LexUriServ.do?uri=COM: 2005:0718:FIN:EN:HTML [Accessed 23 January 2014].

Czemiel Berndtsson, J. (2010). Green roof performance towards management of runoff water quantity and quality: A review. *Ecological Engineering*, 36 (4), p. 351–360. [Online]. Available at: doi:10.1016/j.ecoleng.2009.12.014 [Accessed 22 January 2014].

Dunnett, N. and Kingsbury, N. (2008). *Planting green roofs and living walls.* Portland, OR: Timber Press.

EPA, U. (2016). *US Environmental Protection Agency.* [Online]. Available at: http://www3. epa.gov/ [Accessed 12 February 2016].

Ewing, R. H., Anderson, G., Winkelman, S., Walters, J., and Chen, D. (2008). *Growing cooler the evidence on urban development and climate change.* Washington, D.C.: ULI. [Online]. Available at: http://site.ebrary.com/id/10518814 [Accessed 4 February 2014].

Farr, D. (2008). *Sustainable urbanism : urban design with nature.* Hoboken, N.J.: Wiley.

Geddes, P. (1973). *City development: a report to the Carnegie Dunfermline Trust,* Scottish reprints. Shannon: Irish university press.

Grimm, N. B., Faeth, S. H., Golubiewski, N. E., Redman, C. L., Wu, J., Bai, X., and Briggs, J. M. (2008). Global Change and the Ecology of Cities. *Science*, 319 (5864), p. 756–760. [Online]. Available at: doi:10.1126/science.1150195.

Hamin, E. M. and Gurran, N. (2009). Urban form and climate change: Balancing adaptation and mitigation in the U.S. and Australia. *Habitat International*, 33 (3), p. 238–245. [Online]. Available at: doi:10.1016/j.habitatint.2008.10.005 [Accessed 22 January 2014].

Hoek, G., Brunekreef, B., Verhoeff, A., van Wijnen, J., and Fischer, P. (2000). Daily mortality and air pollution in The Netherlands. *Journal of the Air & Waste Management Association (1995)*, 50 (8), p. 1380–1389.

Howard, E. (1898). *To-morrow A Peaceful Path to Real Reform.* London: Swan Sonnenschein.

International Energy Agency. (2008). *World energy outlook 2008.* Paris; New Milford, Conn.: International Energy Agency ; Turpin Distribution.

Legambiente. (2012). *Mal'aria di città.* [Online]. Available at http://www.legambiente.it/ sites/default/files/docs/dossier_malaria_2012_finale_0.pdf

Luederitz, C., Lang, D. J. and Von Wehrden, H. (2013). A systematic review of guiding principles for sustainable urban neighborhood development. *Landscape and Urban Planning*, 118, p. 40–52. [Online]. Available at: doi:10.1016/j.landurbplan.2013.06.002 [Accessed 23 January 2014].

Ottelé, M., van Bohemen, H. D., and Fraaij, A. L. A. (2010). Quantifying the deposition of particulate matter on climber vegetation on living walls. *Ecological Engineering*, 36 (2), p. 154–162. [Online]. Available at: doi:10.1016/j.ecoleng.2009.02.007 [Accessed 22 January 2014].

Owen, D. (2010). *Green metropolis: why living smaller, living closer, and driving less are the keys to sustainability.* New York: Riverhead Books.

Perini, K. and Magliocco, A. (2014). Effects of vegetation, urban density, building height, and atmospheric conditions on local temperatures and thermal comfort. *Urban Forestry & Urban Greening.* [Online]. Available at: doi:10.1016/j.ufug.2014.03.003 [Accessed 10 April 2014].

Petralli, M., Prokopp, A., Morabito, M., Bartolini, G., Torrigiani, T., and Orlandini, S. (2006). Ruolo delle aree verdi nella mitigazione dell'isola di calore urbana: uno studio nella città di Firenze. *Rivista Italiana di Agrometeorologia*, 1, p. 51–58. [Accessed 22 January 2014].

Powe, N. A. and Willis, K. G. (2004). Mortality and morbidity benefits of air pollution (SO2 and PM10) absorption attributable to woodland in Britain. *Journal of*

Part A

Environmental Management, 70 (2), p. 119–128. [Online]. Available at: doi:10.1016/j. jenvman.2003.11.003 [Accessed 30 January 2014].

Rickson, R. J. (2014). Can control of soil erosion mitigate water pollution by sediments? *Science of the Total Environment*, 468–469, p. 1187–1197. *Scopus* [Online]. Available at: doi:10.1016/j.scitotenv.2013.05.057

Rizwan, A. M., Dennis, L. Y., and Liu, C. (2008). A review on the generation, determination and mitigation of Urban Heat Island. *Journal of Environmental Sciences*, 20 (1), p. 120–128.

Rosenzweig, C., Solecki, W. D., and Slosberg, R. B. (2006). *Mitigating New York City's heat island with urban forestry, living roofs, and light surfaces. New York City regional heat island initiative*. [Online]. Available at: http://gis.fs.fed.us/ccrc/topics/urban-forests/docs/NYSERDA_heat_island.pdf [Accessed 21 February 2014].

Rozbicki, T. and Golaszewski, D. (2003). Analysis of local climate changes in Ursynów in the period 1960–1991 as a result of housing estate development. In: *Proc. 5th Int. Conf. urban climate*, 2, 2003, p. 455–458. [Online]. Available at: http://www.geo.uni.lodz.pl/~icuc5/text/O_32_3.pdf [Accessed 23 January 2014].

Santamouris, M., Papanikolaou, N., Livada, I., Koronakis, I., Georgakis, C., Argiriou, A., and Assimakopoulos, D. N. (2001). On the impact of urban climate on the energy consumption of buildings. *Solar Energy*, 70 (3), p. 201–216. [Online]. Available at: doi:10.1016/S0038-092X(00)00095-5 [Accessed 23 January 2014].

Scholz-Barth, K. (2001). Green Roofs: Stormwater Management From the Top Down. *Environmental Design & Construction, Feature*, January/February 2001. [Online]. Available at: http://www.usgbccc.org/documents/StormWaterManagement.pdf [Accessed 30 January 2014].

Schubert, U. (2005). *Ecocity. Urban Development towards Appropriate Structures for Sustainable Transport*. [Online]. Available at: http://www.rma.at/sites/new.rma.at/files/ECOCITY%20%20_%20Final%20Report.pdf

Seto, K. C., Güneralp, B., and Hutyra, L. R. (2012). Global forecasts of urban expansion to 2030 and direct impacts on biodiversity and carbon pools. *Proceedings of the National Academy of Sciences*, 109 (40), p. 16083–16088. [Online]. Available at: doi:10.1073/pnas.1211658109 [Accessed 28 January 2014].

Susca, T., Gaffin, S. R., and Dell'Osso, G. R. (2011). Positive effects of vegetation: Urban heat island and green roofs. *Environmental Pollution*, 159 (8–9), p. 2119–2126. [Online]. Available at: doi:10.1016/j.envpol.2011.03.007 [Accessed 22 January 2014].

Taha, H. (1997). Urban climates and heat islands: albedo, evapotranspiration, and anthropogenic heat. *Energy and Buildings*, 25 (2), p. 99–103. [Online]. Available at: doi:10.1016/S0378-7788(96)00999-1 [Accessed 23 January 2014].

Tereshchenko, I. E. and Filonov, A. E. (2001). Air temperature fluctuations in Guadalajara, Mexico, from 1926 to 1994 in relation to urban growth. *International Journal of Climatology*, 21 (4), p. 483–494. [Online]. Available at: doi:10.1002/joc.602 [Accessed 23 January 2014].

Tzoulas, K., Korpela, K., Venn, S., Yli-Pelkonen, V., Kaźmierczak, A., Niemela, J., and James, P. (2007). Promoting ecosystem and human health in urban areas using Green Infrastructure: A literature review. *Landscape and Urban Planning*, 81 (3), p. 167–178. [Online]. Available at: doi:10.1016/j.landurbplan.2007.02.001 [Accessed 22 January 2014].

Ulrich, R. (1984). View through a window may influence recovery. *Science*, 224 (4647), p. 224–225. [Accessed 13 February 2014].

United Nations. (2012). *World Urbanization Prospects. The 2011 Revision (United Nations, Department of Economic and Social Affairs, Population Division, New York)*.

Vos, P. E. J., Maiheu, B., Vankerkom, J., and Janssen, S. (2013). Improving local air quality in cities: To tree or not to tree? *Environmental Pollution*, 183, p. 113–122. [Online]. Available at: doi:10.1016/j.envpol.2012.10.021 [Accessed 11 August 2014].

Part A

Wang, X., Zhao, X., Zhang, Z., Yi, L., Zuo, L., Wen, Q., Liu, F., Xu, J., Hu, S., and Liu, B. (2016). Assessment of soil erosion change and its relationships with land use/cover change in China from the end of the 1980s to 2010. *CATENA*, 137, p. 256–268. [Online]. Available at: doi:10.1016/j.catena.2015.10.004.

Wilson, E. O. (1984). *Biophilia*. Cambridge, Mass: Harvard University Press.

Yin, S., Shen, Z., Zhou, P., Zou, X., Che, S., and Wang, W. (2011). Quantifying air pollution attenuation within urban parks: An experimental approach in Shanghai, China. *Environmental Pollution*, 159 (8–9), p. 2155–2163. [Online]. Available at: doi:10.1016/j. envpol.2011.03.009 [Accessed 22 January 2014].

Part A

Chapter 4
Water in Urban Areas: Ecological and Environmental Issues and Strategies

Paola Sabbion

4.1   Urbanisation and the water cycle

Water is among the major morphogenetic agents characterising landscapes. In natural conditions, water efficiently performs environmental basic functions. Moreover, water is an ecological infrastructure that ensures hydrologic, geological, biological, economic, social and cultural functions (Allan and Castillo, 2007). Water is based on interdependent systems, which produce a highly connected network of multi-functional elements, and provide benefits for the community and incentivise ecological restoration. Water systems are indeed involved in a broad range of issues from climate change mitigation to economic development (Pringle, 2003). The outcome document of the UN Conference Rio + 20 is in line with this vision and states that: "Water is at the centre of sustainable development since it is closely linked to a number of major global challenges" (UN, 2012). A directive of the European Parliament (2000/60/EC) also states that: "Water is not a commercial product like any other but, rather, a heritage which must be protected, defended and treated as such" (European Parliament, 2000).

Ancient civilisations have developed in symbiosis with a balanced use of water resources and have benefited greatly from this strategy (crop irrigation, fishing, trade and transport of goods, etc.). Modern water management practices, instead, often neglect traditional water drainage, production, collection and distribution. Water is at stake especially in cities where population growth and urban development cause density, lower permeability and increase flooding risk (White, 2013; Zevenbergen *et al.*, 2012). In modern cities, water infrastructure is often designed as a linear system, a collector to take rainwater and waste out of urban environments as fast as possible. This results in extreme impoverishment of its ecological vital functions (Walsh *et al.*, 2005). During the last century, almost everywhere, waterways have been heavily regimented and artificialised to maximise space for

Urban Sustainability and River Restoration: Green and Blue Infrastructure, First Edition.
Katia Perini and Paola Sabbion.
© 2017 John Wiley & Sons Ltd. Published 2017 by John Wiley & Sons Ltd.

Figure 4.1   Extensive Channelization on the Los Angeles River Featuring Concrete Embankments (photo by William Preston Bowling).

urban growth. In some cases, waterways have been completely fragmented, and have become mere collectors of city waste, which transect deprived and residual urban areas. Channelisation and culverts target river flow control, while width restriction seeks to obtain developable land for settlement and transport infrastructures with serious consequences for hydrogeological, environmental, and landscape systems (Brown *et al.*, 2009; Figure 4.1).

One of the fundamental functions of a healthy hydrological system is to retain water, allowing for stormwater runoff regulation and groundwater redistribution and recharge. The natural water cycle entails rain permeating into the ground and gradually filtering into rivers and groundwater. Forests and land covered with vegetation have a typical *sponge* effect (leaves, branches, shrubs and soil retain water and slow its movement). On the contrary, impervious urban surfaces often act as 'umbrellas' augmenting stormwater runoff. Water tends to flow faster due to lower permeability, river artificiality and rectification which cause the quantity and rate of surface runoff to increase, hydrogeological instability and flooding risk (Shuster *et al.*, 2005; Figure 4.2).

Hydrological disasters and floods cause extensive health and economic damages. The most expensive hydrological disaster occurred in Thailand in 2011 (estimated damages reached $42.1 billion). In 2005–2015 average, the sum of hydrological and meteorological disasters accounted for the greatest share of natural global disasters both for total damage and number of victims (EM-DAT) (Figure 4.3). In Europe, the number of hydrological disasters was the fourth highest since 2004 and showed a 45% increase compared to its decennial average. The most expensive flood, though, occurred in the Jammu and Kashmir region in India ($16 billion) and a similar phenomenon was registered in 2013 in East and

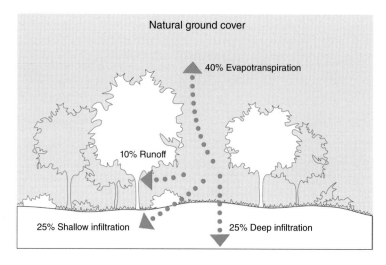

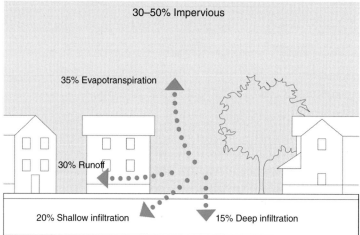

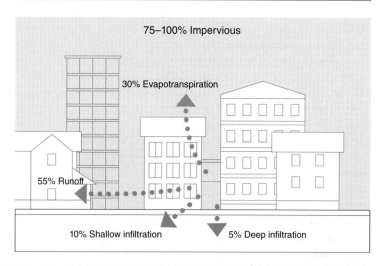

Figure 4.2   Permeability of Undeveloped and Developed Catchment Areas (based on US EPA).

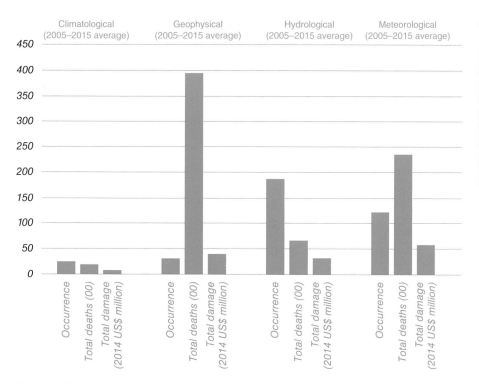

Figure 4.3   The Impact of Natural Disasters By Disaster Subgroup 2005–2015 average, Based on the EM-DAT: OFDA/CRED International Disaster Database.

South Germany ($12.9 billion; Guha-Sapir *et al.*, 2014). In the United States, the Midwest flood (2008, $11 billion), the Calgary region flood (2013, $8.8 billion), and the Mississippi flood (2011, $4.8 billion) are considered severe hydrological disasters in terms of their economic damage.

Conventional stormwater management approaches have often failed to pursue environmental preservation due to the incapacity to address the variations to the flow regime caused by conventional drainage. For example, in many cities (e.g., New York), during heavy rainstorms, combined sewers can receive high flows that treatment plants are unable to handle; the mix of stormwater and untreated wastewater discharges directly into the waterways, causing combined sewer overflows (CSOs).

Moreover, water coming into contact with anthropic surfaces collects toxic substances, fertilizers and pollutants that have a negative impact on ecosystems and fluvial and marine coasts. The reduction of the ecological quality of water is an emerging issue. Waterways in good condition naturally metabolise contaminants and are able to self-purify. Healthy hydrological systems also have a sufficient degree of *connectivity*, and can transfer matter, energy and/or organisms within or between the elements of the hydrological cycle (Jackson and Pringle, 2010). When a river ecosystem is disrupted, however, susceptible species decrease or disappear and the most pollutant-resistant prevail, resulting in less biodiversity and stability. For this reason, it is urgent to "ensure that the good status of surface water and groundwater is achieved and that deterioration in the status of waters is prevented" (European Parliament, 2000).

Since 1948, in the United States, the Clean Water Act (CWA) – and successive Amendments (1972) – have fulfilled these obligations and have governed water pollution, restoring and maintaining chemical, physical, and biological integrity of waters. The European Union has recently established the need to pursue the preservation, protection and improvement of the environmental quality and the rational use of water. European legislation is based on the principles of precaution and preventive action rather than remediation of environmental damage. Innovative aspects of the current European legislation are included in the Framework Directive 60/2000 (European Parliament, 2000) and in the Directive on the Protection of Underground Waters (2006/118/EC). These regulate the integration of management policies on drinking water, bathing, surface and groundwater; water alteration control; definition of environmental quality standards; and identification of significant trends of deterioration/recovery of water bodies. The EU has also established a geographical approach based on natural hydrological boundaries rather than administrative borders. This new regulatory framework outlines quality improvement objectives, defining for the first time ecological aspects as well as chemical aspects of surface waters.

4.2   Perspectives and strategies

Water management should undergo a radical reorganisation, especially within urban environments, where an intervention is most needed to save water resources and to control the biological and chemical status of flows. The concept of city as a self-sufficient system involves new redevelopment projects, based on a more balanced, efficient and competitive use of resources. It is also crucial to improve the urban environmental and ecological heritage. The public and private sectors and local communities should all support this model to contribute to its success. The desired outcome is an integrated approach balancing biophysical and socio-economic conditions with a planning strategy that integrates design, engineering and environmental issues (Feyen *et al.* (eds.), 2008).

Response to floods has changed during the last decades, as there has been a gradual transition from flood *control* to flood *management* (Zevenbergen *et al.*, 2012). Following the devastation produced by Hurricane Katrina in 1995, in the United States, floods have been controlled with dikes and dams. It has been ascertained that the removal of coastal wetlands and intensive settlement on floodplains has insofar contributed to impair the natural mechanisms of river basins, triggering potential catastrophes. Hence, as traditional top-down engineering strategies are not sufficient, more flexible and adaptive approaches are needed to design and plan human activities within ecological systems (Reed and Lister (eds.), 2014).

Laying the groundwork for a risk-management approach is mandatory: "Risk management rather than prevention forms the basis of evolving thinking about integrated flood and water management" (Barton *et al.*, 2015). Approaches and strategies are emerging at various scales (see Chapter 12): integrated catchment management (Blackmore, 1995; Batchelor, 1999); integrated flood risk management (Jha *et al.*, 2012); stormwater Best Management Practices (BMPs) in US and Canada, blue-green cities (Everett and Lamond, 2014) and Sustainable Urban

Drainage Systems (SuDS) in UK (Charlesworth *et al.*, 2003); water sensitive urban design (WSUD) in Australia (Ward *et al.*, 2012); Low Impact Development (LID) in US (Dietz, 2007); Low Impact Urban Development and Design (LIUDD) in New Zealand (Van Roon, 2005); transition town planning (Hopkins, 2014); Integrated Water Resource Management (IWRM); water urbanism (Feyen *et al.* (eds.), 2008) and integrated urban water management (Sharma *et al.*, 2008).

These concepts all stem from an approach that tends to integrate green and blue infrastructure (GBI) with urban planning. This strategy recognises the need to shift from traditional control solutions based on centralised storage and water distribution to new approaches, which focus on lower-risk areas, local collection and distribution, slower flows, and increased permeability. Urban planning employs these practices across various spatial scales oriented to the restoration of river basins and wetlands and the design of habitat corridors (Barton *et al.*, 2015).

The field of water management has been traditionally based on engineering, but has now become far more complex, since water managers have an expanding mandate to consider eco-system preservation and restoration, and protection of endangered species in peri-urban rivers (Furlong *et al.*, 2016; Morley and Karr, 2002). Unlike traditional water management, which is directed to the control of natural forces, the new approaches seek to mimic the processes typically occurring in natural undeveloped catchment areas. Urban stormwater management, therefore, should emphasise the protection of natural hydrologic processes, seeking to restore downstream natural flow regimes and provide essential ecosystem services. As stated by the OECD, UNEP and EU, urban settlements should be adjusted in relation to natural capital and climate change mitigation to lower the threats to hydro-morphology and decrease the impact of floods and droughts on human settlements (European Commission, 2013). Source control techniques for detention/retention of stormwater runoff through infiltration, vegetative uptake and evapotranspiration can reduce the need for stormwater storage and treatment systems.

There are several cities, around the world, where trans-disciplinary conservation of urban ecosystem services and water management are the foundation of urban design. GBI incorporation not only enhances the capacity of these cities to supply water and prevent flooding, but also provides health benefits and a better quality of life. This approach has been adopted over 20 years ago in Portland (Oregon): here catchment-scale green infrastructure, green streets, flood management, river restoration and wastewater services are integrated to deliver improved flood management and water supply. In Malmo (Sweden; Figure 4.4), the regeneration of the

Figure 4.4   Augustenborg, Malmö (photo by Antonina Manzo).

Part A

Augustenborg neighbourhood was at first driven by flood risk management (Kazmierczak and Carter, 2010), and the presence of green infrastructure has also improved the liveability of the city's open spaces.

Some American cities facing deindustrialisation and depopulation are setting an example, as policies are focusing on key redevelopment projects, such as enhancing the quality of accessible waterways. On the one hand, this has led to the discovery and exploitation of important historical heritage sites (e.g., Battery Park and Tidal Basin in New York, Fairmouth Water Works in Philadelphia, Figure 4.5). On the other hand, it has enhanced the construction of new public spaces, often recovering post-industrial and port areas (Figure 4.6).

A very interesting aspect of urban water management is the GBI redesign in cities and surrounding areas, involving ecological corridors and suburban contexts. Restoring urban water systems can be achieved by planning new systems of infiltration, retention, evapotranspiration and water control, through the selection of vegetation and the correct application of compatible construction techniques (see Chapter 6 and 7). This type of recovery addresses the specific hydrological problems of each city, without neglecting formal and spatial dimensions.

The effectiveness of such a virtuous system depends on the efficient use of financial resources, and the ability to engage communities in a shared programme (Feyen *et al.* (eds.), 2008). Policies should focus on long-term achievements, sustainable renewal of the urban environment, setting policy priorities and investments (see cases studies, Chapters 13.1–13.6). Such operations require a series of complex actions and planning to trigger an effective change (Feyen *et al.* (eds.), 2008).

Figure 4.5   Fairmouth Water Works in Philadelphia (photo by Gian Luca Porcile).

Figure 4.6   Hudson River Park, New York.

Therefore, limited financial resources and environmental problems present challenges but, at the same time, new opportunities arise for the development of the urban system through the recovery of its resources.

References

Allan, J. D. and Castillo, M. M. (2007). *Stream Ecology: Structure and function of running waters*. Springer Science & Business Media.

Barton, H., Thompson, S., Burgess, S., and Grant, M. (2015). *The Routledge Handbook of Planning for Health and Well-Being: Shaping a sustainable and healthy future*. Routledge.

Batchelor, C. (1999). Improving water use efficiency as part of integrated catchment management. *Agricultural Water Management*, 40 (2–3), p. 249–263. [Online]. Available at: doi:10.1016/S0378-3774(98)00125-5.

Blackmore, D. J. (1995). Murray-Darling basin commission: A case study in integrated catchment management. *Water Science and Technology*, 32 (5–6), p.15–25. [Online]. Available at: doi:10.1016/0273-1223(95)00642-7.

Brown, R. R., Keath, N., and Wong, T. H. F. (2009). Urban water management in cities: historical, current and future regimes. *Water Science and Technology*, 59 (5), p. 847–855. *Scopus* [Online]. Available at: doi:10.2166/wst.2009.029.

Charlesworth, S. M., Harker, E., and Rickard, S. (2003). A review of sustainable drainage systems (SuDS): A soft option for hard drainage questions? *Geography*, 88 (2), p. 99–107. *Scopus*.

Dietz, M. E. (2007). Low Impact Development Practices: A Review of Current Research and Recommendations for Future Directions. *Water, Air, and Soil Pollution*, 186 (1–4), p. 351–363. [Online]. Available at: doi:10.1007/s11270-007-9484-z.

EM-DAT: The OFDA/CRED International Disaster Database – www.emdat.be – Université Catholique de Louvain – Brussels – Belgium.

European Parliament. (2000). *Directive 2000/60/EC of the European Parliament and of the Council of 23 October 2000 establishing a framework for Community action in the field of water policy.*

Everett, G. and Lamond, J. (2014). *A conceptual framework for understanding behaviours and attitudes around 'Blue-Green' approaches to Flood-Risk Management.* In: 18 June 2014, p. 101–112. [Online]. Available at: doi:10.2495/FRIAR140091 [Accessed 15 December 2015].

European Commission. (2013). *Communication from the Commission to the European Parliament, the Council, the European Economic and Social Committee and the Committee of the Regions. "Green Infrastructure (GI) — Enhancing Europe's Natural Capital".*

Feyen, J., Shannon, K., and Neville, M. (eds.). (2008). *Water and Urban Development Paradigms: Towards an Integration of Engineering, Design and Management Approaches.* Boca Raton, Fla.; London: CRC Press.

Furlong, C., De Silva, S., Guthrie, L., and Considine, R. (2016). Developing a water infrastructure planning framework for the complex modern planning environment. *Utilities Policy*, 38, p. 1–10. [Online]. Available at: doi:10.1016/j.jup.2015.11.002.

Guha-Sapir, D., Hoyois, P., and Below, R. (2014). Annual disaster statistical review 2014. *Centre for Research on the Epidemiology of Disasters (CRED), Institute of Health and Society (IRSS), Université catholique de Louvain – Brussels, Belgium.* [Online]. Available at: http://www.disasters.ir/files/ADSR_2013.pdf [Accessed 12 December 2015].

Hopkins, R. (2014). *The Transition Handbook: From Oil Dependency to Local Resilience.* White River Junction, Vt.: UIT Cambridge Ltd.

Jackson, C. R. and Pringle, C. M. (2010). Ecological Benefits of Reduced Hydrologic Connectivity in Intensively Developed Landscapes. *BioScience*, 60 (1), p. 37–46. [Online]. Available at: doi:10.1525/bio.2010.60.1.8.

Jha, A. K., Bloch, R., and Lamond, J. (2012). *Cities and Flooding: A Guide to Integrated Urban Flood Risk Management for the 21st Century.* The World Bank. [Online]. Available at: http://elibrary.worldbank.org/doi/book/10.1596/978-0-8213-8866-2 [Accessed 15 December 2015].

Kazmierczak, A. and Carter, J. (2010). *Adaptation to climate change using green and blue infrastructure. A database of case studies.* [Online]. Available at: http://orca.cf.ac.uk/64906/1/Database_Final_no_hyperlinks.pdf [Accessed 15 December 2015].

Morley, S. A. and Karr, J. R. (2002). Assessing and restoring the health of urban streams in the Puget Sound Basin. *Conservation Biology*, 16 (6), p. 1498–1509. *Scopus* [Online]. Available at: doi:10.1046/j.1523-1739.2002.01067.x.

Pringle, C. (2003). The need for a more predictive understanding of hydrologic connectivity. *Aquatic Conservation: Marine and Freshwater Ecosystems*, 13 (6), p. 467–471. [Online]. Available at: doi:10.1002/aqc.603.

Reed, C. and Lister, N.-M. (eds.). (2014). *Projective Ecologies.* ACTAR, Harvard Graduate School of Design.

Sharma, A. K., Gray, S., Diaper, C., Liston, P., and Howe, C. (2008). Assessing integrated water management options for urban developments – Canberra case study. *Urban Water Journal*, 5 (2), p. 147–159. [Online]. Available at: doi:10.1080/15730620701736829.

Shuster, W. D., Bonta, J., Thurston, H., Warnemuende, E., and Smith, D. R. (2005). Impacts of impervious surface on watershed hydrology: A review. *Urban Water Journal*, 2 (4), p. 263–275. [Online]. Available at: doi:10.1080/15730620500386529.

UN. (2012). *Report of the United Nations Conference on Sustainable Development. Rio de Janeiro, Brazil, 20–22 June 2012.*

Van Roon, M. (2005). Emerging approaches to urban ecosystem management: The potential of low impact urban design and development principles. *Journal of Environmental Assessment Policy and Management*, 7 (1), p. 125–148. *Scopus* [Online]. Available at: doi:10.1142/S1464333205001943.

Walsh, C. J., Roy, A. H., Feminella, J. W., Cottingham, P. D., Groffman, P. M., and Morgan, I. R. P. (2005). The urban stream syndrome: Current knowledge and the search for a cure. *Journal of the North American Benthological Society*, 24 (3), p. 706–723. *Scopus* [Online]. Available at: doi:10.1899/0887-3593(2005)024\[0706:TUSSCK\]2.0.CO;2.

Ward, S., Lundy, L., Shaffer, P., Wong, T., Ashley, R., Arthur, S., Armitage, N. P., Walker, L., Brown, R., Deletic, A., and Butler, D. (2012). Water sensitive urban design in the city of the future. *WSUD 2012: Water sensitive urban design. Building the water sensitive community, 7th International Conference on Water Sensitive Urban Design*, Barton, A.C.T.: Engineers Australia, 2012: 79–86. [Accessed 15 December 2015].

White, I. (2013). *Water and the City: Risk, Resilience and Planning for a Sustainable Future*. Routledge.

Zevenbergen, C., Cashman, A., Evelpidou, N., Pasche, E., Garvin, S., and Ashley, R. (2012). *Urban Flood Management*. CRC Press.

Part A

Chapter 5
Ecosystem Services in Urban Areas – Social, Environmental, and Economic Benefits

Katia Perini

5.1   Human activities and ecosystems

Terrestrial ecosystems provide a number of vital services to people and society, including biodiversity, food, fibre, water resources, carbon sequestration, and recreation. The future capability of ecosystems to provide these services is determined by changes in socioeconomic characteristics, land use, biodiversity, atmospheric composition, and climate (Costanza *et al.*, 1992; Metzger *et al.*, 2006). Our planet is experiencing a rapid transition due to human activities and this trend is expected to accelerate in the next decades. For example, rising atmospheric carbon dioxide (CO_2) will result in global warming (see Chapter 2).

The importance of the services provided by ecosystems for human well-being seems most evident in cities, as urban centres depend on a healthy natural environment that continuously offers a range of benefits, known as ecosystem services (ES; Derkzen *et al.*, 2015). The latter include drinking water, clean air, healthy food, and protection against floods (TEEB, 2011). Moreover, ES moderate air pollution, noise and heat stress caused by urbanisation and land use changes (Larondelle and Haase, 2013).

According to the urban ecology approach, cities should be considered as ecological systems. Green areas, in fact, play a crucial role and their interconnection is crucial despite being often regarded as separate from human activities (Benedict *et al.*, 2006; van Bueren, 2012). Rosenzweig (2003) proposed the concept of *reconciliation ecology* claiming that diversification of anthropogenic habitats to support biodiversity is particularly relevant to cities as a realistic and practical solution (Francis and Lorimer, 2011). Urban ecosystems and biodiversity can be protected, coordinating and promoting the best management practices on multiple scales (McPhearson *et al.*, 2014). Mapping and modelling ecosystem services helps attain this goal (Crossman *et al.*, 2013).

Urban Sustainability and River Restoration: Green and Blue Infrastructure, First Edition.
Katia Perini and Paola Sabbion.
© 2017 John Wiley & Sons Ltd. Published 2017 by John Wiley & Sons Ltd.

Urban ecosystem services can be divided into four categories (TEEB, 2011): provisioning services, regulating services, habitat (or supporting services), and cultural services. *Provisioning services* concern the material or energy outputs supplied by ecosystems, for example, food, raw materials, fresh water, medicinal resources. *Regulating services* are defined as the services that ecosystems provide by regulating the quality of air and soil. In this category are also included flood and disease control, local climate and air quality regulation, carbon sequestration and storage, moderation of extreme events, waste-water treatment and erosion prevention, maintenance of soil fertility, pollination, and biological control. *Habitat services* pertain to living spaces for plants and animals and enhance the biological diversity of species and the variety of genes within populations. *Cultural services* regard the non-material benefits people obtain from ecosystems, which comprise aesthetic, spiritual, physical and psychological benefits, recreation and tourism (Figure 5.1).

5.2   Green and blue infrastructure supporting ecosystem health

Healthy ecosystems are the foundation of sustainable cities and have a strong impact on human well-being and most economic activities (TEEB, 2011). The 2013 European Commission defines green infrastructure as a "strategically planned network of natural and semi-natural areas with other environmental features designed and managed to deliver a wide range of ecosystem services" (European Commission, 2013; see Chapter 1). Such definition highlights the role of green and blue infrastructure (GBI) in providing ecosystem services, with the scope of delivering a range of environmental benefits, including the maintenance and improvement of ecological functions (Figure 5.2). GBI in cities enhances connectivity among ecological networks (i.e. set of ecosystems of one type are hence linked in a spatially coherent system; see Chapter 6). It preserves green spaces within the urban environment (European Environmental Agency, 2015; Derkzen *et al.*, 2015). A careful design of urban green space is certainly crucial for ecosystem services provision. A more detailed quantification and mapping of the supply of ecosystem services in cities is needed to devise healthier and climate-resilient urban systems.

The growing recognition of the intrinsic value of goods and services provided by vegetation highlights the need to restore damaged ecosystems. Prioritising restoration projects that deliver the greatest benefits can be very important, especially due to the limited resources dedicated to this purpose. This can be achieved by comparing the costs of different restoration projects, objectives and institutional contexts (Scemama and Levrel, 2016). For this reason, ecosystem services provided by GBI and related economic benefits need to be quantified.

5.3   Economic value of urban ecosystems

GBI has multiple benefits, even if it is difficult to quantify them in some cases. GBI integration in the urban context can indeed be a cost-effective strategy (TEEB, 2011). For example, a study based on the city of Los Angeles found that 1 million trees planted over a 35-year period saved $1.33 billion and $1.95

Provisioning services ···············   **Food.** Ecosystems provide the conditions for growing food

Raw materials. Ecosystems provide a great diversity of materials for construction and fuel (e.g. wood, biofuels)

Fresh water. Ecosystems play a vital role in providing cities with drinking water

Medicinal resources. Biodiverse ecosystems provide many plants used as traditional medicines as well as providing raw materials for the pharmaceutical industry.

Regulating services ···············   **Local climate and air quality regulation.** Vegetation lowers the temperature in cities and plays an important role in regulating air quality by removing pollutants from the atmosphere.

Carbon sequestration and storage. Ecosystems regulate the global climate by storing greenhouse gases.

Moderation of extreme events. Ecosystems and living organisms create buffers against natural disasters, thereby preventing or reducing damage from extreme weather events or natural hazards.

Waste-water treatment. Ecosystems filter effluents. Through the biological activity of microorganisms in the soil, most waste is broken down.

Erosion prevention and maintenance of soil fertility. Vegetation cover provides a vital regulating service by preventing soil erosion.

Pollination. Insects and wind pollinate plants which is essential for the development of fruits, vegetables and seeds.

Biological control. Ecosystems are important for regulating pests and vector borne diseases that attack plants, animals and people.

Habitat or Supporting services ······   **Habitats for species.** Habitats provide everything that an individual plant or animal needs to survive: food, water, and shelter.

Maintenance of genetic diversity. Genetic diversity provides the basis for locally well-adapted cultivars and a gene pool for developing commercial crops and livestock.

Cultural services ····················   **Recreation and mental and physical health.** Walking and playing sports in green space is a good form of physical exercise and helps people to relax.

Tourism. Ecosystems and biodiversity play an important role for many kinds of tourism which in turn provides considerable economic benefits.

Aesthetic appreciation and inspiration for culture, art and design. Language, knowledge and the natural environment have been intimately related throughout human history.

Spiritual experience and sense of place. Nature is a common element of all major religions and traditional knowledge, and associated customs are important for creating a sense of belonging.

Figure 5.1   Urban Ecosystem Services (based on TEEB, 2011).

Microclimate regulation
Vegetation mitigates the urban heat island effect

Water regulation
Permeable soils and vegetation reduce stormwater runoff

Pollution reduction and health effects
Urban vegetation can improve air quality with positive effects on human health and wellbeing

Habitat
Green and blue infrastructure can provide living spaces for plant and animal species

Cultural services
Green space in urban areas plays a positive role in enhancing human well-being

Figure 5.2   Example of services provided by GBI in urban areas (based on Elmqvist *et al.*, 2015).

billion for the high and low mortality scenarios, respectively. The average annual savings were estimated to be $38 and $56 for every tree that was planted (McPherson *et al.*, 2011).

The empirical analysis drawn from 25 case studies in the United States, Canada, and China based on the benefits of ecosystem services in urban areas and the resulting monetary value, demonstrates that the ecological restoration and rehabilitation of ecosystems such as rivers, lakes, and woodlands occurring in urban areas, is not only ecologically and socially desirable, but also often economically advantageous (Elmqvist *et al.*, 2015).

Important economic benefits can be obtained by providing regulating services. As described in Chapter 3, vegetation plays a fundamental role in the mitigation of the urban heat island effect. A research conducted by Akbari (2005) shows that such mitigation can reduce the national energy consumption for air conditioning up to 20% in the United States, saving more than $10 billion currently employed for energy consumption. The benefits related to UHI mitigation have also been quantified in Canberra, Australia, where – in addition to carbon sequestration and stormwater run-off reduction – the 400,000 trees planted within the city limits were estimated to provide benefits amounting to $4 million on an annual basis in terms of the value generated or savings occurred in the city (Brack, 2002). In addition, Nowak and Crane (2002) show that the annual gross carbon sequestration provided by trees in the United States amounts to 22.8 million tons of carbon per year, a sequestration service valued at $460 million.

GBI is becoming increasingly popular among cities due to the economic benefits provided by reducing stormwater runoff. For example, the use of wetlands as alternatives to conventional wastewater treatment (see Chapter 6) provides estimated savings between $785–$34,700 per hectare of wetland in the United States (Breaux et al., 1995). The U.S. Environmental Protection Agency demonstrated that in several cities (NYC, Philadelphia, Seattle, etc.) green infrastructure is more cost effective compared to grey alternatives (U.S. EPA, 2013).

Erosion prevention should also be mentioned. In the United States, investments to curb erosion are currently successful, but GBI would provide an estimated cost reduction of $5.24 for every $1 invested (Pimentel et al., 1995). As described in Chapter 4, hydrological disasters and floods cause extensive economic damage. Although GBI in most cases cannot be permanent, this type of intervention is useful as it is specifically designed according to a set context. Another interesting case is located in Vientiane, Lao People's Democratic Republic, where at least 6 times every year frequent heavy rainfall results in overflowing drains and urban flooding, damaging buildings and infrastructure. In this area, wetlands absorb floodwater, dramatically reducing damages, with a value calculated just under $5 million per year (Gerrad, 2011).

Several tools include GBI in urban areas and estimate their effects. For example, in Miami, USA, the CITYgreen tool systematically includes GBI such as parks, urban forests and wetlands into urban planning (TEEB, 2011; Förster, 2011). The ecosystem services provided in Miami relate mainly to stormwater protection, air and water quality improvement and climate regulation (i.e., all regulation services).

Cultural services and eco-tourism can educate people about the importance of biological diversity (TEEB, 2011). A model of how biodiversity stimulates the job market and offers business opportunities is provided by the Limburg case study. This Belgian province is densely populated and, thanks to the efforts of a local non-governmental organization, it is also the site of the country's first national park. The Hoge Kempen National Park protects biodiversity, while creating 400 jobs and stimulating private investment in tourism in a deindustrialised region. Tourists steadily appreciate the recovering nature on the location of former coal mines for its particular landscape and biodiversity values (Schops, 2011).

Ecosystems can inspire culture, art and design and contribute to the sense of place. In Melbourne, liveability and public health is supported by a network of regional parks, trails, foreshores and waterways. Local authorities recognise the health benefits stemming from the access to natural areas, which have been driven by relevant economic investments. Residents are encouraged to increase physical activity by visiting and engaging in activities in parks (Senior, 2011). This example proves that the size of green areas is important as well as the presence of informal green spaces such as allotments and neighbourhood green, which are equally attractive for recreational purposes (Van Herzele and Wiedemann, 2003; Figures 5.3–5.4).

Figure 5.3 Green Infrastructure and Biodiversity in Adelaide, Australia (photo by Lida Cataldi).

Figure 5.4 Recreation Opportunity Offered By Green Infrastructure in Amsterdam, the Netherlands.

References

Akbari, H. (2005). *Energy Saving Potentials and Air Quality Benefits of Urban Heat IslandMitigation.* [Online]. Available at: http://escholarship.org/uc/item/4qs5f42s.pdf [Accessed 22 January 2014].

Benedict, M. A., McMahon, E. T., and Conservation Fund. (2006). *Green infrastructure: linking landscapes and communities.* Washington, DC: Island Press.

Brack, C. L. (2002). Pollution mitigation and carbon sequestration by an urban forest. *Environmental Pollution*, 116, Supplement 1, p. S195–S200. [Online]. Available at: doi:10.1016/S0269-7491(01)00251-2 [Accessed: 11 January 2016].

Breaux, A., Farber, S., and Day, J. (1995). Using Natural Coastal Wetlands Systems for Wastewater Treatment: An Economic Benefit Analysis. *Journal of Environmental Management*, 44 (3), p. 285–291. [Online]. Available at: doi:10.1006/jema.1995.0046 [Accessed 12 January 2016].

Van Bueren, E., Itard, Laure, Visscher, Henk, van Bohemen, Hein. (2012). *Sustainable Urban Environments: An Ecosystem Approach.* Springer Science + Business Media B.V.

Costanza, R., Norton, B. G., and Haskell, B. D. (1992). *Ecosystem health: new goals for environmental management.* Washington, D.C.: Island Press.

Crossman, N. D., Burkhard, B., Nedkov, S., Willemen, L., Petz, K., Palomo, I., Drakou, E. G., Martín-Lopez, B., McPhearson, T., Boyanova, K., Alkemade, R., Egoh, B., Dunbar, M. B., and Maes, J. (2013). A blueprint for mapping and modelling ecosystem services. *Ecosystem Services*, 4, p. 4–14. [Online]. Available at: doi:10.1016/j.ecoser.2013.02.001 [Accessed 5 January 2016].

Derkzen, M. L., van Teeffelen, A. J. A., and Verburg, P. H. (2015). REVIEW: Quantifying urban ecosystem services based on high-resolution data of urban green space: an assessment for Rotterdam, the Netherlands. *Journal of Applied Ecology*, 52 (4), p. 1020–1032. [Online]. Available at: doi:10.1111/1365-2664.12469 [Accessed 9 October 2015].

Elmqvist, T., Setälä, H., Handel, S., van der Ploeg, S., Aronson, J., Blignaut, J., Gómez-Baggethun, E., Nowak, D., Kronenberg, J., and de Groot, R. (2015). Benefits of restoring ecosystem services in urban areas. *Current Opinion in Environmental Sustainability*, 14, p. 101–108. [Online]. Available at: doi:10.1016/j.cosust.2015.05.001 [Accessed 12 January 2016].

European Commission. (2013). *Green Infrastructure (GI) — Enhancing Europe's Natural Capital. Communication from the Commission to the European Parliament, the Council, the European Economic and Social Committee and the Committee of the Regions.* [Online]. Available at: http://eur-lex.europa.eu/LexUriServ/LexUriServ.do?uri=COM: 2013:0249:FIN:EN:PDF.

European Environmental Agency. (2015). *Exploring nature-based solutions. The role of green infrastructure in mitigating the impacts of weather- and climate change-related natural hazards.* [Online]. Available at: file://localhost/Users/katiaperini/Library/ Application%20Support/Zotero/Profiles/rwxgy8et.default/zotero/storage/DSES69X4/ exploring-nature-based-solutions-2014.html.

Förster, J. (2011). Multiple benefits of urban ecosystems: spatial planning in Miami, USA. In: *TEEB Manual for cities: ecosystem services in urban management.* [Online]. Available at: TEEBweb.org.

Francis, R. A. and Lorimer, J. (2011). Urban reconciliation ecology: The potential of living roofs and walls. *Journal of Environmental Management*, 92 (6), p. 1429–1437. [Online]. Available at: doi:10.1016/j.jenvman.2011.01.012 [Accessed: 30 January 2014].

Gerrad, P. (2011). Wetlands reduce damages to infrastructure, Lao People's Democratic Republic. In: *TEEB Manual for cities: ecosystem services in urban management.* [Online]. Available at: teebweb.org.

Van Herzele, A. and Wiedemann, T. (2003). A monitoring tool for the provision of accessible and attractive urban green spaces. *Landscape and Urban Planning*, 63 (2), p. 109–126. [Online]. Available at: doi:10.1016/S0169-2046(02)00192-5 [Accessed 5 January 2016].

Larondelle, N. and Haase, D. (2013). Urban ecosystem services assessment along a rural–urban gradient: A cross-analysis of European cities. *Ecological Indicators*, 29, p. 179–190. [Online]. Available at: doi:10.1016/j.ecolind.2012.12.022.

McPhearson, T., Hamstead, Z. A., and Kremer, P. (2014). Urban Ecosystem Services for Resilience Planning and Management in New York City. *Ambio*, 43 (4), p. 502–515. [Online]. Available at: doi:10.1007/s13280-014-0509-8 [Accessed 5 January 2016].

McPherson, E. G., Simpson, J. R., Xiao, Q., and Wu, C. (2011). Million trees Los Angeles canopy cover and benefit assessment. *Landscape and Urban Planning*, 99 (1), p. 40–50. [Online]. Available at: doi:10.1016/j.landurbplan.2010.08.011.

Metzger, M. J., Rounsevell, M. D. A., Acosta-Michlik, L., Leemans, R., and Schröter, D. (2006). The vulnerability of ecosystem services to land use change. *Agriculture, Ecosystems & Environment*, 114 (1), p. 69–85. [Online]. Available at: doi:10.1016/j.agee.2005.11.025 [Accessed 22 January 2014].

Nowak, D. J. and Crane, D. E. (2002). Carbon storage and sequestration by urban trees in the USA. *Environmental Pollution*, 116 (3), p. 381–389. [Online]. Available at: doi:10.1016/S0269-7491(01)00214-7 [Accessed 11 January 2016].

Pimentel, D., Harvey, C., Resosudarmo, P., Sinclair, K., Kurz, D., McNair, M., Crist, S., Shpritz, L., Fitton, L., Saffouri, R., and Blair, R. (1995). Environmental and economic costs of soil erosion and conservation benefits. *Science (New York, N.Y.)*, 267 (5201), p. 1117–1123. [Online]. Available at: doi:10.1126/science.267.5201.1117.

Rosenzweig, M. L. (2003). *Win-win ecology how the earth's species can survive in the midst of human enterprise*. Oxford; New York: Oxford University Press.

Scemama, P. and Levrel, H. (2016). Using Habitat Equivalency Analysis to Assess the Cost Effectiveness of Restoration Outcomes in Four Institutional Contexts. *Environmental Management*, 57 (1), p. 109–122. [Online]. Available at: doi:10.1007/s00267-015-0598-6 [Accessed 5 January 2016].

Schops, I. (2011). Developing the first national park in Belgium together with stakeholders. In: *TEEB Manual for cities: ecosystem services in urban management*. [Online]. Available at: teebweb.org.

Senior, J. (2011). *An Example of recreational services by city parks in Melbourne, Australia, in TEEB Manual for cities: ecosystem services in urban management*. [Online]. Available at: TEEBweb.org.

TEEB. (2011). TEEB Manual for cities: ecosystem services in urban management. In: UNEP and the European Union (ed.), *The economics of ecosystems and biodiversity. Manual for cities: Ecosystem services in urban management*.

US EPA. (2013). *Case Studies Analyzing the Economic Benefits of Low Impact Development and Green Infrastructure Programs Case Studies Analyzing the Economic Benefits of Low Impact Development and Green Infrastructure Programs*. Washington, D.C.

Part A

Part B
Strategies and Techniques

Urban Sustainability and River Restoration: Green and Blue Infrastructure, First Edition.
Katia Perini and Paola Sabbion.
© 2017 John Wiley & Sons Ltd. Published 2017 by John Wiley & Sons Ltd.

Chapter 6
Green and Blue Infrastructure – Vegetated Systems

Paola Sabbion

6.1   The role of GBI vegetation

Vegetation plays a key role in the implementation of green and blue infrastructure (GBI) because it provides a wide range of ecosystem services (as described in Chapters 1–5). GBI involves multiple environmental benefits and curbs climate change (through energy use reduction; climatic modification; temperature decrease; shading; evapotranspiration; wind speed modification). It also contributes to air quality improvement (emission avoidance; carbon sequestration; pollutant removal); water cycle re-naturalisation (canopy interception; flow control; flood reduction; soil infiltration and storage; water quality improvement); soil improvement (permeability increase; soil stabilisation; nutrient cycling; waste decomposition); biodiversity enhancement (habitat and corridor creation; species diversity fostering); food production (productive agricultural land and urban agriculture development); other economic benefits (property value rise; ecosystem service value; commercial vitality); social benefits (human health and well-being improvement; physical, social and psychological side-effects; community and cultural vitality; visual and aesthetic beautification.

GBI proves to be so effective also thanks to vegetation performing a number of hydrologic functions within the natural water cycle. For this reason, vegetation has become an important component of the Water Sensitive Urban Design (WSUD) strategies in Australia and of the Best Management Practices (BMPs) and Low Impact Development (LID) in the United States. These systems and related guidelines seek to replicate the natural water cycle in urban areas (see also Chapters 7 and 12). Hydrologic functions provided by trees and plants are canopy interception, stemflow, soil infiltration, evapotranspiration, hydraulic lift/redistribution, groundwater recharge, and conveyance of large storms (Figure 6.1). Water quality can similarly be improved by natural systems filtering pollutants (Benedict and McMahon, 2001).

Urban Sustainability and River Restoration: Green and Blue Infrastructure, First Edition.
Katia Perini and Paola Sabbion.
© 2017 John Wiley & Sons Ltd. Published 2017 by John Wiley & Sons Ltd.

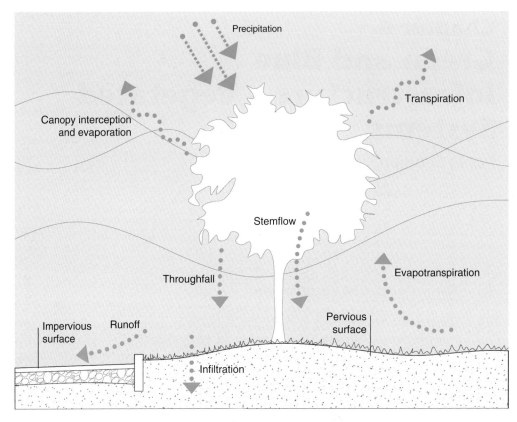

Figure 6.1   Role of Vegetation in the Natural Hydrologic Cycle.

Vegetation plays an important role with regard to biofiltration, as it enhances the capacity of soils to remove pollutants through a combination of biological, chemical, and physical processes (Riser-Roberts, 1998; Pilon-Smits, 2005). All these benefits can restore the ecological condition of urban rivers reduce overflow and flood risk, and increase water quality to enhance and protect biodiversity.

Selection of vegetation employed for GBI is based on the appropriateness of a plant according to the site conditions and programmatic requirements (its specific horticultural needs, its role on the site and in a larger plant community). A viable selection considers on-site climate, soils and hydric conditions as well as potential interactions between species, and future maintenance needs. For example, on a site that is likely to accumulate excess water it is necessary to identify and grow plants coming mostly from wetland communities. If the soil is contaminated by organic and inorganic pollutants, species to address phytoremediation should be selected (Calkins, 2011).

6.2   Multifunctional ecological systems in urban areas

The ecological structure of landscapes, according to ecologists, consists of matrix patches (the dominant feature) and relevant connecting corridors. Large patches should be preserved in urban areas to increase biodiversity and form new connections between the remnant patches and ecological/habitat corridors (Barnes, 1999). Corridors are often termed as *habitat corridors*, wildlife corridors, or ecological structures. Planning habitat corridors, linking patches with surrounding environments, can contribute to increase biodiversity and ecosystem health (see Chapter 5). Developing ecological networks revolves around a set of ecosystems, linked in a spatially coherent interconnection through the flows of organisms, and interacting with the landscape matrix in which they are embedded. This is a means of alleviating the ecological impacts of habitat fragmentation. For this reason, biodiversity conservation strategies are an integral part of sustainable landscape promotion (Opdam *et al.*, 2006). The elements and components of green infrastructure allow the improvement of ecosystem health, defined as the occurrence of normal ecosystem processes and functions, free from distress and degradation, maintaining organisation and autonomy over time and resilience to stress (Lu and Li, 2003). Heterogeneous habitats, which are characterised by species diversity and relative species and genes differentiation, are considered more resilient than homogeneous habitats (Loreau *et al.*, 2002). Heterogeneous habitats can influence the health of urban ecosystems by contributing to their resilience, organisation, and vigour (Tzoulas *et al.*, 2007). Biodiversity and ecosystem health are the key elements for the implementation of ecosystem services at every scale (Vergnes *et al.*, 2013).

GBI may provide the physical basis for ecological networks. *Ecological* and *habitat corridors*, in particular, are considered as landscape elements, which can counteract the negative effects of habitat fragmentation. Many countries have developed their own legal definitions of *corridor*, emphasising different objectives and approaches to biodiversity conservation (Jongman *et al.*, 2004) and identifying landscape management policies to protect and develop corridors within green frameworks from local to regional scales (Bryant, 2006; EEA, 2012; Jongman *et al.*, 2004; Vergnes *et al.*, 2013).

Ecological corridors usually have a linear structure – as they can be found on linear pieces of land, which are different from the surrounded matrix (Forman, 1995) – where plants and animals can travel from one area to another, increasing the movement of organisms among patches in fragmented landscapes or among landscape elements in a mosaic of habitat types (Hess and Fischer, 2001; Bailey, 2007; Gilbert-Norton *et al.*, 2010; Vergnes *et al.*, 2013; Figure 6.2). The restoration of natural riparian systems and wetlands found in river and stream corridors is one of the best practices to implement the natural equilibrium of flow, sediment movement, temperature, and biodiversity (see Chapter 8). The restoration process re-establishes the general structure, function, and dynamics of the ecosystem (National Research Council, 1992). Corridors can be part of ecological or habitat networks, but are sometimes held to be equivalent to greenways and green belts (Hilty *et al.*, 2006): many GBI elements work as habitat corridors, even if they have not been explicitly designed for this aim. For example, roadside vegetation, fencerows, domestic gardens, parks and greenways may fulfil the function of corridors to facilitate the connectivity for individual species or groups of species. Clearly, it is less feasible that entire ecological communities can benefit from corridors not purposely retained or restored to appropriate habitat conditions (Hilty *et al.*, 2006).

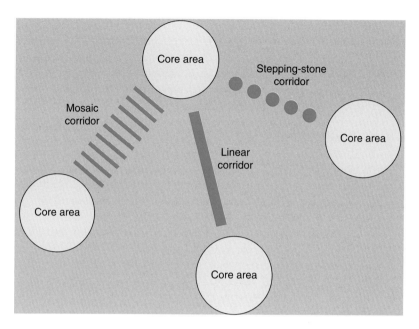

Figure 6.2 Ecological Network Scheme (Including Core Areas and Habitat Corridors) (based on Farina, 2001).

GBI may include *greenways*, which can be systematically planned to reduce private transportation and, consequently, lessen their impact on the city environment (Hamin and Gurran, 2009; Figure 6.3). *Greenway* is a term generally referred to linear multifunctional areas composed of vegetation (trees and shrubs or grasses), which are more natural than the surrounding environs (Mason *et al.*, 2007). Many scholars identify Frederick Law Olmsted as the founder of the *greenway movement* on account of his design of the Boston Emerald Necklace, which was devised to link a system of parks through the city of Boston (Fábos, 2004). As Fábos states, greenways provide a range of benefits, including preservation of environmental resources, wildlife habitat and ecological relations, floodplain protection, recreation and transportation, urban beautification, increased historical, cultural, and property value of urban and rural areas (Fábos, 1995). Current global greenway planning generally focuses on multiple purposes: control of urban expansion; edge buffering; scenic, economic, recreational benefits, and sometimes also addresses biodiversity conservation (Ahern, 1995). In the last decades, greenways have become a popular infrastructure, mitigating some of the negative effects of development in North America, Europe and Asia where hundreds of projects have been completed (Bryant, 2006; Jongman, 1995; Searns, 1995; Figure 6.4).

Greenways can have further ecological benefits in terms of enhancing biodiversity and creating linear systems for wildlife habitats. Even if greenways are often described as habitat corridors and generally foster species protection, the level of their contribution to wildlife conservation is unclear (Schiller and Horn, 1997; Sinclair *et al.*, 2005). Urban and suburban areas can be biologically rich, but generally the heavily built-up urban core does not support as many species – especially those that are native – as less urbanised areas (Alvey, 2006). Street planting often lacks species diversity, limiting

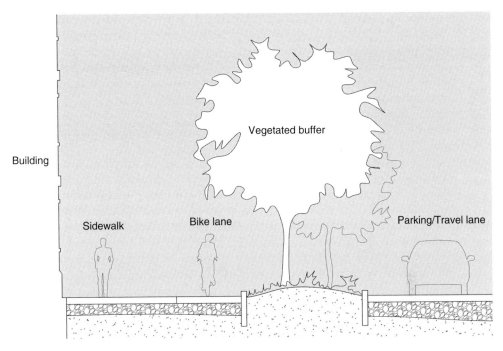

Building

Vegetated buffer

Sidewalk   Bike lane   Parking/Travel lane

Figure 6.3   Greenway Scheme.

Figure 6.4   Hudson River Park Greenway, NYC, New York.

biodiversity and exposing street tree populations to the threat of species-specific diseases. Urban planners have to investigate characteristics and environmental factors to contribute to greenway wildlife habitat values (Mason *et al.*, 2007). Ecologists and conservation biologists can play an important role in this endeavour by conducting research on wildlife-greenway relationships and disseminating their findings among land use planners (Miller and Hobbs, 2000; Broberg, 2003; Mason *et al.*, 2007). Researchers agree that greenway width, habitat quality within the greenway, and adjacent land use are the dominant factors affecting a greenway's value as wildlife habitat (Mason *et al.*, 2007; Rodewald and Bakermans, 2006).

Trees and vegetation can be efficiently used to reduce runoff and to counteract soil erosion in greenways, increasing the rate or volume of water infiltration into the soil. A part of the rainfall held in the canopy, flows slowly to the ground (Xiao and McPherson, 2002) where the plant roots increase the capacity and rate of rainfall infiltration, improving subsurface hydraulic conductivity and reducing surface flows (Bartens *et al.*, 2008). Street greening is also a growing practice in the United States and streets are progressively designed to manage and treat stormwater runoff. *Green streets* have been defined as "a constructed ecological network" (Thompson and Sorvig, 2007) based on vegetation potential or stormwater treatment. Green streets are usually planned together with other sustainable design practices, such as pedestrian and cycle paths; traffic moderation; and the scenic amelioration of streetscapes (Thompson and Sorvig, 2007). The design of green streets has been implemented especially in cities such as Portland (Podobnik, 2011; Sharifi, 2016), Seattle (City of Seattle, 2008), New York City (New York Department of Design and Construction, 2005) and Chicago (City of Chicago, nd), where a great number of permeable pavements and natural drainage projects with a subsoil infiltration system is currently being planned. Greenways can be effectively devised along urban rivers to reduce runoff, improve water quality, reduce soil erosion, and improve river conditions while providing recreational amenities, as demonstrated in the case of the Bronx River (NYC, see Chapters 9.1 and 13.1).

Greenways and open spaces can incorporate and connect BMP features for the mitigation of environmental impacts associated with runoff, integrating blue and GBI. These practices may create a hydrologic regime more similar to pre-development conditions, where total runoff volume is reduced through infiltration and storage (consequently reducing the impact of urban impervious surfaces on rivers); peak flows are lowered also through infiltration and flow retardance caused by increased channel roughness (Davis *et al.*, 2012; Figure 6.5).

Treatment BMPs are of particular interest since they provide connections among GBI. They can include vegetative biofilters (Filter Strip - Buffer Strip - Wet and Dry Vegetated Swales - Bioretention/Rain gardens), infiltration systems (Permeable Pavements - Infiltration Trench - Infiltration Pond - Bioretention/Rain gardens), and ponds (Detention and Retention basins - Dry Extended Detention Basin - Wet Retention Pond - Wetland Pond; EPA, 2004; Figure 6.6).

6.3   Vegetative biofilters

Buffer strips are linear areas consisting of gravel or pervious pavement that absorb stormwater in urban areas. They have greater aesthetic appeal if integrated with

Figure 6.5   New Kronsberg Settlement, Hannover (Germany): a Combination of Ponds, Trenches, Swales Integrated in Public Spaces (photo by Emanuele Sommariva).

sidewalks, curbs and other features. Usually buffer strips are combined with vegetated filter strips to prevent channelization and erosion. The most suitable plants for filter strips are low-maintenance herbaceous species which must be able to tolerate periodic inundation and pollutants (New York Department of Design and Construction, 2005).

Vegetative buffers strips are areas of land with a vegetative cover, which are designed to withstand runoff as overland sheet flow from upstream development. Dense vegetative cover facilitates sediment attenuation and pollutant removal. Filter strips are used to treat runoff from pervious surfaces such as roads, highways, roof downspouts, and small parking lots. They are effective for overland sheet flow, but provide little treatment for concentrated high volume flows; filter strips are often used as pre-treatment for other practices, such as infiltration basins.

Vegetated swales or bioswales are shallow trenches, open grass-lined channels or slopes used to slow the speed of surface runoff and allow stormwater to infiltrate into the ground instead of flowing directly into sewers. Bioswales are bio-filters for silt, pollutants and debris and can be a viable opportunity for the enhancement of wildlife habitat (City of Chicago, nd). Vegetated swales are used for both infiltration and filtration to provide pre-treatment before stormwater runoff is discharged into treatment systems (e.g., bioretention systems or other BMPs).

Part B

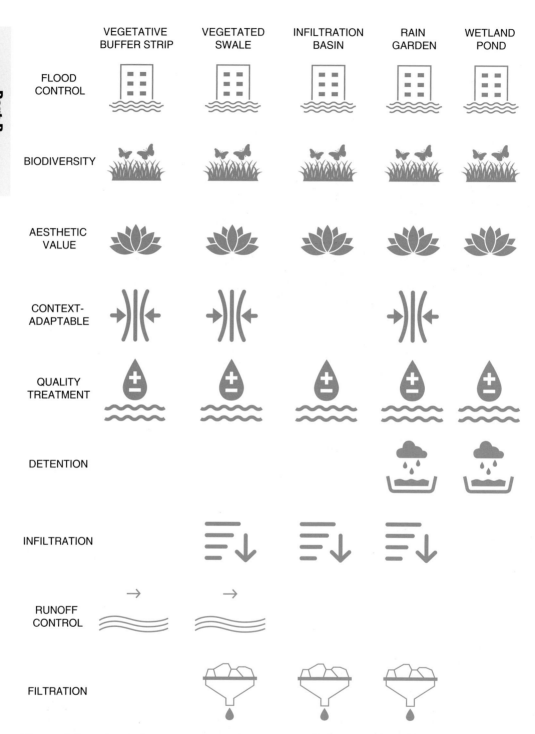

Figure 6.6   BMPs Performance Scheme (based on Mazzarello and Raimondo, 2015).

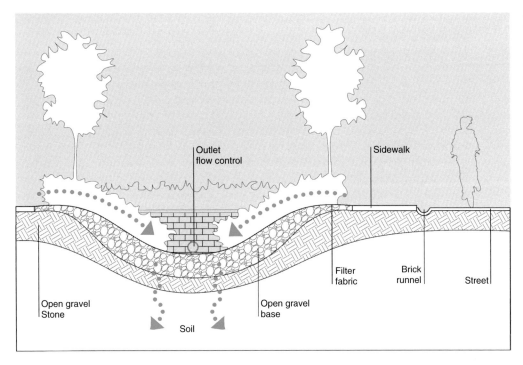

Figure 6.7   Section of a Vegetated Swale.

Swales have several advantages over conventional stormwater management practices, especially for their capacity to decrease peak flows, remove pollutants, and lower capital costs (promoting runoff infiltration they reduce the rate and the quantity of stormwater entering sewer systems and, consequently, this can moderate storm sewer piping and detention requirements).

However, vegetated swales are typically ineffective with high volumes/high flow velocity that can erode the vegetated cover. Some other limitations in the use of bioswales may occur in areas with very flat or steep topography, on undrained or erosive soils, and where it is difficult to maintain a dense vegetative cover. Negative environmental impacts of vegetated swales may include risk of pollutants infiltration through the swale into local groundwater. Finally, standing water in vegetated swales can result in odour and mosquito breeding (EPA, 1999; Figure 6.7).

6.4   Infiltration basins

Infiltration ponds or basins are dry ponds designed to allow water infiltration, often constructed as end-of-pipe BMPs to capture a defined volume of stormwater runoff and transform the water into groundwater flow. Filtration through the underlying soils and absorption remove pollutants. Infiltration ponds can also efficiently eliminate fine sediment, trace metals, nutrients, and bacteria.

Part B

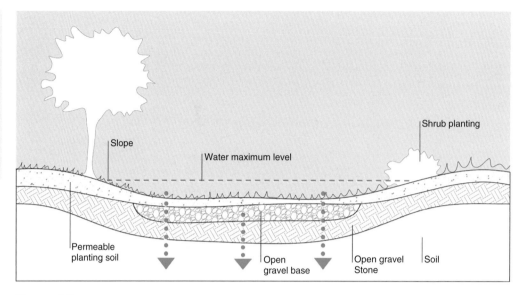

Figure 6.8   Section of an Infiltration Basin.

Vegetation plays a key role, increasing the infiltration capacity of the basin and impeding the erosion of the basin banks and floor. Infiltration ponds contribute to the groundwater recharge and the preservation of the natural water balance of the site. They can be useful to control the water volume and can often provide protection for the volume of the channel. Infiltration ponds, moreover, can not only reduce flood risk, but also curb thermal impacts on streams (EPA, 1999).

Infiltration ponds are typically used in residential watersheds, but are not recommended in karst areas, industrial parks, high-density areas, and polluted or chemical storage areas. They are not appropriate for treating heavy loads of sediment and pollutants due to potential clogging of the basin infiltration floor. The success of an infiltration pond depends on runoff pre-treatment in the overall design and on effective maintenance (Figure 6.8).

6.5   Bioretention Systems

Bioretention Systems (e.g., Rain Gardens) utilise soils and both shrubs and herbaceous plants to remove pollutants from stormwater runoff. Bioretention systems incorporate shallow depressions of the landscape that temporarily store and readily infiltrate runoff. These level depressions include both rain gardens and bioretention cells that provide stormwater treatment, removing fine sediments, heavy metals, phosphorous, nitrogen, hydrocarbons, bacteria, and organics through filtration, sedimentation, plant uptake, and biological processes (EPA, 1999). A rain garden relies solely on soils with good percolation rates, while bioretention cells typically include a rock chamber, subdrain, and modified soil mix. In bioretention cells, stormwater runoff collected in the upper layer of the system is filtered through the surface vegetation, mulch layer, pervious soil layer, and base layers

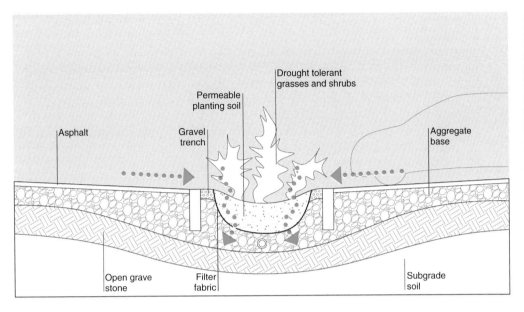

Figure 6.9   Section of a Rain Garden in a Parking Lot.

which are temporarily stored in a stone aggregate, and released over a period of few days by infiltration into the underlying soils or to an outlet through a perforated pipe subdrain. Bioretention systems are also able to provide shade and wind breaks, absorb noise, and improve landscapes (EPA, 1999).

Plants in bioretention cells enhance infiltration and provide evapotranspiration. Native species are more resistant to moisture changes and phytopathology and provide a greater uptake of runoff water and pollutants. Deep-rooted native plants (grasses and forbs) are recommended to provide high infiltration rates and aerobic conditions which are necessary to microbial activity for processing pollutants. Bioretention systems can be successfully used even on sites with limiting soils if a subdrain-system is provided. This system can be applied to both new and existing conditions, especially in urban areas, to manage the quantity and quality of water runoff volume from residential, commercial or industrial sites. It is suitable for highly impervious areas, such as parking lots, road medians, and street right-of-ways. It is not recommended for areas with slopes greater than 20%. Clogging may be a problem, particularly if the bioretention system receives runoff with high sediment loads that can cause premature failure. Integrated upstream treatment (i.e., perimeter grass filter strip or grass swale) could be needed to capture sediment. Finally, high entrance velocities and concentrated flows may need special design considerations (DNR, 2009; Figure 6.9).

6.6   Wetland ponds

Wet retention basins or wetland ponds contain a permanent pool of water with wetland vegetation, and are designed to remove pollutants from stormwater, providing water quality treatment. Runoff from each rain event is detained and treated in the pond until it is displaced by runoff from the next storm (EPA, 1999).

The natural physical, biological, and chemical processes of ponds work to remove pollutants. Sedimentation processes remove particulates, organic matter, and metals, while dissolved metals and nutrients are removed through biological uptake. In general, a higher level of nutrient removal and a more precise control of stormwater quantity can be achieved in wet detention ponds, while it is difficult to obtain similar results in other BMPs such as dry ponds, infiltration trenches, or sand filters. It is advisable to increase the settling area of sediments through the addition of a sediment forebay to enhance the effective removal of pollutants. Heavier sediments will drop out of suspension as runoff passes through the sediment forebay, while lighter sediments will settle as the runoff is retained in the permanent pool. A second common modification is the construction of shallow ledges along the edge of the permanent pool. The latter can be used to grow aquatic plants that can impede flow and trap pollutants. The ledges also have several other functions, which include preventing accidental drowning and providing easy access to the permanent pool for maintenance (EPA, 1999).

Moreover, temporary storage can be provided above the permanent pool elevation in wet ponds. Wetland ponds are typically used in low-density areas, and are not recommended for high-density residential urban areas. The advantages of wet ponds include a moderate to high removal of urban pollutants, as well as wildlife habitat and aesthetic/recreational value. Limitations of wet pond use are its low drainage, the need for base flow or supplemental water (ponds should not be constructed in areas where there is insufficient precipitation or on highly permeable-soils), mosquito breeding risk, the need of flat land and stable slopes, potential thermal impacts in downstream water (DNR, 2009). Highly developed areas may preclude the installation of a pond and the local climate (i.e., temperature) may affect the biological uptake. Finally, ponds require regular maintenance. Cleaning and maintaining the permanent pool is particularly important to prevent the emersion of trapped sediments. The accumulation of sediments in the pond reduces its storage capacity and performance. Therefore, the bottom silts in the permanent pools should be removed at least every 2 to 5 years (EPA, 2004; Figure 6.10).

6.7   Green roofs

Green roofs, which allow the growth of vegetation on built areas, can be interesting solutions providing most of the benefits of GBI especially with regard to the urban landscape design. Green roof areas on top of parking lots or car tunnels can provide a dense urban area with a park. An interesting example is the Madrid Rìo Project, described in Chapter 9.3, where a large green area is built on top of a motorway, allowing pines and other species to be planted.

Green roofs can reduce stormwater runoff, although urban thick substrate layers are more effective, reaching up to a 95% runoff reduction, while green roofs reach a 60% to 85% reduction depending on the type of green roof and vegetation (Kosareo and Ries, 2007; Scholz-Barth, 2001). Green roofs also improve water quality, although some roofing materials may add chemicals or

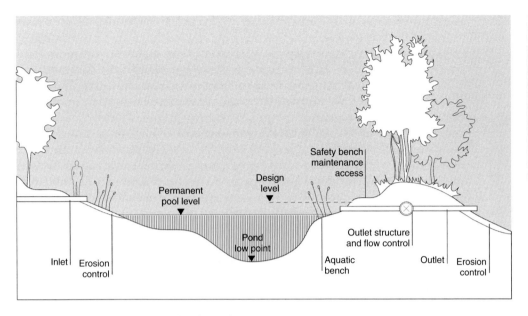

Figure 6.10   Section of a Wetland Pond.

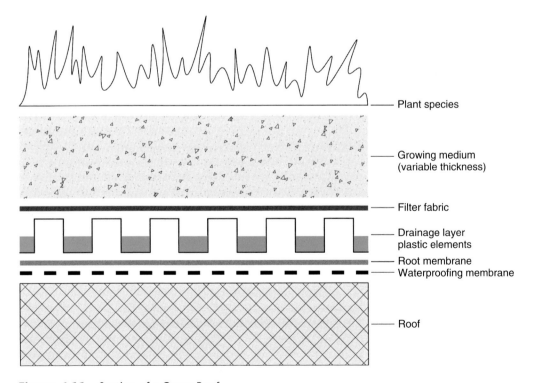

Figure 6.11   Section of a Green Roof.

metal compounds to the runoff water (Bianchini and Hewage, 2012). Other materials, such as used or reused waste, could replace the current use of polymers to enhance overall sustainability of green roofs, since green roof materials often use polymers for all the layers except as a growing medium.

The many products available on the market offer several integrated solutions for proper drainage, waterproofing, and roof protection depending on the vegetation type, such as grass and bigger or smaller shrubs. These are commonly classified in intensive, semi-intensive and extensive solutions and have different uses, stratigraphy and vegetation. For every type of green roof substrate thickness (given by the plant species used), maintenance needed, system weight, obtainable microclimatic benefits, aesthetic, costs, and use are different (Dunnett and Kingsbury, 2008; Perini, 2013). Intensive green roofs can create gardens at several heights, with a 30-100 cm (or more) thick substrate. Such systems are the ones used to green parking lot roofs and other grey infrastructures.

References

Ahern, J. (1995). Greenways as a planning strategy. *Landscape and Urban Planning*, 33 (1–3), p. 131–155. [Online]. Available at: doi:10.1016/0169-2046(95)02039-V.

Alvey, A. A. (2006). Promoting and preserving biodiversity in the urban forest. *Urban Forestry & Urban Greening*, 5 (4), p. 195–201. [Online]. Available at: doi:10.1016/j.ufug.2006.09.003.

Bailey, S. (2007). Increasing connectivity in fragmented landscapes: An investigation of evidence for biodiversity gain in woodlands. *Forest Ecology and Management*, 238 (1–3), p. 7–23. [Online]. Available at: doi:10.1016/j.foreco.2006.09.049.

Barnes, T. G. (1999). *A Guide to Urban Habitat Conservation Planning. For-74, Cooperative Extension Service, Kentucky State University, College of Agriculture.*

Bartens, J., Day, S. D., Harris, J. R., Dove, J. E. and Wynn, T. M. (2008). Can Urban Tree Roots Improve Infiltration through Compacted Subsoils for Stormwater Management? *Journal of Environment Quality*, 37 (6), p. 2048. [Online]. Available at: doi:10.2134/jeq2008.0117.

Benedict, M. A. and McMahon, E. T. (2001). *Green infrastructure: smart conservation for the 21st century*. [Online]. Available at: http://www.sprawlwatch.org/greeninfrastructure.pdf.

Bianchini, F. and Hewage, K. (2012). Probabilistic social cost-benefit analysis for green roofs: A lifecycle approach. *Building and Environment*. [Online]. Available at: http://www.sciencedirect.com/science/article/pii/S036013231200193X [Accessed 22 January 2014].

Broberg, L. (2003). Conserving ecosystems locally: a role for ecologists in land-use planning. *BioScience*, 53 (7), p. 670–673. [Online]. Available at: doi:10.1641/0006-3568(2003)053[0670:CELARF]2.0.CO;2.

Bryant, M. M. (2006). Urban landscape conservation and the role of ecological greenways at local and metropolitan scales. *Landscape and Urban Planning*, 76 (1–4), p. 23–44. [Online]. Available at: doi:10.1016/j.landurbplan.2004.09.029.

Calkins, M. (2011). *The Sustainable Sites Handbook: A Complete Guide to the Principles, Strategies, and Best Practices for Sustainable Landscapes*. John Wiley & Sons.

City of Chicago, Daley, R. M.-M., Byrne, T. G., and Attarian, J. L. (nd). *The Chicago Green Alley Handbook. An Action Guide to Create a Greener, Environmentally Sustainable Chicago*. City of Chicago, Streetscape & Urban Design Program, Department of Transportation.

City of Seattle. (2008). *Seattle's Natural Drainage Systems*. Seattle Public Utilities.

Davis, A. P., Stagge, J. H., Jamil, E., and Kim, H. (2012). Hydraulic performance of grass swales for managing highway runoff. *Water Research*, 46 (20), p. 6775–6786. [Online]. Available at: doi:10.1016/j.watres.2011.10.017.

DNR. (2009). *Iowa Stormwater Management Manual*. Iowa Department of Natural Resources.

Dunnett, N. and Kingsbury, N. (2008). *Planting green roofs and living walls*. Portland, Or. Timber Press.

EEA. (2012). *Annual report 2011and Environmental statement 2012*.

EPA. (1999). *Storm Water Technology Fact Sheet: Vegetated Swales*. United States Environmental Protection Agency, Office of Water Washington, D.C., 832-F-99-006.

EPA. (2004). *Stormwater Best Management Practice Design Guide*: National Risk Management Research, Laboratory Office of Research and Development, U.S. Environmental Protection Agency.

Fábos, J. G. (1995). Introduction and overview: the greenway movement, uses and potentials of greenways. *Landscape and Urban Planning*, 33 (1–3), p. 1–13. [Online]. Available at: doi:10.1016/0169-2046(95)02035-R.

Fábos, J. G. (2004). Greenway planning in the United States: its origins and recent case studies. *Landscape and Urban Planning*, 68 (2–3), p. 321–342. [Online]. Available at: doi:10.1016/j.landurbplan.2003.07.003.

Farina, A. (2001). *Ecologia del paesaggio: principi, metodi e applicazioni*. UTET.

Forman, R. T. T. (1995). *Land Mosaics: The Ecology of Landscapes and Regions*. Cambridge University Press.

Gilbert-Norton, L., Wilson, R., Stevens, J. R. and Beard, K. H. (2010). A Meta-Analytic Review of Corridor Effectiveness. *Conservation Biology*, 24 (3), p. 660–668. [Online]. Available at: doi:10.1111/j.1523-1739.2010.01450.x.

Hamin, E. M. and Gurran, N. (2009). Urban form and climate change: Balancing adaptation and mitigation in the U.S. and Australia. *Habitat International*, 33 (3), p. 238–245. [Online]. Available at: doi:10.1016/j.habitatint.2008.10.005 [Accessed 22 January 2014].

Hess, G. R. and Fischer, R. A. (2001). Communicating clearly about conservation corridors. *Landscape and urban planning*, 55 (3), p. 195–208.

Hilty, J. A. et al. (2006). *Corridor Ecology: The Science and Practice of Linking Landscapes for Biodiversity Conservation*. Washington, DC: Island Press.

Jongman, R. H. G. (1995). Nature conservation planning in Europe: developing ecological networks. *Landscape and Urban Planning*, 32 (3), p. 169–183. [Online]. Available at: doi:10.1016/0169-2046(95)00197-O.

Jongman, R., Külvik, M. and Kristiansen, I. (2004). *European ecological networks and greenways*. *Landscape and Urban Planning* 68:305–319.

Kosareo, L. and Ries, R. (2007). Comparative environmental life cycle assessment of green roofs. *Building and Environment*, 42 (7), p. 2606–2613. [Online]. Available at: doi:10.1016/j.buildenv.2006.06.019 [Accessed 22 January 2014].

Loreau, M., Naeem, S. and Inchausti, P. (2002). *Biodiversity and Ecosystem Functioning: Synthesis and Perspectives*. Oxford University Press.

Lu, F. and Li, Z. (2003). A model of ecosystem health and its application. *Ecological Modelling*, 170 (1), p. 55–59. [Online]. Available at: doi:10.1016/S0304-3800(03)00300-4 [Accessed: 19 February 2014].

Mason, J., Moorman, C., Hess, G. and Sinclair, K. (2007). Designing suburban greenways to provide habitat for forest-breeding birds. *Landscape and Urban Planning*, 80 (1–2), p. 153–164. [Online]. Available at: doi:10.1016/j.landurbplan.2006.07.002.

Mazzarello, M. and Raimondo, M. (2015). *Infrastrutture verdi: una gestione alternativa delle acque meteoriche*. University of Genoa.

Miller, J. R. and Hobbs, N. T. (2000). Recreational trails, human activity, and nest predation in lowland riparian areas. *Landscape and Urban Planning*, 50 (4), p. 227–236. [Online]. Available at: doi:10.1016/S0169-2046(00)00091-8.

Part B

National Research Council (NRC). (1992). *Restoration of Aquatic Ecosystems: Science, Technology, and Public Policy*. Washington, D.C.: National Academies Press. [Online]. Available at: http://www.nap.edu/catalog/1807 [Accessed 9 November 2015].

New York Department of Design and Construction. (2005). *High performance infrastructure guidelines: best practices for the public right-of-way : New York City, October 2005*. [New York]: New York City Department of Design + Construction : Design Trust for Public Space.

Opdam, P., Steingröver, E. and Rooij, S. van. (2006). Ecological networks: A spatial concept for multi-actor planning of sustainable landscapes. *Landscape and Urban Planning*, 75 (3–4), p. 322–332. [Online]. Available at: doi:10.1016/j.landurbplan.2005.02.015 [Accessed 6 February 2014].

Perini, K. (2013). *Progettare il verde in città: una strategia per l'architettura sostenibile*. Milano: F. Angeli.

Pilon-Smits, E. (2005). Phytoremediation. *Annual Review of Plant Biology*, 56 (1), p.15–39. [Online]. Available at: doi:10.1146/annurev.arplant.56.032604.144214.

Podobnik, B. (2011). Assessing the social and environmental achievements of New Urbanism: Evidence from Portland, Oregon. *Journal of Urbanism*, 4 (2), p. 105–126. *Scopus* [Online]. Available at: doi:10.1080/17549175.2011.596271.

Riser-Roberts, E. (1998). *Remediation of Petroleum Contaminated Soils: Biological, Physical, and Chemical Processes*. CRC Press.

Rodewald, A. D. and Bakermans, M. H. (2006). What is the appropriate paradigm for riparian forest conservation? *Biological Conservation*, 128 (2), p. 193–200. *Scopus* [Online]. Available at: doi:10.1016/j.biocon.2005.09.041.

Schiller, A. and Horn, S. P. (1997). Wildlife conservation in urban greenways of the mid-southeastern United States. *Urban Ecosystems*, 1 (2), p. 103–116. [Online]. Available at: doi:10.1023/A:1018515309254.

Scholz-Barth, K. (2001). Green Roofs: Stormwater Management From the Top Down. *Environmental Design & Construction, Feature*, January/February 2001. [Online]. Available at: http://www.usgbccc.org/documents/StormWaterManagement.pdf [Accessed 30 January 2014].

Searns, R. M. (1995). The evolution of greenways as an adaptive urban landscape form. *Landscape and Urban Planning*, 33 (1–3), p. 65–80. [Online]. Available at: doi:10.1016 /0169-2046(94)02014-7.

Sharifi, A. (2016). From Garden City to Eco-urbanism: The quest for sustainable neighborhood development. *Sustainable Cities and Society*, 20, p. 1–16. [Online]. Available at: doi:10.1016/j.scs.2015.09.002.

Sinclair, K. E., Hess, G. R., Moorman, C. E. and Mason, J. H. (2005). Mammalian nest predators respond to greenway width, landscape context and habitat structure. *Landscape and Urban Planning*, 71 (2–4), p. 277–293. [Online]. Available at: doi:10.1016/j.landurbplan.2004.04.001.

Thompson, J. W. and Sorvig, K. (2007). *Sustainable Landscape Construction: A Guide to Green Building Outdoors*. Washington: Island Press.

Tzoulas, K., Korpela, K., Venn, S., Yli-Pelkonen, V., Kaźmierczak, A., Niemela, J. and James, P. (2007). Promoting ecosystem and human health in urban areas using Green Infrastructure: A literature review. *Landscape and Urban Planning*, 81 (3), p. 167–178. [Online]. Available at: doi:10.1016/j.landurbplan.2007.02.001 [Accessed 22 January 2014].

Vergnes, A., Kerbiriou, C. and Clergeau, P. (2013). Ecological corridors also operate in an urban matrix: A test case with garden shrews. *Urban Ecosystems*, 16 (3), p. 511–525. [Online]. Available at: doi:10.1007/s11252-013-0289-0.

Xiao, Q. and McPherson, E. G. (2002). Rainfall interception by Santa Monica's municipal urban forest. *Urban Ecosystems*, 6 (4), p. 291–302.

Part B

Chapter 7
Green and Blue Infrastructure – Unvegetated Systems

Katia Perini

7.1 Unvegetated green and blue infrastructure

Stormwater management in urban areas is of great importance to prevent flood risks and environmental quality. For this reason, different green and blue management strategies should be integrated in urban settings. Even if vegetation provides many benefits, as described in Chapter 6, unvegetated green and blue infrastructure (GBI) can offer interesting solutions when vegetated systems cannot be used due to maintenance problems or lack of space, specific conditions of the urban context or other limitations. The unvegetated GBI systems can effectively reduce stormwater runoff, improving water quality, and can help to process high water volumes. Integrating water squares, trenches, and pervious paving in urban areas can indeed reduce water-related issues, and these elements can be located in mono-functional spaces or under-used areas to improve urban aesthetics. These systems, in fact, can be devised on most impervious surfaces, including parking lots and private local access roads, with limited or lighter traffic, as well as heavy-traffic roads and emergency lanes (Newman et al., 2013). GBI is usually set in contexts which are not fully used, as parking areas that are designed for peak traffic but are mostly not used at their full capacity every day (Brattebo and Booth, 2003). These systems can be also combined with vegetated systems and comprise water squares, porous paving/pervious paving and infiltration trenches. These elements can be combined in series to form treatment trains to manage stormwater from its source to restore the natural drainage system.

Urban Sustainability and River Restoration: Green and Blue Infrastructure, First Edition.
Katia Perini and Paola Sabbion.
© 2017 John Wiley & Sons Ltd. Published 2017 by John Wiley & Sons Ltd.

7.2   Water squares

Water squares combine water storage and creation of public spaces. Both functions are important in dense urban areas. These unvegetated systems consist of one or more paved basins (similar to pools), usually dry, and accessible for recreational uses, as basketball courts or skateparks. When medium rainfall occurs, water can be filtered and stored in water tanks, while during intense events a significant amount of water can be collected in visible basins. Water squares allow introducing this water collected during storms in the water management system, reducing the risk of collapse (European Commission, 2016; Longo *et al.*, 2016). Rainfall water remains in the water squares until the drain system condition normalises and then reaches the underground piping system (De Urbanisten, 2016). The latter can be designed with several basins, allowing for its progressive filling. In general, intense events occur once or twice per year, therefore, the recreational function is prevalent. Water cannot be stored for more than 32 hours due to hygienic reasons (Longo et al., 2016). In addition, water is filtered before flowing into squares, with a consequent water quality improvement. This "twofold strategy" offers the opportunity of investing money for water storage facilities while providing enjoyable public spaces and recreational areas in neighbourhoods (De Urbanisten, 2016).

The multidisciplinary group De Urbanisten, in collaboration with Marco Vermeulen Studio, launched water square systems at the second International Architecture Biennale held in Rotterdam in 2005. This exhibition, titled *The Flood*, focused on water and urban design to achieve climate change adaptation in the Netherlands and around the world (IABR, 2005). The water square project was developed thanks to the involvement of the Rotterdam Municipality and was based on the creation of dynamic and attractive urban areas to stimulate economic and social development.

This project demonstrated that the economic resources allocated for the construction of traditional stormwater infrastructure could be invested on water squares, which are visible, usable, accessible structures in public spaces with functional and aesthetic characteristics (Longo *et al.*, 2016). These water storage facilities are devised around a central paved sports field delimited by bleachers. Rainfall is directed to the basins through steel gutters running along the square (European Commission, 2016). In case of heavy rains, the square is gradually filled by rainfall water, reaching different filling levels up to the retention capacity of $1,700\,m^3$ (De Urbanisten, 2016). The water square project was first planned in 2006–2007 and later became an integrated part of the city policy in the *Rotterdam Waterplan 2*. After a pilot study in 2008–2009, the designers delivered the graphic novel *De Urbanisten and the Wondrous Water square* to inform a wider public (De Urbanisten, 2016; Dutch Water Sector, 2012).

Rotterdam's first water square system, Benthemplein, was opened in 2013 and features outdoor sports venues, green areas and even a theatre (European Commission, 2016). This is the first water square system ever built. The system has been designed as a meeting place while managing rainfall and curbing potential floods in Rotterdam's sewage system, reducing the impact of urban rainwater on the Maas River. It encompasses three different basins, having different depths, which are progressively filled with filtered rainwater during storm events. A self-watering system for the nearby vegetated areas is also included.

Figure 7.1   Rotterdam Water Square, the Netherlands.

Figure 7.2   Rotterdam Water Square, the Netherlands.

The case of this water square is important because it responds to the need of Rotterdam and the Schieland and Krimpenerwaard District Water Board (the south Holland water board) to achieve water and climate goals (European Commission, 2016).

7.3   Porous paving/pervious paving

As described in Chapter 5, impervious surfaces in urban areas are responsible for high levels of stormwater runoff. Impervious pavements cover the majority of parking areas, roadways, and roofs (Torres *et al.*, 2015). Pervious pavements can be a sustainable alternative to conventional paving to allow water infiltration and effective means to address important environmental issues (Pervious Pavement, 2011; Barrett *et al.*, 2009). Porous paving systems are recommended as Best Management Practices (BMPs) by the U.S. Environmental Protection Agency (EPA) to meet stormwater regulations.

Permeable pavement systems (PPS) can be successfully used in case of increased urban runoff and decreased water quality due to traffic runoff pollution (Brattebo and Booth, 2003). In fact, water can pass through porous paving and subsurface flow, it can then be filtered before reaching the drainage systems or joining the groundwater (Melbourne Water, 2016a). PPS can be integrated in dense urban areas to face important water management issues by reducing the amount of stormwater from impervious surfaces (diminishing peaks), increasing groundwater recharges, improving water quality while maintaining other functions. Physical screening, separation processes and rapid sedimentation of gross pollutants and coarse sediments are primary and secondary treatments which ensure water quality improvement (Melbourne Water, 2016a). When water penetrates through porous paving layers, nonpoint source pollution (NPS, identified among the

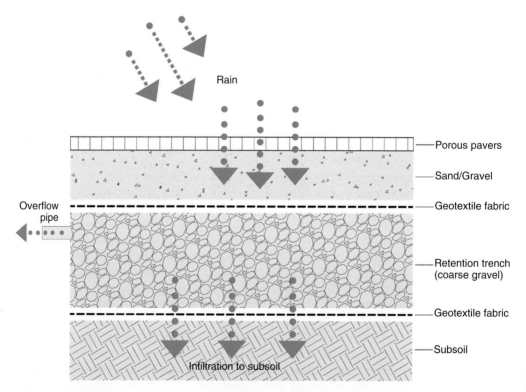

Figure 7.3   Section of a Porous paving/pervious paving.

causes of water quality degradation in the United States) control can be obtained, since NPS pollution derives from precipitation, land runoff, drainage and seepage (Barrett *et al.*, 2009).

PPS typically consist of concrete block pavers designed to create infiltration channels so that water can reach the storage area beneath, i.e. sand/gravel sub-base over natural soil. Water then infiltrates the surrounding soil or is gradually released into drainage systems and, later, into watercourses (Newman *et al.*, 2013; Melbourne Water, 2016a). A subsoil drainage is needed below the sub-base to allow stormwater overflow in the drainage system if the soil is impermeable. Other materials for the surface layer can be used - as pervious asphalt or porous asphalt paving and pervious concrete pour (in situ) or precast concrete porous grid paving - to mitigate the impacts of stormwater runoff in urban areas (Pratt, 1995; Melbourne Water, 2016b). Plastic porous paving is mostly used in modular blocks with cavities filled with gravel, sand, or soil and grass on a sand or gravel base. Rainfall drains through these cavities into the sand/gravel layer and hence into a geotextile layer. In some cases, retention trenches can be placed below. An overflow drives water to the drainage system. Porous paving, moreover, can be more suitable to plant grass in hot climates, compared to concrete grid pavers, which can overheat causing damages to the vegetation (Melbourne Water, 2016a). Concrete, although, can provide more interesting solutions in terms of structural performance. According to Barrett *et al.* (2009) and to the American Concrete Institute (2010), a thin layer of Portland cement paste and a coarse aggregate (with a thickness which depends on the amount of cement used) preserves structural performance. Aggregate coating thickness affects porosity and mechanical properties. The size of the coarse aggregate and the volume, size and distribution of voids and amount of cement has an impact on infiltration performances (American Concrete Institute, 2010; Montes *et al.*, 2005). Voids can be designed to facilitate penetration or can be the result of entrained air in the mortar (i.e., cementitious material), which surrounds the aggregate (Kevern et al., 2010). According to Montes et al. (2005), interruption of fluid flow can occur (*inactive porosity*) with very compact or small course aggregate (<5 mm) which create small voids trapping the fluid due to the effects of surface tension and capillary action.

Porous paving/pervious pavers retain pollutants (close to source) reduce rain water run-off, lessen flood peaks and increase groundwater input. Some disadvantages, although, can lead to limits in the use of these systems as the reduced traffic load they can support, occasional unsatisfactory performances and risk of groundwater contamination due to possible pavement clogging. In addition, these systems are only suitable for mildly sloped sites (Melbourne Water, 2016a).

7.4   Infiltration trenches

Maimone *et al.* (2011), Ku *et al.* (1992), Alectia (2016) and Göbel *et al.* (2004) present several case studies based on infiltration trenches at the urban scale, showing that integrating widespread stormwater infiltration allows increasing groundwater levels. This function is crucial, especially with low soil conductivity and with shallow groundwater tables. In general, different types of infiltration systems have different uses. The most common are simple gravel-filled trench systems or rain gardens. In the second case scenario (described in Chapter 6), the maximum pollutant removal is achieved prior to infiltration and plant action (Melbourne Water, 2016a).

Infiltration trenches can successfully improve water quality (via rainwater treatment) and reduce peak flows in sewer systems, recharging groundwater. An infiltration trench is a shallow excavation filled with gravel, rubble or stone and lined with a geotextile and backfilled. Such layer creates temporary subsurface storage of stormwater runoff (Stormwater Management, n.d.; SuDS Wales, 2016a). These long thin soakaways allow for the runoff to gradually infiltrate into the subsoil. Treatments include a physical screening sedimentation for coarse and fine infiltration (i.e., primary treatment), biological pollutant uptake (secondary treatment), heavy metals and retentions (tertiary treatment; Melbourne Water, 2016a). The sewer system and this treatment facility reduce the volume of water that is discharged into watercourses, and some of the impacts related to excess flows and pollutants can also be mitigated (Dublin Drainage, n.d.).

Rainwater flows into trenches from adjacent impermeable surfaces, receiving lateral and point source inflows, and then infiltrates into the surrounding soils. Overflows in some conditions are required to process water exceeding the system capacity during extreme rainfall events (SuDS Wales, 2016a).

Infiltration trenches are used in several countries and are among the Water Sensitive Urban Design (WSUD) strategies (Fletcher *et al.*, 2014; Locatelli *et al.*, 2015; Wong and Brown, 2009). According to Dublin Drainage, these systems are

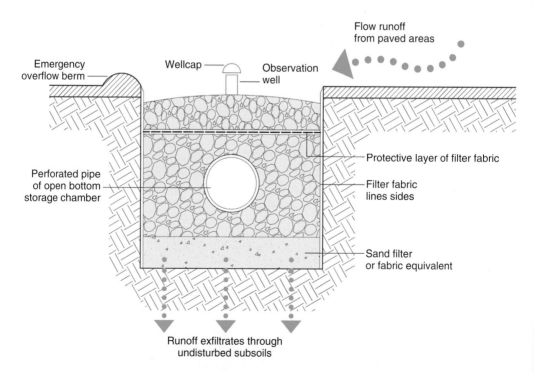

Figure 7.4   Section of an Infiltration Trench.

extensively used in Scotland: the Scottish Environment Protection Agency (SEPA) drafted a SuDS database, showing a high percentage of this type of systems. Other interesting examples come from the city of Malmö, in Sweden, where infiltration trenches covered by grass, filter water when it passes through the soil, and reduce stormwater runoff in residential areas. In Essen, in Germany, successful applications also employ overflows to remove rainwater during extreme storm events.

Some important aspects should be considered when designing infiltration trenches. First of all, soils below the infiltration systems should be permeable, with a clay and a silt-clay content respectively lower than 20% and 40% (BRE, 1991; Bettess, 1996). Swale or filter strips can be used as pre-treatment devices to reduce flow incoming velocities and coarser sediments. According to Dublin Drainage, these devices should be placed at least at 1.5 m above the maximum groundwater level. Rainwater can be retained and treated in the resulting voids by filling the trenches with clean stones wrapped in a geo-textile layer. The choice of materials should be based on potential pollution removal and evaporation capacity (Melbourne Water, 2016a). Underdrained trenches can work as an overflow to avoid problems deriving from possible clogging. The construction of a chamber below can also increase treatment storage and exfiltration potential (Melbourne Water, 2016a). Building elevated banks, so that water can pool and once collected seep into the porous soil, can be important to reduce the risk of overflow as well (Stormwater Management, n.d.). In addition, inspection tubes, especially in the case of long trenches, can be very useful to avoid malfunctioning (Pratt et al., 2002).

Trench design should also consider some dimensional limitations: these systems cannot treat more than 5-hectare areas. In fact, infiltration trenches combined with other source control techniques, as treatment trains, are suitable to serve 2–3 ha. Such systems should be built at least 5 m from buildings or roads, far away from drinking water wells, drainfields and septic tanks. In addition, sediment erosion and soil compaction should be limited during construction and surrounding areas (especially upstream) should be stabilised (Dublin Drainage, n.d.; SuDS Wales, 2016a).

These systems provide a wide range of benefits, first of all, stormwater quality enhancement. After rainwater flows on impervious (urban) surfaces trenches collect several pollutants by processing surface flows, especially when these systems are built along roads or parking lots. Trenches reduce car-related pollutants also thanks to the microbial biofilms of the soil which digest organic pollutants (Stormwater Management, n.d.). Furthermore, according to Xiao et al. (2007), Holman-Dodds et al. (2003), and Elliott and Trowsdale (2007), by constructing several infiltration systems in the urban environment, peak flows can be reduced as well as combined sewer overflows (Roldin et al., 2012). Concomitant use of vegetated filter strips can play an important role as it can reduce runoff rates and volumes, besides improving water quality. Another important advantage of trenches is the limited space required for their installation. Such systems can work in small areas, along streets and at regional scale (Melbourne Water, 2016a).

However, even if infiltration trenches do not need surface areas, integrating these systems in urban areas can be difficult due to the presence of infrastructure and buildings. Other limiting factors are economic aspects, groundwater levels, and local drinking water assets (Göbel et al., 2004; Locatelli et al., 2015). Further disadvantages include the absence of positive aesthetic effects and possible underground contamination, especially if soils are coarse. Moreover, infiltration trenches cannot be used where groundwater is contaminated and in natural areas with not more than a 15%-gradient slope (Melbourne Water, 2016a). In addition, infiltration trenches cannot be employed as a unique system to treat industrial or agricultural pollution hotspots, as the latter are more toxic compared to commercial and residential hotspots. Therefore, infiltration trenches should not be used near farms or industries to avoid the risk that chemical pollutants could reach the groundwater (Stormwater Management, n.d.). Since these systems infiltrate water in the ground, the effectiveness in terms of pollutant treatment has to be carefully taken into account. For example, in the case of soluble pollutants as hydrocarbons, nitrates, salts and organic compounds, these systems may not be effective (Dublin Drainage, n.d.). Another possible issue regards the required time for obtaining pollutant removal: if water flows too fast, polluted water may infiltrate in the ground (with potential high risks if water is pumped for drinking). Infiltration trenches require regular maintenance and inspection to avoid the risk of clogging due to pollutants and sediments. To reduce this risk also pre-treatment of inflows can be very useful (SuDS Wales, 2016a). These systems may need to be replaced every 5 years due to clogging (Dublin Drainage, n.d.).

Local conditions, especially soil characteristics and the distance of sources of runoff, highly influence the performances of infiltration trenches (Locatelli *et al.*, 2015; SuDS Wales, 2016a). Finally, it should also be mentioned that in some countries/regions, infiltration is not permitted in urban areas to avoid potential threat to residents.

7.5   Treatment train

A treatment train uses several combined treatment types to boost water outcomes (Melbourne Water, 2016a). It can include non-vegetated and vegetated systems (see Chapter 6). The expression Stormwater Treatment Train has been used since the mid-1980s to refer to the management of a quantity and quality of stormwater runoff employing multiple GBI Systems. It concerns prevention and source control, pollutant removal, and stormwater volume regulation from local to regional scale (Minnesota Pollution Control Agency, 2016). In fact, the treatment train includes four stages (SuDS Wales, 2016b): prevention, source control, site control, and regional control.

From one stage to the next, water is conveyed through different systems: pipes, swales and linear wetlands (SuDS Wales, 2016b). The most effective treatment trains are those that allow on-site runoff, while maintaining or rebuilding natural hydraulic, physical, biological, and chemical processes (Rushton, 2002).

Systems included in treatment trains are selected considering a range of aspects (e.g. available space, required regulations, environment, etc.). In addition, each GBI System utilises one or more components, which helps to remove pollutants (through a combination of hydraulic, physical, biological, and chemical methods), contributing to effectively remove all pollutants (Minnesota Pollution Control Agency, 2016). Different type of pollutants (e.g., sediments and nutrients) that must be removed can require different systems in sequence. Therefore, treatment train design should be aimed at identifying the most effective sequence, in particular when pre-treatment is required to remove pollutants which can affect the system's performances (as described in the case of infiltration trenches; Melbourne Water, 2016a).

At the watershed scale, the management of stormwater starts from Pollution Prevention (achieved through ordinances, urban regulations, and public education), and continues through Source Controls (monitoring and removing illicit discharge, control of shop floor cleaning and other street-level practices that can increase the phosphorus percentage in runoff water, etc.), onsite stormwater practices (rain gardens, permeable pavement, infiltration trenches, etc.), and regional practices (infiltration ponds or basins, wetlands, etc.; Minnesota Pollution Control Agency, 2016).

Treatment trains can successfully improve water quality in large areas or at watershed scale. However, on-site design can be more adequate since the first system is in general the one that provides the highest level of pollutant reduction. Treatment train planning should hence consider that the successive sequence of systems receives cleaner water (or at least with fewer pollutants; Scholes *et al.*, 2008). This allows ensuring the protection of wetland systems from gross pollutants and coarse sediments (Melbourne Water, 2016a).

Hydraulic and physical processes remove larger solids and associated pollutants during storm events, while biological and chemical processes that treat finer solids and dissolved pollutants occur between storms (Scholes *et al.*, 2008; Wong et al., 2002). A complete treatment train can lead to important results, including: minimising the rate of runoff, employing a hydraulic process; removing bulk solids thanks to a physical process; removing settleable solids and floatables by means of a physical process; removing suspended and colloidal solids thanks to a physical, biological or chemical process; and removing colloidal, dissolved, volatile, and pathogens thanks to a biological or chemical process (Strecker, 2006).

The management train concept rests on the division of a catchment area into sub-catchments. Each sub-area is characterised by different drainage strategies, drainage capacity and land uses. Working on-site at the local scale will reduce the quantity that has to be managed at any point, and above all reduces the need for conveying the water in pipes off the site (Susdrain, 2012). Dividing catchments into smaller sections is important to control the whole catchment, facilitate a normal hydrological cycle and develop better open and green spaces in cities.

Stormwater treatment train design and development is a complex process taking into consideration project goals, available budget and site conditions. According to the Minnesota Pollution Control Agency (2016), the development of a stormwater treatment train requires several steps. This is a non-linear process because the results of one stage may lead to reconsider earlier decisions about siting, sizing or feasibility of the project. Assessing the project goals and site conditions is usually the first step. The site conditions include constraints and regulatory requirements that affect stormwater systems and the purpose of the project are related to runoff volume control and drainage issues, water quality or both. The project should thus vary in terms of its topography and site conditions depending on the amount and quality of impervious surface, drainage area, runoff, soils, and climate conditions.

After assessing the site's conditions, it is important to evaluate pollutant removal strategies. Secondly, it is crucial to identify the best combination of practices to manage the pollutants identified in the previous step. The third step is to evaluated site constraints that can influence the choice of location and size. This selection process considers available space; access for maintenance; infiltration limitations due to soil type; soil contamination; groundwater depth; presence of infrastructure and utility conflicts; regulatory requirements; and compatibility with other uses such as green and public spaces (Minnesota Pollution Control Agency, 2016). The fourth step consists in choosing an individual component. If the component is not appropriate to respond to the site needs (e.g. pollutant removal capacity) or conditions, alternative components should be located. At this point of the process, the systems need to be accurately measured or it is necessary to return to previous steps of the process to select alternative components (Minnesota Pollution Control Agency, 2016).

Prevention practices – for example, preventing runoff by reducing impermeable areas, good housekeeping measures for reducing pollution – are at the basis of the treatment train systems. These prevention techniques are achieved through the progression of local source controls to larger catchment sites and regional

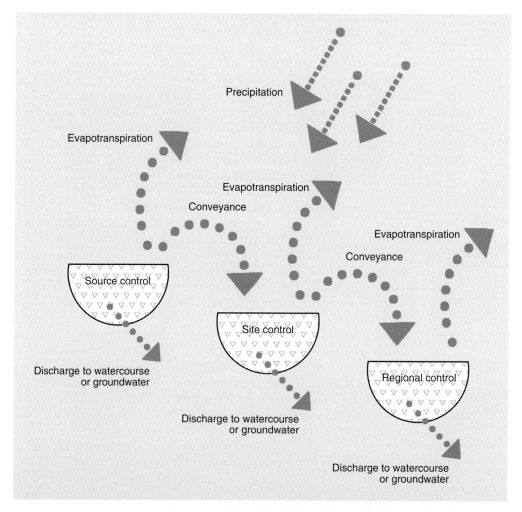

Figure 7.5   Example of Treatment Trains (based on SuDS Wales, 2016b).

controls. As a general principle, it is better to deal with runoff locally, "returning the water to the natural drainage system as near to the source as possible" (Susdrain, 2012). Water should be slowly conveyed elsewhere only if it cannot be managed on site. This can occur if water requires additional treatment before being disposed or if the volume of runoff generated is greater than the capacity of the natural drainage system. In those cases, excess flows needs to be routed offsite. At the end of the process, the series of drainage techniques positively affects runoff flow and quality in a similar way to natural catchments. Treatment train design requires the control of different options, and the skill to balance advantages and disadvantages of costs, benefits and risks in each step of the process. The risk of flooding should always be balanced with the costs of protecting an area from different levels of floods (Susdrain, 2012). Review construction and operation criteria to ensure that treatment train operates as designed and that it is properly maintained is a final, but important step.

References

Alectia. (2016). *Quantitative hydrological effects of urbanization and stormwater infiltration in Copenhagen, Denmark*. [Online]. Available at: http://www.alectia.com/en/phds/quantitative-hydrological-effects-of-urbanization-and-stormwater-infiltration-in-copenhagen-denmark-en/ [Accessed 12 May 2016].

American Concrete Institute. (2010). *522R-10 Report on Pervious Concrete*. Farmington Hills, MI. [Online]. Available at: https://www.concrete.org/store/productdetail.aspx?ItemID=52210&Format=PROTECTED_PDF [Accessed 11 May 2016].

Barrett, M. E., Malina, J. F., Charbeneau, R. J. and Ward, G. H. (2009). *Characterization of highway runoff in the Austin, Texas area*. Technical Report, Center for Research in Water Resources, University of Texas at Austin. [Online]. Available at: https://repositories.lib.utexas.edu/handle/2152/6742 [Accessed 11 May 2016].

Bettess, R. (1996). *Infiltration drainage - manual of good practice*. CIRIA. [Online]. Available at: http://www.ciria.org/ItemDetail?iProductCode=R156&Category=BOOK [Accessed 12 May 2016].

Brattebo, B. O. and Booth, D. B. (2003). Long-term stormwater quantity and quality performance of permeable pavement systems. *Water Research*, 37 (18), p. 4369–4376. [Online]. Available at: doi:10.1016/S0043-1354(03)00410-X [Accessed 6 May 2016].

BRE. (1991). *Soakaway design Digest 365*. Building Research Establishment, Watford, Herts. [Online]. Available at: http://forterra.co.uk/plugins/downloads/files/BRE365.pdf [Accessed 12 May 2016].

De Urbanisten. (2016). *Water squares*. [Online]. Available at: http://www.urbanisten.nl/wp/?portfolio=waterpleinen [Accessed 3 May 2016].

Dublin Drainage. (n.d.). *Infiltration trenches & soak-aways*. [Online]. Available at: http://www.uksuds.com/information/Infiltration_Trenches_Soakaways.pdf [Accessed 5 May 2016].

Dutch Water Sector. (2012). Wayss & Freytag/BAM Techniek to build 35 km underground waste water tunnel for German water board. *Dutch Water Sector*. [Online]. Available at: http://www.dutchwatersector.com/news-events/news/1967-wayss-freytag-bam-techniek-to-build-35-km-underground-waste-water-tunnel-for-german-water-board.html [Accessed 10 April 2016].

Elliott, A. H. and Trowsdale, S. A. (2007). A review of models for low impact urban stormwater drainage. *Environmental Modelling and Software*, 22 (3), p. 394–405. *Scopus* [Online]. Available at: doi:10.1016/j.envsoft.2005.12.005.

European Commission. (2016). *European Green Capital.* [Online]. Available at: http://ec.europa.eu/environment/europeangreencapital/rotterdams-water-square/ [Accessed 3 May 2016].

Fletcher, T. D., Shuster, W., Hunt, W. F., Ashley, R., Butler, D., Arthur, S., Trowsdale, S., Barraud, S., Semadeni-Davies, A., Bertrand-Krajewski, J.-L., Mikkelsen, P. S., Rivard, G., Uhl, M., Dagenais, D. and Viklander, M. (2014). SUDS, LID, BMPs, WSUD, and more - The evolution and application of terminology surrounding urban drainage. *Urban Water Journal,* p. 1–18. *Scopus.*

Göbel, P., Stubbe, H., Weinert, M., Zimmermann, J., Fach, S., Dierkes, C., Kories, H., Messer, J., Mertsch, V., Geiger, W. F., and Coldewey, W. G. (2004). Near-natural stormwater management and its effects on the water budget and groundwater surface in urban areas taking account of the hydrogeological conditions. *Journal of Hydrology,* 299 (3-4), p. 267–283. *Scopus* [Online]. Available at: doi:10.1016/j.jhydrol.2004.08.013.

Holman-Dodds, J. K., Bradley, A. A. and Potter, K. W. (2003). Evaluation of hydrologic benefits of infiltration based urban storm water management. *Journal of the American Water Resources Association,* 39 (1), p. 205–215. *Scopus.*

IABR. (2005). *The 2nd IABR: The Flood.* [Online]. Available at: http://iabr.nl/en/editie/the-flood [Accessed 11 May 2016].

Kevern, J. T., Wang, K., and Schaefer, V. R. (2010). Test Methods for Characterizing Air Void Systems in Portland Cement Pervious Concrete. In: Wang, K. (ed.), *Recent Advancement in Concrete Freezing-Thawing (F-T),* 100 Barr Harbor Drive, PO Box C700, West Conshohocken, PA 19428-2959: ASTM International, p. 119-119-16. [Online]. Available at: http://www.astm.org/doiLink.cgi?STP49086S [Accessed 11 May 2016].

Ku, H., Hagelin, N., and Buxton, H. (1992). Effects of urban storm-runoff control on ground-water recharge in Nassau County, New York. *Ground Water,* 30 (4), p. 507–514. *Scopus.*

Locatelli, L., Mark, O., Mikkelsen, P. S., Arnbjerg-Nielsen, K., Wong, T., and Binning, P. J. (2015). Determining the extent of groundwater interference on the performance of infiltration trenches. *Journal of Hydrology,* 529, Part 3, p.1360–1372. [Online]. Available at: doi:10.1016/j.jhydrol.2015.08.047 [Accessed 5 May 2016].

Longo, G., Moretti, S., Nario, L., and Papalia, I. (2016). *Strategie alternative di gestione delle acque meteoriche. Caso studio Genova San Fruttuoso.* Università degli Studi di Genova Scuola Politecnica: Dipartimento di Scienze per l'Architettura.

Maimone, M., O'Rourke, D., Knighton, J., and Thomas, C. (2011). Potential Impacts of Extensive Stormwater Infiltration in Philadelphia. *Environmental Engineer and Scientist: Applied Research and Practice,* 14, p. 29–39. [Accessed 12 May 2016].

Melbourne Water. (2016a). *Infiltration trenches.* [Online]. Available at: http://www.melbournewater.com.au/planning-and-building/stormwater-management/wsud_treatments/pages/infiltration-trenches.aspx [Accessed 5 May 2016].

Melbourne Water. (2016b). *Porous paving.* [Online]. Available at: http://www.melbournewater.com.au/planning-and-building/stormwater-management/wsud_treatments/pages/porous-paving.aspx [Accessed 11 May 2016].

Minnesota Pollution Control Agency. (2016). *Using the treatment train approach to BMP selection - Minnesota Stormwater Manual.* [Online]. Available at: http://stormwater.pca.state.mn.us/index.php/Using_the_treatment_train_approach_to_BMP_selection [Accessed 5 May 2016].

Montes, F., Valavala, S. and Haselbach, L. (2005). A New Test Method for Porosity Measurements of Portland Cement Pervious Concrete. *Journal of ASTM International,* 2 (1), p. 12931. [Online]. Available at: doi:10.1520/JAI12931 [Accessed 11 May 2016].

Newman, A. P., Aitken, D. and Antizar-Ladislao, B. (2013). Stormwater quality performance of a macro-pervious pavement car park installation equipped with channel drain based oil and silt retention devices. *Water Research*, 47 (20), p. 7327–7336. [Online]. Available at: doi:10.1016/j.watres.2013.05.061 [Accessed 3 May 2016].

Pervious Pavement. (2011). *Pervious Pavement: Pervious Concrete for Green, Sustainable Porous and Permeable Stormwater Drainage*. [Online]. Available at: http://www.perviouspavement.org/ [Accessed 3 May 2016].

Pratt, C. J. (1995). A review of source control of urban stormwater runoff. In: *Journal of the Institution of Water and Environmental Management*, 9, 1995, Institution of Water and Environmental Management, p.132–139. [Online]. Available at: http://cat.inist.fr/?aModele=afficheN&cpsidt=3497918 [Accessed 11 May 2016].

Pratt, C., Wilson, S., and Cooper, P. (2002). *Source control using constructed pervious surfaces. Hydraulic, structural and water quality performance issues (C582)*. CIRIA. [Online]. Available at: http://www.ciria.org/ItemDetail?iProductCode=C582&Category=BOOK [Accessed 12 May 2016].

Roldin, M., Mark, O., Kuczera, G., Mikkelsen, P. S., and Binning, P. J. (2012). Representing soakaways in a physically distributed urban drainage model - Upscaling individual allotments to an aggregated scale. *Journal of Hydrology*, 414-415, p. 530–538. *Scopus* [Online]. Available at: doi:10.1016/j.jhydrol.2011.11.030.

Rushton, B. (2002). *Enhanced Parking Lot Design for Stormwater Treatment*. In: 2002, ASCE, p. 1–16. [Online]. Available at: http://cedb.asce.org/CEDBsearch/record.jsp?dockey=0133415 [Accessed 18 May 2016].

Scholes, L., Revitt, D. M., and Ellis, J. B. (2008). A systematic approach for the comparative assessment of stormwater pollutant removal potentials. *Journal of Environmental Management*, 88 (3), p. 467–478. [Online]. Available at: doi:10.1016/j.jenvman.2007.03.003.

Stormwater Management. (n.d.). *Infiltration Trenches*. [Online]. Available at: http://www.esf.edu/ere/endreny/GICalculator/InfiltrationIntro.html [Accessed 5 May 2016].

Strecker, E. (2006). Critical Assessment of Stormwater Treatment and Control Selection Treatment. *Water Intelligence Online*, 5, p.9781843397410. [Accessed 18 May 2016].

SuDS Wales. (2016a). *Infiltration trenches « SuDS Wales – Sustainable Drainage Systems*. [Online]. Available at: http://www.sudswales.com/types/source-control/infiltration-trenches/ [Accessed 5 May 2016].

SuDS Wales. (2016b). *The SuDS Treatment Train: SuDS Wales – Sustainable Drainage Systems*. [Online]. Available at: http://www.sudswales.com/education/background/the-suds-treatment-train/ [Accessed 5 May 2016].

Susdrain. (2012). *SuDS management train*. [Online]. Available at: http://www.susdrain.org/delivering-suds/using-suds/suds-principles/management-train.html [Accessed 5 May 2016].

Torres, A., Hu, J. and Ramos, A. (2015). The effect of the cementitious paste thickness on the performance of pervious concrete. *Construction and Building Materials*, 95, p. 850–859. [Online]. Available at: doi:10.1016/j.conbuildmat.2015.07.187 [Accessed 3 May 2016].

Wong, T. H. F. and Brown, R. R. (2009). The water sensitive city: Principles for practice. *Water Science and Technology*, 60 (3), p. 673–682. *Scopus* [Online]. Available at: doi:10.2166/wst.2009.436.

Wong, T. H., Fletcher, T. D., Duncan, H. P., Coleman, J. R., and Jenkins, G. A. (2002). A model for urban stormwater improvement conceptualisation. *Global Solutions for Urban Drainage*,813.[Online].Availableat:http://ascelibrary.org/doi/pdf/10.1061/40644(2002)115 [Accessed 18 May 2016].

Xiao, Q., McPherson, E. G., Simpson, J. R., and Ustin, S. L. (2007). Hydrologic processes at the urban residential scale. *Hydrological Processes*, 21 (16), p. 2174–2188. *Scopus* [Online]. Available at: doi:10.1002/hyp.6482.

Part B

Chapter 8
Urban River Restoration
Paola Sabbion

8.1 Watershed processes and functions

In natural conditions, rivers fulfil a range of geomorphological, hydrological and biological processes including water transport and storage, erosion and sediment transport. Waterways distribute nutrients and organic matter and provide habitats for animal and plant species. Rivers and floodplains are influenced by watershed-scale hydrologic processes as also by flow attributes, such as the main channel roughness and floodplain flood storage capacity. The riverbed form and the channel roughness regulate flow velocity. Roughness is considerably higher in mountain rivers as boulders and cobblestones cause high turbulence and reduce flow velocity. Suspended sediments in lowland rivers are conversely very small, thus, river form and vegetation roughness have a greater influence on in-channel flow velocity. Vegetated areas with high roughness values can slow discharge, even if over-bank flooding occurs. Typically, in large rivers, both grain and vegetation roughness has little influence. Flow resistance, in fact, can be mainly attributed to channel meandering and roughness. Irregular riverbeds, meander bends, pools, and wood accumulation significantly decrease water velocity. Floodplain ponds, lakes and wetlands slow flows, reducing the flood downstream discharge by storing an important amount of water (Roni and Beechie (eds.), 2012).

Stream flow also influences ecological processes occurring in floodplain systems, such as riparian forests and aquatic habitats (Ward *et al.*, 2002; Doyle *et al.*, 2005; Moore and Richardson, 2012). Channel features (depth, velocity, roughness) and riparian vegetation contribute to increase habitat and biological diversity, supporting the establishment and maintenance of communities of species (Poff *et al.*, 1997; Richter *et al.*, 2003). In particular, floodplain storage lentic habitats (with still water) provide the ideal conditions for the river wildlife's feeding and spawning (Pretty *et al.*, 2003; Stanford *et al.*, 2006). Undamaged rivers

Urban Sustainability and River Restoration: Green and Blue Infrastructure, First Edition.
Katia Perini and Paola Sabbion.
© 2017 John Wiley & Sons Ltd. Published 2017 by John Wiley & Sons Ltd.

are among the most diverse and complex ecosystems and are characterised by specific dynamic processes (Jungwirth *et al.*, 2002). Changing riverine landscapes are connected to the stream flow, which determines continuous habitat variations. The pattern and distribution of habitat types, though, remain substantially stable (Ward *et al.*, 2002; Beechie *et al.*, 2006). River variations include discharge, bank erosion, bar deposition (lateral channel migration), floodplain establishment and channel switching. River modifications determine the thermal and chemical properties of a waterflow and, hence, control the biological diversity of floodplain habitats (Poole, 2002; Stanford, 2007).

Channel structure and floodplain interactions influence the transport and storage of inorganic sediments and organic matter. The latter is primarily produced within streams (e.g., aquatic plants, algae, mosses) and in riparian areas (e.g., leaf litter, seeds, terrestrial invertebrates; Richardson *et al.*, 2010). Channel complexity disrupts the transport of organic matter and increases its in-stream consumption rate. The rates of retention within the stream reach depend on structural characteristics of the channel. Larger particles, such as leaves, can be easily trapped by wood or cobbles (Richardson *et al.*, 2009). Smaller particles, such as seeds, settle instead in backwaters or are captured by aquatic and riparian vegetation (Gurnell *et al.*, 2008; Hoover *et al.*, 2010). The in-stream biological processes contribute to influence the structure and function of stream ecosystems, including habitat selection, feeding, competition, and predation (Roni and Beechie (eds.), 2012).

Intact river environments provide a variety of ecosystem services (supporting, regulating, provisioning and cultural services, see Chapter 4), which unfortunately have not always been considered in the decision making regarding urban planning and catchment systems development (Georgiou and Turner, 2012; Gilvear *et al.*, 2013).

8.2   Degraded river ecosystems

Anthropogenic alterations to river flows and forms are implemented to devise flood control management, enhance water resources and hydroelectric power as, also, to meet agricultural, industrial, and navigation needs. River systems, moreover, have been heavily modified by urban growth and municipal demands for water. Floodplains are consistently stressed by extensive exploitation and high rates of pollution. Rivers have often been used as channels for waste such as sewage waste and toxic chemical disposal, causing diffused pollution. Dredging, intensive fishing, riparian and aquatic vegetation removal, flow regime changes and alien species introduction have reduced the natural complexity of riverine landscapes and induced the loss of its ecological functions (Ward and Stanford, 1995; Ward, 1998). River integrity is at risk due to human activities, which are not compatible with the original ecosystem functioning, and affect the flow, quality and structure of watercourses. Primary ecosystem processes are, thus, negatively affected by these processes and degraded rivers provide less ecosystem goods and services (Gilvear *et al.*, 2013; Figure 8.1).

In North America and Europe, intensive exploitation of rivers started over 500 years ago and increased with the advent of mechanisation in the late nineteenth century and twentieth century (Newson, 2001). According to recent studies,

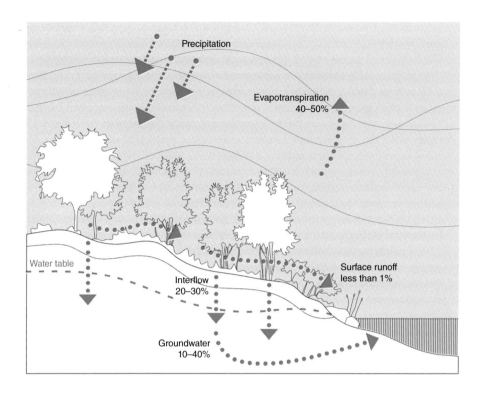

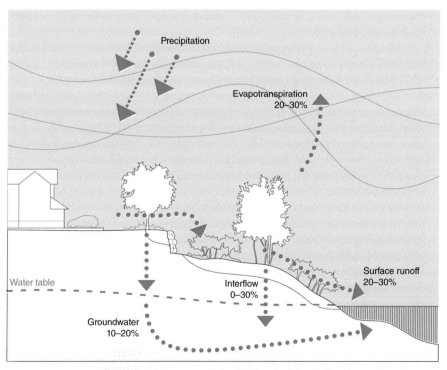

Figure 8.1   Before and After Development Conditions in a Drainage Basin (based on Washington State Department of Ecology).

almost 80% of the world's population is currently exposed to high levels of threats from water security and degraded riverine habitats (Vörösmarty *et al.*, 2010). The World Water Council estimates that more than half of the world's rivers are polluted or at risk of running dry. Moreover, less than 20% of the world's freshwaters are considered pristine. Habitat loss is indicated as the primary cause of extinction in aquatic ecosystems (UN Water, 2009; Roni and Beechie (eds.), 2012). Anthropogenic activities have directly and indirectly altered the river environments, leading to important changes in watershed processes, habitat conditions and ecological integrity (Karr and Chu, 2006; Allan, 2004). Direct alterations affect reach-scale processes. Channel engineering practices - such as channel diversion for irrigation purposes, channel size reduction, hydroelectric dams construction, and flood control mechanisms - interrupt downstream water and the transport of sediments and organic matter. In heavily dammed rivers, the time and capacity of sediment delivery is significantly reduced and, this has a strong impact on the establishment of riparian vegetation, the biota of the river and its habitat conditions (Richter and Thomas, 2007). Levee construction and bank armouring – which simplify the channel cross-section – reduce floodplain habitats and biological diversity by eliminating flood flows (especially when levees are in place), bank erosion (especially when bank armouring occurs), channel migration, connectivity and river–floodplain interactions. These processes also affect the formation of floodplain channels and riparian ecosystem conditions. Channelisation of watercourses significantly reduces organic matter transport and storage and results in habitat simplification, since channel roughness and heterogeneity contribute to the retention of organic matter (Roni and Beechie (eds.), 2012).

Furthermore, humans can trigger indirect alterations on riverine ecosystems due to changes in land use within the catchment area. These variations affect runoff watershed-scale processes, as well as erosion and nutrient delivery, leading to a loss in stream flow balance, water quality, and biological interactions (Karr, 1991). Manipulating channel roughness and filling wetlands to convert lands for agriculture or urban development modifies habitat diversity and biological capacity (e.g., channel dredging and wood removal from channels; Roni and Beechie (eds.), 2012). Alterations to the natural habitat conditions occur by removing riparian vegetation for grazing, agricultural practices and construction of impervious surfaces (roads, pavements, roof tops). This results in increased bank erosion and higher nutrient and pollutant inflow within the stream reach (Sweeney *et al.*, 2004). Deforestation also increases surface erosion and reduces the interception and evapotranspiration of vegetation, leading to soil compaction and decreased infiltration capacity (Booth and Jackson, 1997). The most consistent effect within urban catchments is an increased impervious surface cover that alters the hydrology and geomorphology of streams (Paul and Meyer, 2001). Subsurface flow, intercepted by impervious surface within the catchment area, rapidly runs into watercourses and a more rapid runoff can result in increased flood risk (Jones and Grant, 1996). Moreover, urbanisation and road construction increase sediment supply in the streamflow. Pollutants - including pesticides; urban and industrial waste; metals; and agricultural land nutrients, such as nitrogen and phosphorous – can be delivered to streams either from the point source (urban wastewater treatment plants or sewage) or non-point sources (ditches, surface runoff, groundwater) affecting riverine habitats and biota (Roni and Beechie (eds.), 2012; Figure 8.2).

Part B

ECOLOGICAL IMPACT OF HUMAN-INDUCED ALTERATIONS

Food (energy) source	Water quality	Habitat structure	Flow regime	Biotic interactions
Alteration in type, amount and particle size of organic material	Increased turbidity and suspended solids	Decreased stability of substrate and banks due to erosion and sedimentation	Increased extreme flows (magnitude, frequency)	Altered dynamics of competition, predation
Decreased coarse particulate organic matter	Increased nutrients (nitrogen, phosphorus)	Habitat uniformity	Increased maximum flow velocity'	Shift in species composition
Increased algal production and fine particulate organic matter	Altered pH	Decreased heterogeneity for spawning, nursery and hiding (pools, riffles, woody debris)	Decreased minimum flow velocity	Increased frequency of exotic species

Figure 8.2   Ecological Impacts of Human-Induced Alterations (based on Karr, 1991).

8.3   Techniques and strategies for river restoration

In recent decades, interest in river restoration has considerably increased, along with the growing emphasis on the value of river functions and the ecosystem services provided by waterways (Lemons and Victor, 2008). The term *restoration* refers to rehabilitation, enhancement, improvement, mitigation, and reclamation strategies (Roni and Beechie (eds.), 2012). There is widespread agreement that urban areas should adapt to climate change, reintegrating the natural water-cycle, and creating *water sensitive cities* (Brown *et al.*, 2009; Sharma *et al.*, 2008; Kazmierczak and Carter, 2010; Ward *et al.*, 2012; Everett and Lamond, 2014). As stated by the British Department for Environment, Food and Rural Affairs, the process of *making space for water* is gaining reputation in academic literature and policies (DEFRA, 2005; McBain *et al.*, 2010). Inundation is now addressed not only erecting structural defences but also developing resilience to flooding (Bowker, 2007). It is globally recognised that returning rivers and catchments to a more natural state is a key strategy to improve the quality of the environment and biodiversity. River rehabilitation provides an opportunity to restore ecosystem services that have been degraded and lost. Additionally, the natural functions of watershed settlements become more balanced. River rehabilitation regards biodiversity conservation (supporting); sustainable flood management (regulating); physical habitat quality restoration (regulating); fisheries enhancement (cultural/provisioning); pollution control (regulating); and also cultural awareness (recreation and amenity; Gilvear *et al.*, 2013; Figure 8.3).

In Europe, strategies to stabilise non-cohesive riverbanks relying on planting and bioengineering approaches have been underway since the beginning of the twentieth century. Recently, both the United States (1 $billion estimated annual expenses) and European countries (especially Denmark and England) are investing considerable resources on river and watershed restoration (Bernhardt *et al.*, 2007; Boon *et al.* (eds.), 2000).

Part B

Long-term ecosystem services efficacy

Rehabilitation measure	Intermediate ecosystem processes and form	Biodiversity	Sustainable flood management	Physical habitat quality	Fisheries enhancement	Diffuse pollution control	Cultural (recreation and amenity)
Remeandering	Increased hydraulic diversity / Decrease in channel slope / Habitat heterogeneity / Landscape evolution	***	*	***	**	–	***
Buffer strip creation and riparian revegetation/woodland	Improved riparian habitat / Reduced soil erosion / Nutrient uptake / Shading of channel / Leaf litter input to river	***	*	**	*	*	**
Flood embankment removal	Increased floodplain storage / Increased floodplain inundation / Opening up of old channels and backwaters / Landscape evolution	**	***	**	*	–	*
Culvert removal	Increased ease of fish passage / Increased hydraulic diversity / Naturalness	–	–	**	***		*
Weir removal	Increased ease of fish passage / Downstream sediment conveyance re-established / Naturalness	***	*	***	***	–	*
Reconnecting old channels	Creation nursery areas for fish / Refugia for plants and animals / Increase in spawning habitat / Habitat heterogeneity / Landscape evolution	***	–	***	**	–	*
Bank protection removal	Channel instability / Bankside habitat / Naturalness	*	–	***	*	–	*
Restored floodplain forests	Increased floodplain roughness / Habitat structural diversity / Coarse woody debris inputs to river / Leaf litter input to river / Habitat heterogeneity / Landscape evolution	***	***	***	*	*	**

Ecosystem services:
- Biodiversity
- Sustainable flood management
- Physical habitat quality
- Fisheries enhancement
- Diffuse pollution control
- Cultural (recreation and amenity)

Long-term ecosystem services efficacy:
- – None or uncertain benefit
- * Moderate benefit
- ** Good benefit
- *** High benefit

Figure 8.3   Examples of Rehabilitation Measures, Intermediate Ecosystem Processes and Form and Long-Term Ecosystem Services Benefits Efficacy (based on Gilvear et al., 2013).

Several river restoration techniques have focused on single aspects, in particular fish habitat improvement. Only few comprehensive regional riverine restoration plans are currently devised (FISRWG, 1998; Holmes *et al.*, 2001). River reclamation within heavily urbanised areas can help to change people's perception of public green spaces and resources, but it often has little effect on natural processes and habitats. Growing urbanisation and climate change, in fact, threaten urban aquatic ecosystems leading to a constant habitat loss. Hence, in this context, the protection of high quality habitats needs to be an urban restoration priority. In recent years, the concept of *process-based* river restoration has been gaining importance. According to Beechie *et al.* (2010), this integrated social-ecological approach adopts holistic techniques to address root causes of ecosystem degradation and establish a new balance between socio-economic needs and sustainable watershed management (Brierley and Fryirs (eds.), 2004; Kondolf *et al.*, 2006; Bennett *et al.*, 2009). In addition, it focuses on avoiding anthropogenic interference in natural processes, enhancing the resilience of river–floodplain ecosystems to future disturbances (Sear, 1994; Beechie *et al.*, 2010). This ensures that restoration plans and actions support sustainable recovery without requiring continual human intervention and maintenance. The aim of *process based* restoration is to "re-establish normative rates and magnitudes of physical, chemical, and biological processes that create and sustain river and floodplain ecosystems" (Beechie *et al.*, 2010). This process is based on the analysis of multiple causes and socio-economic contexts at local, regional, and national levels to maximise the restoration benefits over short, medium and long-term timescales (Roni and Beechie (eds.), 2012; Gilvear *et al.*, 2013).

The best combination strategies to restore the ecological values of waterbodies, in fact, devise regulatory frameworks and planning policies to decrease anthropic pressure. This allows the self-regulation of natural systems, runoff reduction and habitat and water quality improvement (see Chapters 10, 11 and 12). In particular, the choice of river restoration techniques depends on the specific watershed assessment, its issues and objectives. Techniques can be settled at different scales of intervention. Strategies that focus on habitat improvement of instream or riparian processes (e.g., channel re-meandering, planting, fencing, grazing removal) are designed at the reach scale, while techniques restoring connectivity (e.g., barrier removal, levee setbacks, fish passage) or sediment and hydrologic processes (e.g., stormwater runoff regulating, instream flow) can be tailored at the watershed scale. Restoration strategies vary also in terms of time: in-stream habitat improvement and restoration of connectivity can result in rapid improvements, while techniques as road removal or riparian planting may take years to be effective. Long-term and short-term strategies can be implemented to provide initial benefits while enhancing the system's resilience capacity (Roni and Beechie (eds.), 2012).

Riparian habitat improvement is based on increasing complexity and diversity of the watercourse by restoring the natural sinuosity and creating structures (i.e., pools, riffles, new floodplain habitats) to improve the biotic productivity of the ecosystem. Re-meandering – which envisages straightening and narrowing channels – is especially useful in agricultural landscapes (Vought and Lacoursière, 2010). At the reach scale, riparian buffers can improve bank stability and instream conditions, previously damaged by fencing and intensive grazing (Armour *et al.*, 1991; Belsky *et al.*, 1999; Robertson and Rowling, 2000;

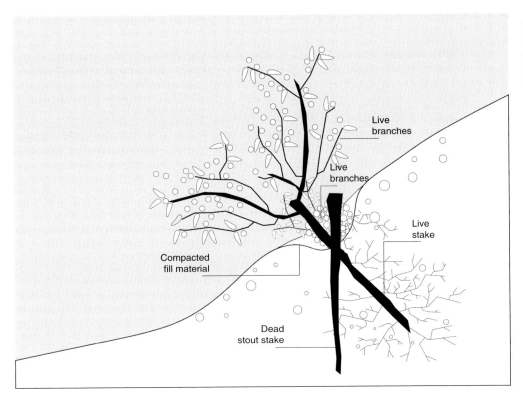

Figure 8.4   An Example of Bioengineering Approaches to Bank Stabilisation.

Izaak Walton League, 2006; FISRWG, 1998). In urban areas, where waterways have often been piped and buried to make space for urban settlements, there is widespread need to uncover rivers and redesign their banks (Holmes and Nielsen, 1998). In developed watersheds, cement banks cause habitat loss. Thus, restoration practices focus mainly on bank re-naturalisation by eliminating hard structures and designing new vegetated banks and meanders with trees and bushes within channels. Bioengineering techniques stabilise banks reducing erosion while improving riparian or in-stream habitat. This approach employs a combination of natural materials such as wood (e.g., logs, trees, fascines), living plants (live bush stakes, live branches, willow bundles, cuttings), rocks, and natural fibre mat (coir fabric, turf) to control slope erosion until riparian vegetation grows and naturally stabilises the banks (Boccalaro, 2012; Izaak Walton League, 2006; Principato, 2011; Figure 8.4).

The effectiveness of these structures to protect banks and prevent channel movement may nevertheless interfere with some watershed-scale processes with regard to connectivity, sediment, and hydrology. Typical objectives of restoration plans are: reducing or restoring sediment supply, runoff and hydrology, especially in settlement areas. Common strategies and techniques include natural drainage systems, resurfacing, bank stabilisation, addition or removal of culverts, addition of cross-drains and road improvements to reduce impervious surfaces (Bagley, 1998; Novotny et al., 2010).

8.4   Restoring connectivity within urbanised areas

Intervening in settled or heavy urbanised areas involves working on river connectivity. Anthropic pressure, in fact, usually affects the connectivity of watersheds as it decreases the capacity of physical, chemical, and biological/ecological processes (Paul and Meyer, 2001). In many cities, programmes to restore water bodies are activated on a short-term basis, in particular, to stabilise incising streams and to protect near-stream properties and infrastructures (Brooks et al., 2002; Nilsson et al., 2003; Walsh et al., 2005). Functional short-term objectives within urban channels count the elimination of pollution sources, channel morphology reconstruction, and habitat provision for self-sustaining biota. Complete long-term stream rehabilitation is not always possible under urban constraints. However, this should not preclude potential future gains, as some ecological benefits may be achieved by local-scale stream habitat enhancement (i.e., see Figure 8.5; Booth, 2005; Walsh et al., 2005).

Watercourses register an upstream-downstream connection (longitudinal connectivity), floodplain and riparian area connection (lateral connectivity) and hyporheic zone and subsurface area connection (vertical connectivity). Connectivity is also influenced by the incision of lateral channels, which are isolated from floodplains due to urbanisation. Restoring connectivity implies reactivating the transport of organic material, sediment, and nutrients as well as reconnecting lateral habitats. It also allows for the natural migration of channels through a range of techniques that often include the removal or modification of disconnection infrastructures such as of dams, culverts, levees (Fullerton et al., 2010; Cowx and Van Zyll de Jong, 2004).

Figure 8.5   Cheonggyecheon River Restoration, Seoul.

Dam removal and the restoration of a natural hydrologic regime primarily address the longitudinal connectivity of stream and floodplain habitats. Reconnection techniques include dams, culverts and bridges removal and reinstating the natural morphology and topography of rivers through channel reconstruction and riparian planting (Roni *et al.*, 2005; Roni and Beechie (eds.), 2012).

Over the last decades, retrofitting or replacing culverts and other types of road crossing to restore longitudinal connectivity has been the focus of numerous restoration plans in both Europe and North America (Bernhardt *et al.*, 2005). Replacement or removal of culverts leads to rapid fish colonisation. Moreover, a variety of fish passage structures can be used to effectively restore migration corridors and longitudinal habitat connectivity (Roni *et al.*, 2008; Zitek *et al.*, 2008). Connectivity can be limited by banks stabilised with cement, riprap and rock. Removing bank armouring, when possible, can be an effective method to restore channel migration and other floodplain processes. Lateral connectivity enhancement typically seeks to restore links between the river channel and its floodplain to increase water retention, the exchange between surface and subsurface flow, organic matter retention, natural erosional/sediment deposition and channel migration processes, which create habitat diversity. Levee removal, lowering or setback, allows a river to migrate or meander freely and connect to the adjacent floodplain for full recovery of all or most riverine functions (including retention and the natural exchange of water, wood, sediment, seed and nutrients between floodplains and main streams; fine sediment deposition; channel migration; diversification of riparian conditions and habitat types; Roni *et al.*, 2005, 2008). Adjacent land use also influences water expansion limits and the portions of the floodplain that are inundated. Land exploitation has indeed an impact on soil erosion and sediment deposition (Cowx and Van Zyll de Jong, 2004). Flood control often calls for other restoration techniques to adjust channel morphology, such as re-meandering or restructuring the channel (Roni and Beechie (eds.), 2012).

In the most urbanised areas, watershed connectivity restoration depends on reducing the impact of paved roads and impervious surfaces employing green and blue infrastructure (GBI; see Chapters 6–7). Impervious surfaces, in fact, affect on aquatic ecosystems causing the dramatic increase in frequency and magnitude of peak flows and channel incision. Moreover, urbanisation simplifies the instream habitat, decreases water quality and biotic diversity and production (Walsh *et al.*, 2005; Reich and Lake, 2015). Several studies show that, if impervious surface cover (ISC) in catchment areas increases by 10–20%, runoff registers a twofold increase; when ISC increases by 35–50% runoff registers a threefold increase; and when ISC increases by 75–100% surface runoff registers more than a fivefold increase. These changes lead to an alteration of hydrology, sediment supply and water quality (Riley and Leopold, 1998; Paul and Meyer, 2001). Additionally, studies evaluating stream flows through watersheds with varying levels of urban development show that biological conditions decline as impervious areas increase (Booth *et al.*, 2004).

Extreme floods can impair stream restoration efforts, thus, it is necessary to cope with more frequent and extreme hydrological events. In urban settlements, efforts focus mainly on stormwater runoff control and treatment aiming at improving or restoring natural hydrology, balancing sediment supply, and lowering pollutant levels. These goals are achieved devising stormwater storage and

Part B

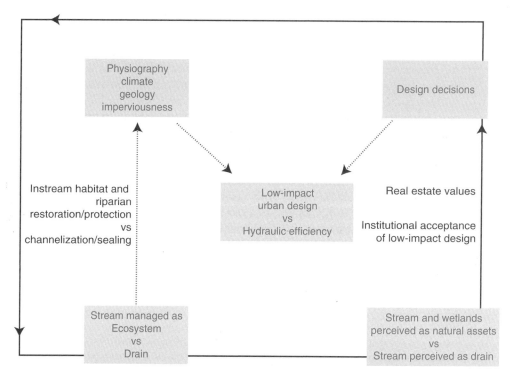

Figure 8.6   A conceptual Model of Stormwater Management in Relation to Stream Ecology and Urban Ecology (based on Grimm *et al.*, 2000; Walsh *et al.*, 2005).

delaying its arrival into water bodies, reducing the amount of impervious surfaces and filtering or treating stormwater to improve water quality (Reich and Lake, 2015). In particular, as stated by Bastien *et al.* (2012), blue-green approaches to Flood Risk Management can be useful to shift from the idea of flood defence to water management with a particular attention to biodiversity and cultural values (Wright *et al.*, 2011; Kenyon, 2007; Werritty, 2006; Johnson and Priest, 2008). In urbanised environments, stormwater management and GBI can effectively reduce density and surface sealing thus recharging the urban groundwater aquifer and reducing soil erosion (Davis and McCuen, 2005). In a long-term perspective, GBI also reduces costs compared to grey infrastructure. A variety of vegetated (detention, retention, basins or ponds; bioswales, rain gardens; wetlands) and unvegetated (rainwater cisterns; highflow bypass channels; porous paving or pervious pavers) systems can be designed to reduce runoff and increase infiltration (see Chapters 6-7). These techniques can be useful in new settlements as well as in existing urban areas. Studies state that retrofitting existing housing developments with rain gardens and vegetated swales reduces storm flows up to 90% (Nassauer and Faust, 1998).

Furthermore, GBI may create an ecosystem which is more self-sustaining and resilient to perturbation (Palmer *et al.*, 2005). The challenge is to better understand interactions between catchments and stream processes in urban areas and also integrate strategies with social, economic, community and political drivers (Walsh *et al.*, 2005). The field of urban stream restoration is dominated by physical

Part B

scientists and engineers and rarely extends beyond stormwater management and bank stabilisation. Re-establishing channel geomorphology and a dynamic equilibrium with the landscape, instead, should be a primary goal (Riley and Leopold, 1998). Urban stream restoration offers the opportunity to integrate physical, chemical and biological processes to rehabilitate impaired ecosystems. It is a unique chance to consider aesthetics and human attitudes toward the landscape and blend ecological and social sciences with landscape design to further the creation of sustainable cities (Paul and Meyer, 2001).

References

Allan, J. D. (2004). Landscapes and Riverscapes: The Influence of Land Use on Stream Ecosystems. *Annual Review of Ecology, Evolution, and Systematics*, 35, p. 257–284.

Armour, C. L., Duff, D. A. and Elmore, W. (1991). Position statement on the effects of livestock grazing on riparian and stream ecosystems. *Fisheries*, 16 (1), p. 1–56. [Online]. Available at: doi:10.1577/1548-8446-16-1.

Bagley, S. (1998). *The road-ripper's guide to wildland road removal.* Wildlands Center for Preventing Roads.

Bastien, N. R. P., Arthur, S., and McLoughlin, M. J. (2012). Valuing amenity: public perceptions of sustainable drainage systems ponds. *Water and Environment Journal*, 26 (1), p. 19–29. [Online]. Available at: doi:10.1111/j.1747-6593.2011.00259.x.

Beechie, T. J., Liermann, M., Pollock, M. M., Baker, S., and Davies, J. (2006). Channel pattern and river-floodplain dynamics in forested mountain river systems. *Geomorphology*, 78 (1–2), p. 124–141. [Online]. Available at: doi:10.1016/j.geomorph.2006.01.030.

Beechie, T. J., Sear, D. A., Olden, J. D., Pess, G. R., Buffington, J. M., Moir, H., Roni, P., and Pollock, M. M. (2010). Process-Based Principles for Restoring River Ecosystems. *BioScience*, 60 (3), p. 209–222. [Online]. Available at: doi:10.1525/bio.2010.60.3.7.

Belsky, A. J., Matzke, A. and Uselman, S. (1999). Survey of livestock influences on stream and riparian ecosystems in the western United States. *Journal of Soil and Water Conservation*, 54 (1), p.419–431.

Bennett, E. M., Peterson, G. D., and Gordon, L. J. (2009). Understanding relationships among multiple ecosystem services. *Ecology Letters*, 12 (12), p. 1394–1404. *Scopus* [Online]. Available at: doi:10.1111/j.1461-0248.2009.01387.x.

Bernhardt, E. S., Palmer, M. A., Allan, J. D., and Brooks, S. (2005). *Synthesizing U.S. River Restoration Efforts*. 308, p. 636–637.

Bernhardt, E. S., Sudduth, E. B., and Palmer, M. A. (2007). Restoring rivers one reach at a time: results from a survey of U.S. *Science*, 308, p. 636–637. *Scopus*.

Boccalaro, F. (2012). *Difesa delle coste e ingegneria naturalistica: manuale di ripristino degli habitat lagunari, dunari, litoranei e marini.* Flaccovio Dario.

Boon, P. J., Davies, B. R., and Geoffrey Petts, E. (eds.). (2000). *Global Perspectives on River Conservation: Science, Policy and Practice.* [Accessed 19 January 2016].

Booth, D. B. (2005). Challenges and prospects for restoring urban streams: a perspective from the Pacific Northwest of North America. *Journal of the North American Benthological Society*, 24 (3), p. 724–737. [Online]. Available at: doi:10.1899/04-025.1.

Booth, D. B. and Jackson, C. R. (1997). Urbanization of Aquatic Systems: Degradation Thresholds, Stormwater Detection, and the Limits of Mitigation1. *JAWRA Journal of the American Water Resources Association*, 33 (5), p. 1077–1090. [Online]. Available at: doi:10.1111/j.1752-1688.1997.tb04126.x.

Booth, D. B., Karr, J. R., Schauman, S., Konrad, C. P., Morley, S. A., Larson, M. G., and Burges, S. J. (2004). Reviving Urban Streams: Land Use, Hydrology, Biology, and Human

Behavior1. *JAWRA Journal of the American Water Resources Association*, 40 (5), p. 1351–1364. [Online]. Available at: doi:10.1111/j.1752-1688.2004.tb01591.x.

Bowker, P. (2007). *Flood Resistance and Resilience Solutions: An R&D Scoping Study*. Defra: London.

Brierley, G. J. and Fryirs, K. A. (eds.). (2004). The River Styles Framework. In: *Geomorphology and River Management*, Blackwell Publishing, p. 241–242. [Online]. Available at: http://onlinelibrary.wiley.com/doi/10.1002/9780470751367.part3/summary [Accessed 18 January 2016].

Brooks, S. S., Palmer, M. A., Cardinale, B. J., Swan, C. M., and Ribblett, S. (2002). Assessing Stream Ecosystem Rehabilitation: Limitations of Community Structure Data. *Restoration Ecology*, 10 (1), p. 156–168. [Online]. Available at: doi:10.1046/j.1526-100X.2002.10117.x.

Brown, R. R., Keath, N., and Wong, T. H. F. (2009). Urban water management in cities: historical, current and future regimes. *Water Science and Technology*, 59 (5), p. 847–855. *Scopus* [Online]. Available at: doi:10.2166/wst.2009.029.

Cowx, I. G. and Van Zyll de Jong, M. (2004). Rehabilitation of freshwater fisheries: tales of the unexpected? *Fisheries Management and Ecology*, 11 (3-4), p. 243–249. [Online]. Available at: doi:10.1111/j.1365-2400.2004.00410.x.

Davis, A. P. and McCuen, R. H. (2005). *Stormwater Management for Smart Growth*. New York: Springer-Verlag. [Online]. Available at: http://link.springer.com/10.1007/0-387-27593-2 [Accessed 19 January 2016].

DEFRA. (2005). *Making Space for Water. Developing a new Government strategy for flood and coastal erosion risk management in England*. DEFRA, London.

Doyle, M. W., Stanley, E. H., Strayer, D. L., Jacobson, R. B., and Schmidt, J. C. (2005). Effective discharge analysis of ecological processes in streams. *Water Resources Research*, 41 (11), p.16. [Online]. Available at: doi:10.1029/2005WR004222.

Everett, G. and Lamond, J. (2014). *A conceptual framework for understanding behaviours and attitudes around 'Blue-Green' approaches to Flood-Risk Management*. In: 18 June 2014, p. 101-112. [Online]. Available at: doi:10.2495/FRIAR140091 [Accessed 15 December 2015].

FISRWG. (1998). *Stream Corridor Restoration: Principles, Processes, and Practices*. (Federal Interagency Stream Restoration Workin Group) GPO Item No. 0120- A. USDA, Washington, DC.

Fullerton, A., Burnett, K., Steel, E., Flitcroft, R., Pess, G., Feist, B., Torgersen, C., Miller, D., and Sanderson, B. (2010). Hydrological connectivity for riverine fish: measurement challenges and research opportunities. *Publications, Agencies and Staff of the U.S. Department of Commerce*. [Online]. Available at: http://digitalcommons.unl.edu/usdeptcommercepub/265.

Georgiou, S. and Turner, R. K. (2012). *Valuing ecosystem services: the case of multi-functional wetlands*. Routledge.

Gilvear, D. J., Spray, C. J., and Casas-Mulet, R. (2013). River rehabilitation for the delivery of multiple ecosystem services at the river network scale. *Journal of Environmental Management*, 126, p. 30–43. [Online]. Available at: doi:10.1016/j.jenvman.2013.03.026.

Grimm, N. B., Grove, J. G., Pickett, S. T. A., and Redman, C. L. (2000). Integrated Approaches to Long-Term Studies of Urban Ecological Systems. *BioScience*, 50 (7), p. 571–584. [Online]. Available at: doi:10.1641/0006-3568(2000)050[0571:IATLTO]2.0.CO;2.

Gurnell, A., Thompson, K., Goodson, J., and Moggridge, H. (2008). Propagule deposition along river margins: linking hydrology and ecology: Propagule deposition along river margins. *Journal of Ecology*, 96 (3), p. 553–565. [Online]. Available at: doi:10.1111/j.1365-2745.2008.01358.x.

Holmes, N., Ward, D., and Jose, P. (2001). *The New Rivers and Wildlife Handbook*. Sandy, Bedfordshire: The Royal Society for the Protection of Birds.

Hoover, T. M., Marczak, L. B., Richardson, J. S., and Yonemitsu, N. (2010). Transport and settlement of organic matter in small streams. *Freshwater Biology*, 55 (2).

Izaak Walton League. (2006). *A Handbook for Stream Enhancement & Stewardship*. Blacksburg, Va. : Gaithersburg, Md: McDonald and Woodward Publishing Company.

Johnson, C. L. and Priest, S. J. (2008). Flood Risk Management in England: A Changing Landscape of Risk Responsibility? *International Journal of Water Resources Development*,24(4),p.513–525.[Online].Availableat:doi:10.1080/07900620801923146.

Jones, J. A. and Grant, G. E. (1996). Peak Flow Responses to Clear-Cutting and Roads in Small and Large Basins, Western Cascades, Oregon. *Water Resources Research*, 32 (4), p. 959–974. [Online]. Available at: doi:10.1029/95WR03493.

Jungwirth, M., Muhar, S., and Schmutz, S. (2002). Re-establishing and assessing ecological integrity in riverine landscapes. *Freshwater Biology*, 47 (4), p. 867–887. [Online]. Available at: doi:10.1046/j.1365-2427.2002.00914.x.

Karr, J. R. (1991). Biological Integrity: A Long-Neglected Aspect of Water Resource Management. *Ecological Applications*, 1 (1), p. 66–84. [Online]. Available at: doi:10.2307/1941848.

Karr, J. R. and Chu, E. W. (2006). Seven foundations of biological monitoring and assessment. *Biologia Ambientale*, 20 (2), p. 7–18.

Kazmierczak, A. and Carter, J. (2010). *Adaptation to climate change using green and blue infrastructure. A database of case studies*. [Online]. Available at: http://orca.cf.ac.uk/64906/1/Database_Final_no_hyperlinks.pdf [Accessed 15 December 2015].

Kenyon, W. (2007). Evaluating flood risk management options in Scotland: A participant-led multi-criteria approach. *Ecological Economics*, 64 (1), p. 70–81. [Online]. Available at: doi:10.1016/j.ecolecon.2007.06.011.

Kondolf, G. M., Boulton, A. J., O'Daniel, S., Poole, G. C., Rahel, F. J., Stanley, E. H., Wohl, E., B\a ang Asa, Carlstrom, J., and Cristoni, C., others. (2006). Process-based ecological river restoration: visualizing three-dimensional connectivity and dynamic vectors to recover lost linkages. *Ecology and Society*, 11 (2), p. 5.

Lemons, J. and Victor, R. (2008). *Uncertainty in River Restoration, in: River Restoration: Managing the Uncertainty in Restoring Physical Habitat*. Darby, S. and Sear, D. (eds.). Chichester, West Sussex, England: John Wiley & Sons Ltd.

McBain, W., Wilkes, D., and Retter, M. (2010). *Flood Resilience and Resistance for Critical Infrastructure*. CIRIA. London.

Moore, R. D. and Richardson, J. S. (2012). Natural disturbance and forest management in riparian zones: comparison of effects at reach, catchment, and landscape scales. *Freshwater Science*, 31 (1), p. 239–247. [Online]. Available at: doi:10.1899/11-030.1.

Nassauer, J. I. and Faust, C. (1998). Urban Ecological Retrofit. *Landscape Journal*, 17 (Special Issue), p. 15–17. [Online]. Available at: doi:10.3368/lj.17.Special_Issue.15.

Newson, M. (2001). New approaches to river management, edited by A.J.M. Smits, P.H. Nienhuis and R.S.E.W. Leuven. Backhuys, Leiden, 2000. ISBN 90-5782-058-7. *Aquatic Conservation: Marine and Freshwater Ecosystems*, 11 (6), p. 487–487. [Online]. Available at: doi:10.1002/aqc.488.

Nilsson, C., Pizzuto, J. E., Moglen, G. E., Palmer, M. A., Stanley, E. H., Bockstael, N. E., and Thompson, L. C. (2003). Ecological Forecasting and the Urbanization of Stream Ecosystems: Challenges for Economists, Hydrologists, Geomorphologists, and Ecologists. *Ecosystems*, 6 (7), p. 659–674. [Online]. Available at: doi:10.1007/s10021-002-0217-2.

Part B

Novotny, V., Ahern, J., and Brown, P. (2010). *Water Centric Sustainable Communities: Planning, Retrofitting and Building the Next Urban Environment.*

Palmer, M. a., Bernhardt, E. s., Allan, J. D., Lake, P. s., Alexander, G., Brooks, S., Carr, J., Clayton, S., Dahm, C. N., Follstad Shah, J., Galat, D. L., Loss, S. G., Goodwin, P., Hart, D. d., Hassett, B., Jenkinson, R., Kondolf, G. m., Lave, R., Meyer, J. l., O'donnell, T. k., Pagano, L., and Sudduth, E. (2005). Standards for ecologically successful river restoration. *Journal of Applied Ecology*, 42 (2), p. 208–217. [Online]. Available at: doi:10.1111/j.1365-2664.2005.01004.x.

Paul, M. J. and Meyer, J. L. (2001). Streams in the Urban Landscape. *Annual Review of Ecology and Systematics*, 32 (1), p. 333–365. [Online]. Available at: doi:10.1146/annurev.ecolsys.32.081501.114040.

Poff, N. L., Allan, J. D., Bain, M. B., Karr, J. R., Prestegaard, K. L., Richter, B. D., Sparks, R. E., and Stromberg, J. C. (1997). The natural flow regime. *BioScience*, 47 (11). [Online]. Available at: http://asu.pure.elsevier.com/en/publications/the-natural-flow-regime-a-paradigm-for-river-conservation-and-res [Accessed 18 January 2016].

Poole, G. C. (2002). Fluvial landscape ecology: addressing uniqueness within the river discontinuum. *Freshwater Biology*, 47 (4), p. 641–660. [Online]. Available at: doi:10.1046/j.1365-2427.2002.00922.x.

Pretty, J. L., Harrison, S. S. C., Shepherd, D. J., Smith, C., Hildrew, A. G., and Hey, R. D. (2003). River rehabilitation and fish populations: assessing the benefit of instream structures. *Journal of applied ecology*, 40 (2), p. 251–265.

Principato, G. (2011). *Tecniche di ingegneria naturalistica negli interventi idraulico-forestale.* Parco Nazionale della Sila.

Reich, P. and Lake, P. S. (2015). Extreme hydrological events and the ecological restoration of flowing waters. *Freshwater Biology*, 60 (12), p. 2639–2652. [Online]. Available at: doi:10.1111/fwb.12508.

Richardson, J. S., Hoover, T. M., and Lecerf, A. (2009). Coarse particulate organic matter dynamics in small streams: towards linking function to physical structure. *Freshwater Biology*, 54 (10), p. 2116–2126.

Richardson, J. S., Zhang, Y., and Marczak, L. B. (2010). Resource subsidies across the land–freshwater interface and responses in recipient communities. *River Research and Applications*, 26 (1), p. 55–66. [Online]. Available at: doi:10.1002/rra.1283.

Richter, B. D., Mathews, R., Harrison, D. L., and Wigington, R. (2003). Ecologically sustainable water management: managing river flows for ecological integrity. *Ecological applications*, 13 (1), p. 206–224.

Richter, B. D. and Thomas, G. A. (2007). Restoring environmental flows by modifying dam operations. *Ecology and society*, 12 (1), p. 12.

Riley, A. and Leopold, L. B. (1998). *Restoring Streams in Cities: A Guide for Planners, Policymakers, and Citizens.* Washington, D.C: Island Press.

Robertson, A. i. and Rowling, R. w. (2000). Effects of livestock on riparian zone vegetation in an Australian dryland river. *Regulated Rivers: Research & Management*, 16 (5), p. 527–541. [Online]. Available at: doi:10.1002/1099-1646(200009/10)16:5 < 527::AID-RRR602 > 3.0.CO;2-W.

Roni, P. and Beechie, T. (eds.). (2012). *Stream and Watershed Restoration: A Guide to Restoring Riverine Processes and Habitats.* Chichester, West Sussex; Hoboken, NJ: Wiley-Blackwell.

Roni, P., Hanson, K., and Beechie, T. (2008). Global Review of the Physical and Biological Effectiveness of Stream Habitat Rehabilitation Techniques. *North American Journal of Fisheries Management*, 28 (3), p. 856–890. [Online]. Available at: doi:10.1577/M06-169.1.

Roni, P., Quimby, E. and Society, A. F. (2005). *Monitoring Stream and Watershed Restoration.* CABI.

Sear, D. A. (1994). River restoration and geomorphology. *Aquatic Conservation: Marine and Freshwater Ecosystems*, 4 (2), p. 169–177. [Online]. Available at: doi:10.1002/aqc.3270040207.

Sharma, A. K., Gray, S., Diaper, C., Liston, P., and Howe, C. (2008). Assessing integrated water management options for urban developments – Canberra case study. *Urban Water Journal*, 5 (2), p. 147–159. [Online]. Available at: doi:10.1080/15730620701736829.

Stanford, J. A. (2007). CHAPTER 1 - Landscapes and Riverscapes. In: Hauer, F. R. and Lamberti, G. A. (eds.), *Methods in Stream Ecology*, San Diego: Academic Press, p. 3–21. [Online]. Available at: http://www.sciencedirect.com/science/article/pii/B9780123329080500036 [Accessed 18 January 2016].

Stanford, J. A., Frissell, C. A., and Coutant, C. C. (2006). 5 - The Status of Freshwater Habitats. In: Williams, R. N. (ed.), *Return to the River*, Burlington: Academic Press, p. 173–248. [Online]. Available at: http://www.sciencedirect.com/science/article/pii/B9780120884148500084 [Accessed 18 January 2016].

Sweeney, B. W., Bott, T. L., Jackson, J. K., Kaplan, L. A., Newbold, J. D., Standley, L. J., Hession, W. C., and Horwitz, R. J. (2004). Riparian deforestation, stream narrowing, and loss of stream ecosystem services. *Proceedings of the National Academy of Sciences of the United States of America*, 101 (39), p. 14132–14137. [Online]. Available at: doi:10.1073/pnas.0405895101.

UN Water. (2009). *Water in a Changing World – World Water Development Report 3. World Water Assessment Program, United Nations Education*. Scientific and Educational Organization. [Online]. Available at: http://www.unesco.org/water/wwap/wwdr/wwdr3/ [Accessed 18 January 2016].

Vörösmarty, C. J., McIntyre, P. B., Gessner, M. O., Dudgeon, D., Prusevich, A., Green, P., Glidden, S., Bunn, S. E., Sullivan, C. A., Liermann, C. R., and Davies, P. M. (2010). Global threats to human water security and river biodiversity. *Nature*, 467 (7315), p. 555–561. [Online]. Available at: doi:10.1038/nature09440.

Vought, L. B.-M. and Lacoursière, J. O. (2010). Restoration of Streams in the Agricultural Landscape. In: Eiseltová, M. (ed.), *Restoration of Lakes, Streams, Floodplains, and Bogs in Europe*, Wetlands: Ecology, Conservation and Management 3, Springer Netherlands, p. 225–242. [Online]. Available at: http://link.springer.com/chapter/10.1007/978-90-481-9265-6_12 [Accessed 19 January 2016].

Walsh, C. J., Roy, A. H., Feminella, J. W., Cottingham, P. D., Groffman, P. M., and Morgan, I. R. P. (2005). The urban stream syndrome: Current knowledge and the search for a cure. *Journal of the North American Benthological Society*, 24 (3), p. 706–723. *Scopus* [Online]. Available at: doi:10.1899/0887-3593(2005)024\[0706:TUSSCK\]2.0.CO;2.

Ward, J. V. (1998). Riverine landscapes: Biodiversity patterns, disturbance regimes, and aquatic conservation. *Biological Conservation*, 83 (3), p. 269–278. [Online]. Available at: doi:10.1016/S0006-3207(97)00083-9.

Ward, J. V. and Stanford, J. A. (1995). Ecological connectivity in alluvial river ecosystems and its disruption by flow regulation. *Regulated Rivers: Research & Management*, 11 (1), p. 105–119.

Ward, J. V., Tockner, K., Arscott, D. B., and Claret, C. (2002). Riverine landscape diversity. *Freshwater Biology*, 47 (4), p. 517–539. [Online]. Available at: doi:10.1046/j.1365-2427.2002.00893.x.

Ward, S., Lundy, L., Shaffer, P., Wong, T., Ashley, R., Arthur, S., Armitage, N. P., Walker, L., Brown, R., Deletic, A., and Butler, D. (2012). Water sensitive urban design in the city of the future. *WSUD 2012: Water sensitive urban design. Building the water sensitive community*, 7th International Conference on Water Sensitive Urban Design, Barton, A.C.T.: Engineers Australia, 2012: 79–86. [Accessed 15 December 2015].

Part B

Werritty, A. (2006). Sustainable flood management: oxymoron or new paradigm? *Area*, 38 (1), p. 16–23. [Online]. Available at: doi:10.1111/j.1475-4762.2006.00658.x.

Wright, G. B., Arthur, S., Bowles, G., Bastien, N., and Unwin, D. (2011). Urban creep in Scotland: stakeholder perceptions, quantification and cost implications of permeable solutions. *Water and Environment Journal*, 25 (4), p. 513–521. [Online]. Available at: doi:10.1111/j.1747-6593.2010.00247.x.

Zitek, A., Schmutz, S., and Jungwirth, M. (2008). Assessing the efficiency of connectivity measures with regard to the EU-Water Framework Directive in a Danube-tributary system. *Hydrobiologia*, 609 (1), p. 139–161. [Online]. Available at: doi:10.1007/s10750-008-9394-0.

Chapter 9.1
The Bronx River, USA – Strategies and Techniques
Katia Perini

9.1.1 Context

The Bronx River flows through the New York City (NYC) borough of the Bronx and Southern Westchester County in New York State (Figure 9.1.1). Its corridor begins near Valhalla, in New York, and the river crosses south for 37 km through Westchester and Bronx Counties before emptying into the East River (Bronx River Alliance, 2006a). The Bronx is a low-income, polluted neighbourhood in

Urban Sustainability and River Restoration: Green and Blue Infrastructure, First Edition.
Katia Perini and Paola Sabbion.
© 2017 John Wiley & Sons Ltd. Published 2017 by John Wiley & Sons Ltd.

Figure 9.1.1   The New York City Section of the Bronx River (United States, NY).

the northern part of the city and it has long been characterised by many environmental and social inequities (Loria, 2009; Maantay, 2000).

The actions and initiatives implemented by public and private actors over the past 40 years have allowed the construction of the Bronx River Greenway. This trail along the river was devised for recreational use and environmental preservation and it clearly improves the ecological conditions within the neighbourhood and the river watershed (Figure 9.1.2).

The Bronx River winds its way through areas with different types of land use and physical characteristics (Figure 9.1.2). The neighbourhood around the Bronx River is characterised by industries to the south and residential and parkland areas in the central and northern segments (Bronx River Alliance, 2006a; New York City Department of Environmental Protection, 2010; New York City Department of Environmental Protection, 2015). The southern segment of the Bronx River, the estuary section in the Hunts Point peninsula, is mostly dedicated to industrial, parkland and residential use and also features some commercial, institutional and vacant parts (Figure 9.1.3). The access to the riverfront is extremely limited along this stretch, with the exception of the Hunts Point Riverside Park, which is a small green area.

The southern portion of the Bronx River has undergone an important makeover in recent years, and the waterfront is increasingly more accessible for citizens, even though the presence of the Amtrak railway line and the Sheridan Expressway hinder further renovation. The railway line and the expressway, in fact, hold a prominent place along the Bronx River and clearly influence the visual impact and the use of this area as they run on a north-south axis along the southern segment of the River for about 1.5 km (Figure 9.1.4).

Along the northern portion of the Bronx River, the building stock comprises a mixture of detached and semi-detached homes, townhouses, brownstones, and

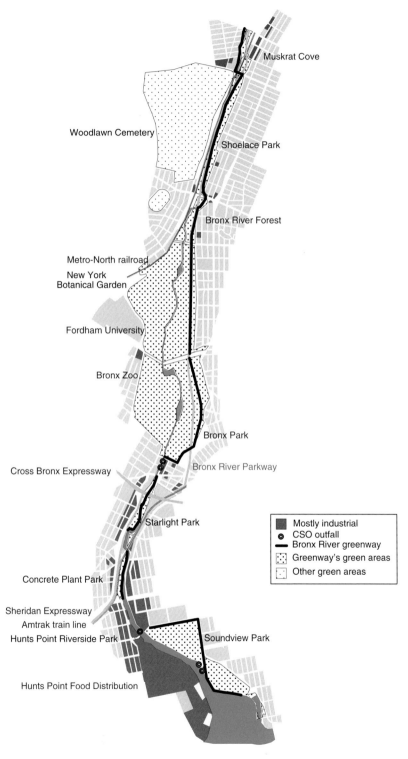

Figure 9.1.2   The Bronx River Area Land Use and the Bronx River Greenway.

Figure 9.1.3   The Hunts Point Peninsula in the Bronx District.

Figure 9.1.4   Infrastructures Along the Bronx River.

multi-storey, multifamily apartment buildings. More mixed uses can also be found closer to the Bronx Park as commercial structures and industrial buildings are set alongside residential areas on most of the east bank of the River. The central section of the Bronx River area is dominated by the Bronx Park, an extensive parkland that includes the New York Botanical Garden and the Bronx Zoo. The Bronx Park borders with a mostly residential area, also featuring some industries and the Bronx River Parkway that runs parallel to the River (Figure 9.1.5). Finally, the northern edge of the Bronx River's eastern shore is distinguished almost exclusively by residential zoning.

In conclusion, the densely populated section of the Bronx River that flows through industrial areas shows a range of problems typical of urban rivers, while the northern part flowing through Bronx Park is mostly naturalised and well vegetated.

Human activities implemented over 400 years along the Bronx River have had a very high impact on the river ecology and on the environment. The Bronx River has been used for human activities at least since the time of the Mohegan Indians, who inhabited the mainland peninsula that came to be called the Bronx, and used its numerous freshwater waterways – including the Bronx River, known then as Aquehung or "River of High Bluffs" – for drinking water, food, transportation, waste removal, and recreation (Kadt, 2011).

In 1639, a Dutch immigrant named Jonas Bronck purchased this land from the Mohegans. The valley remained vegetated and the river water was considered "pure and wholesome". In 1798, the Bronx River was even proposed as the source

Figure 9.1.5   The Bronx River Parkway and the Bronx River.

of New York City's drinking water (New York City Department of Environmental Protection, 2010). However, in the 1680s, the construction of a dam (now known as the 182nd Street Dam), affected the health of the River, slowing the water flow, reducing fish passage and strongly affecting the ecosystems (Griffin, 2009). In the 1840s, the railroad construction turned the valley into an industrial corridor for the production of tobacco, paint, cotton, and rubber products. Since then, the Bronx River has been used for waste discharge and as a source of water for industrial processes. By the beginning of the eighteenth century, 12 mills were manufacturing paper, flour, pottery, tapestries, barrels, and snuff, powered by water from the River (Kadt, 2011).

In the early 1900s, the construction of sewers that discharged into the Bronx River worsened its water quality. In the same period, New York City's demand for water continued to rise and the construction of the Kensico Dam diverted the upper reaches of the Bronx River into the reservoir, cutting its flow by approximately 25% (New York City Department of Environmental Protection, 2010). Mills operated along the Bronx River until 1934, decreasing its water quality. Dams harnessing the Bronx River's power hindered anadromous fish from spawning upstream (Greenburgh Nature Center and Scarsdale Historical Society, 1983). The damage caused by industrial production lasted a century, and had major negative effects also on human health, as demonstrated by a study conducted in 2003 by Consolidated Edison (Con Ed) and the New York State Department for Environmental Conservation (DEC). This study found that hazardous waste produced in the power plant in the early 1900s, could be a cause of cancer and asthma (Nolan, 2003).

When mills started to close, however, the water quality of the Bronx River became an even greater concern due to the creation of combined sewer systems (CSS) and separate stormwater conveyance systems that discharged into the waterway (Kadt, 2011). Urbanisation led to increased population and more loading from the sewage network and industries. The construction of sewer systems and physical changes also affected the surface topography and the watershed imperviousness (New York City Department of Environmental Protection, 2015).

Some areas have not been urbanised (e.g., the 268-acres Bronx Park has prevented urban development on either side of the river), but many large-scale projects have been realised, including highway connections that divide the Bronx (New York City Department of Environmental Protection, 2010).

This historical overview shows how the Bronx River rapidly turned from a beautiful and flourishing resource to a contaminated conduit for industrial and residential waste. In this area, there are still many pending ecological and environmental issues related to transportation and industry, although public interest is growing. "As the twentieth century becomes the twenty-first, people are returning to the Bronx River, drawn back to a place that has remained true to itself in a region where much else has changed" (Bronx River Alliance, 2016).

9.1.2   Ecological and environmental issues

The urbanisation around the Bronx River (with exception of the Bronx Park) has increased annual stormwater runoff to the water body and has all but eliminated any natural response mechanism (e.g., tidal marshes, buffer zones) that could have helped to absorb the hydraulic load (New York City Department of Environmental Protection, 2010). According to McDonnell and Larson (2004), impervious surfaces, such as rooftops, parking lots, and roads, cover more than 60% of the River's upland areas and inhibit the watershed's natural hydrological function. This results in disturbed flow patterns within the river channel that cause flash floods, erosion, low habitat value, high water temperatures, low base flow, and excessive sedimentation (Bronx River Alliance, 2006a). This is not the only problem related to human activities; other examples provide further insights such as the dams located in the Bronx Park section that work as barriers for fish passage, floating waste, and sewage, which lower dissolved oxygen (DO) levels and damage aquatic organisms.

Habitat degradation and poor water quality prevent the growth of flora and fauna and violate health standards. These waters are hence unsuitable for public recreation. The City's sewage system plays an important role in polluting the Bronx River. During storm events, combined sewer overflows (CSO) discharge untreated sewage, stormwater, and other pollutants into the River (Bronx River Alliance, 2006a). Combined sewer systems are designed to collect rainwater run-off, domestic sewage and industrial wastewater in the same pipe. During periods of heavy rainfall or snow melt, if the wastewater volume in a combined sewer system exceeds its capacity, excess wastewater can be discharged directly into nearby water bodies (U.S. EPA, 2016). Every year, 100 billion liters of raw sewage and polluted stormwater flow into New York City's waterways via combined sewer overflows (Bronx River Alliance, 2016).

There are numerous discharges to each section of the Bronx River, in total 108 along the freshwater shoreline and 112 pipes along the saline shoreline (New York City Department of Environmental Protection, 2015). Discharges have an impact on water quality, as demonstrated by a wide monitoring campaign comprising over 3,800 individual water quality measurements. Results showed low dissolved oxygen (DO) concentrations in the lower portion of the River. In addition, temperatures in the northern part of the River tend to have lower median and mean water temperatures, an observation consistent with the greater impervious cover and stormwater and combined sewer overflow discharges downstream that introduce warmer runoff into the river (Bronx River Alliance, 2015). Another important aspect is the presence of invasive vegetation, which limits the diversity of the vegetative community, contributes to bank instability, and excludes trees from the riverbank, thus limiting the supply of large woody debris necessary to create certain habitats (Bronx River Alliance, 2006a; Kriesberg, 2013).

9.1.3 Strategies, techniques and results

The strategies implemented to improve ecological and environmental conditions in (and for) the Bronx River address operation and maintenance procedures and related planning efforts to maximise CSO capture and reduce contaminants in the combined sewer system for a better water quality. Green solutions are employed as control tools and can effectively restore site hydrology to capture, infiltrate, evaporate, and detain stormwater runoff reducing both its volume and peak overflow rate. Consequently, a lower volume of stormwater reaches the combined sewer system, while the water quality is improved (the "first flush" contains the highest concentration of nitrogen, other nutrients, and urban pollutants). Such solutions include rain gardens, vegetated buffers, grassed swales, green roofs, and increased tree cover (New York City Department of Environmental Protection, 2010). These contribute to the improvement of hydrology in reducing erosion, sedimentation, and habitat disturbance. The New York City Department of Environmental Protection (2015) claims that Green Infrastructure (GI) penetration rates would manage 14% of the impervious surfaces within the Bronx River combined sewer service area by 2030. Biodiversity also plays an important role. Ecological goals include protecting and improving the aquatic and riparian vegetation and animal biological diversity through the targeted removal of invasive vegetation, and increasing habitat connectivity (Bronx River Alliance, 2006a). The invasive Japanese knotweed species grows very fast and tall, so that nothing else can grow in its surroundings; and, thus, planting native species can re-establish native habitats for the benefit of plants and animals.

In general, the initiatives implemented, have sought to restore the habitat and wildlife and foster a healthy ecosystem, providing support for fishes, birds and biodiversity within the river basin (Kriesberg, 2013). As explained, the Bronx River shows different characteristics. Long stretches of natural shoreline characterise the northern part (in the Bronx), and altered shorelines can be found in the heavily industrialised areas set in the southern part. This imbalance has influenced both design strategies for the restoration, and related results.

The integration of green infrastructure in the areas bordering the Bronx River is strongly related to the Bronx River Greenway, a multi-use path which covers the length of the river on both east and west shorelines on a north-south axis (Bronx River Alliance). The Greenway stretches for 37 km and includes several parks, connections (in general 'grey' connections for bikes and pedestrians), and also features some critical interruptions (Figure 9.1.2). Most of the green areas have been built or renovated along with the Greenway construction to exploit ecological, environmental as well as social and recreational positive effects.

Since 2006, on account of the Bronx River Greenway project, new green spaces in the neighbourhood have been inaugurated and existing parks have been enlarged, connecting some areas which were separated by highways, railroads, and other barriers. The Greenway design aims to follow ecological performance guidelines related to landscape (e.g., ecological connectivity and habitat diversity increase, enhancement of public amenities and quality of life, control of invasive plant species), stormwater management, hardscape (e.g., increase of smart access to the river, replacement of informal circulation networks with bike and pedestrian connections), streetscape, and sustainable maintenance practices (Bronx River Alliance, 2006b).

The Bronx River Greenway starts (in the southern section) from the Soundview Park, the largest park along the Bronx River, a former landfill that was closed in the 1960s. The Soundview Park bikeway (constructed from 2001 to 2011) offers a continuous riverside route, providing access points to the water along the Bronx River, and overlook seating areas (Bronx River Alliance, 2011, 2006b; Patrick Rocchio, 2010). In recent years, the Soundview Lagoons, located at the southeastern end of the park, have been cleaned up to restore the natural habitat (New York City Department of Environmental Protection, 2010).

The north-west path of the Bronx River Greenway has not been connected yet to its adjacent green area on the opposite side of the river, the Hunts Point Riverside Park, which has recently been transformed into the first waterfront park constructed in the South Bronx over more than 60 years (Bronx River Alliance, 2004). At the present time, the Greenway connection between the Hunts Point Riverside Park and Concrete Plant Park, as well as the link between the Soundview Park and Concrete Park, have not been realised. However, federal funding addressed for the construction of two bicycle/pedestrian bridges and approximately 1.2 km of pathway between Concrete Plant and Starlight Parks demonstrate the project is progressing (Schumer, 2015).

Concrete Plant Park is a waterfront park, which is accessible along the western shoreline of the Bronx River and which was completed in 2009 (Figure 9.1.6). Formerly, it was an abandoned concrete plant. Half of the existing structures of the cement manufacturing facility, which closed in 1987, were maintained as relics of the site's industrial history (Asaba, 2008), and the park contains facilities supporting and linking existing and planned multiuse pedestrian greenways with other bicycle and pedestrian routes as well as a canoe and kayak launch site. The requalification of the area included ecological restoration of the mudflats through large-scale salt marsh grass planting, and the construction of an aquatic nursery (New York City Department of Environmental Protection, 2010).

Further upriver is Starlight Park, which has not been connected to Concrete Plant Park yet. Starlight Park is located between the Bronx River and the Sheridan Expressway and was developed in the 1960s when the Expressway was built. The park was scarcely used and in poor condition. High levels of contamination were

Figures 9.1.6   The Concrete Plant Park.

Figure 9.1.7 Bridge Connecting Starlight Park and Bronx Park.

found in 2003 when soil excavated for the creation of a drainage system was tested. This site, as was discovered, had formerly housed a manufactured gas plant. After remedial work, including the removal and safe disposal of contaminated soil (Bronx River Alliance, 2006b), the park reopened in 2013 (Gonzalez, 2012).

The Bronx Park is set further upriver from Starlight Park and comprises the New York Botanical Garden (opened in 1891) and the Bronx Zoo (opened in 1899; Bronx River Alliance, 2006b), and is characterised by long stretches of natural shoreline (Figure 9.1.7).

Shoelace Park is a narrow section of Bronx Park, which has a canoe and kayak launch site serving for public canoe tours and river wide events (Figure 9.1.8). During the last few years, improvements to this area were completed, such as the installation of a rain garden and swales (Bronx River Alliance, 2011). Native trees, plants, and shrubs, as well as green infrastructure elements, were also added along with a link between Bronx Park and Shoelace Park (Sanchez, 2011). Rain gardens were installed and native trees and shrubs were planted also to improve the last Greenway section, Muskrat Cove, aiming to stabilise its stormwater pipe and improve the conditions in the surrounding areas (Bronx River Alliance, 2013).

A 37-kilometre greenway with few interruptions has been installed, with very important environmental, ecological, and social effects in the underserved Bronx neighbourhood and on a formerly degraded river. The improvement in water quality and the actions implemented have led to important results, such as a significant and measurable biodiversity increase (Milosheff, 2010).

Figure 9.1.8　Bronx Park, New York City.

Figure 9.1.9　Shoelace Park on the Bronx River Greenway, the Bronx, New York City.

Over the past few years, ecological and environmental improvements have been registered together with the enhancement of neighbourhood conditions and land value in the watershed areas due to the opening of the Greenway (Bronx River Alliance, 2006b). However, accessibility, ecological, and environmental issues related to transportation and industries are yet to be tackled and any future plan will also be entrenched on citizens' and volunteers' engagement (as described in Chapter 13.1).

References

Asaba, J. (2008). $10 million facelift for Concrete Park. *Bronx Times*. [Online]. Available at: http://www.bxtimes.com/stories/2008/26/doc485bf4f356e5d260584041.html [Accessed 4 April 2014].

Bronx River Alliance. (2004). *Annual report*. [Online]. Available at: http://www.bronxriver. org/.

Bronx River Alliance. (2006a). *Bronx River Ecological Restoration and Management Plan*. [Online]. Available at: http://www.bronxriver.org/puma/images/usersubmitted/greenway_ plan/FULLwEcoPlan.pdf.

Bronx River Alliance. (2006b). *Bronx River Greenway Plan*. [Online]. Available at: http:// www.bronxriver.org/puma/images/usersubmitted/greenway_plan/BronxRiverGreenway Plan.pdf.

Bronx River Alliance. (2011). *Annual report*.

Bronx River Alliance. (2013). *News & Announcements - Bronx River Alliance. New Raingardens for Muskrat Cove*. [Online]. Available at: http://bronxriver.org/news [Accessed 17 June 2016].

Bronx River Alliance. (2015). *Citizen Science on the Bronx River: An Analysis of Water Quality Data*. [Online]. Available at: http://bronxriver.org/puma/images/usersubmitted/ file/citizenscience_waterquality_ds_final.pdf.

Bronx River Alliance. (2016). *Bronx River Alliance - homepage*. [Online]. Available at: http://www.bronxriver.org/ [Accessed 24 November 2015].

Gonzalez, D. (2012). *City Room*. [Online]. Available at: http://cityroom.blogs.nytimes. com/2012/12/28/a-long-closed-park-is-soon-to-reopen-improved-yet-still-hard-to-reach/ [Accessed 29 May 2014].

Greenburgh Nature Center and Scarsdale Historical Society. (1983). *Bronx River Retrospective: 300 Years of Life Along the Bronx River Valley*. Greenburgh Nature Center.

Griffin, D. (2009). *How To Polute A River*. [Online]. Available at: http://bronxrivereducation. edublogs.org/2009/11/24/how-to-pollute-a-river-part-1/.

Kadt, M. de. (2011). *The Bronx River: an environmental & social history*. Charleston, SC: History Press.

Kriesberg, R. (2013). *Personal communication in: Katia Perini, 2014. Urban areas and green infrastructure. Research report, published by Urban Design Lab Columbia University ISNB 978-09822174-5-0*. [Online]. Available at: http://urbandesignlab. columbia.edu/files/2015/04/3_Urban_Areas_Green_Infrastructure.pdf.

Loria, K. (2009). *Sustainable South Bronx*. [Online]. Available at: http://cooperator.com/ articles/1916/1/Sustainable-South-Bronx/Page1.html [Accessed 2 April 2014].

Maantay, J. (2000). *Industrial Zoning Changes and Environmental Justice in New York City: An historical, Geographical and Cultural Analysis*. Doctoral dissertation, Rutgers University, New Brunswick.

McDonnell, T. C. and Larson, M. (2004). *Estimating pollutant loading to the Bronx River*. NYC Parks and Recreation Department: Natural Resrouces Group. New York, NY.

Milosheff, P. (2010). Alewife Return To The Bronx River. *The Bronx Times*. [Online]. Available at: http://www.bronx.com/news/local/891.html [Accessed 11 November 2015].

New York City Department of Environmental Protection. (2010). *Waterbody/Watershed Facility Plan Bronx River*. [Online]. Available at: http://www.hydroqual.com/projects/ltcp/wbws/bronx_river/bronx_river_cover.pdf.

New York City Department of Environmental Protection. (2015). *Combined Sewer Overflow Long Term Control Plan for Bronx River*. [Online]. Available at: http://www.nyc.gov/html/dep/pdf/cso_long_term_control_plan/bronx-river-ltcp-201506.pdf.

Nolan, C. (2003). Sludge slows park cleanup. Columbia University Graduate School of Journalism. *Bronx Beat*.

Patrick Rocchio. (2010). Hunts Point Park wins Bruner Award. *The Bronx Times*. [Online]. Available at: http://www.bronx.com/.

Sanchez, K. (2011). NYC parks cut ribbon on new entrance to Shoelace Park. *Bronx Times*. [Online]. Available at: http://www.bxtimes.com/stories/2012/30/30_shoelace_2012_07_26_bx.html [Accessed 4 April 2014].

Schumer, C. (2015). *Schumer, Gellibrand, Serrano, De Blasio announce $10 million in federal dot funding to complete final link along Bronx River Greenway*. [Online]. Available at: http://www.schumer.senate.gov/newsroom/press-releases/schumer-gillibrand-serrano-de-blasio-announce-10-million-in-federal-dot-funding-to-complete-final-link-along-bronx-river-greenway-federal-investment-means-thousands-of-south-bronx-residents-will-be-better-connected-to-other-neighborhoods-in-the-bronx-via-bicycle-and-pedestrian-bridges [Accessed 10 November 2015].

U.S. EPA. (2016). *National Pollutant Discharge Elimination System (NPDES)*. Collections and Lists. [Online]. Available at: https://www.epa.gov/npdes [Accessed 17 June 2016].

Part B

Chapter 9.2
Los Angeles River, USA – Strategies and Techniques

Paola Sabbion

9.2.1 Context

The Los Angeles River (L.A. River) flows for 77 km through the Greater Los Angeles County Region. It originates in the San Fernando Valley, starting in the Simi Hills and Santa Susana Mountains and winds its way between the Transverse and Peninsular Ranges to its mouth in Long Beach, on the Pacific Coast of the United States (Figure 9.2.1). Most of the Los Angeles River watershed is highly developed. The soils have been heavily transformed. Lowland areas have been

Urban Sustainability and River Restoration: Green and Blue Infrastructure, First Edition.
Katia Perini and Paola Sabbion.
© 2017 John Wiley & Sons Ltd. Published 2017 by John Wiley & Sons Ltd.

Figure 9.2.1   The Los Angeles River Basin.

filled, while hills have largely been cut and the soil transported and deposited along the streams to channelise the river banks and used to raise the grade of low lying areas and for the construction of new roads, bridges, and railroads. Factories have been set up along the riverbanks to provide development opportunities, blocking physical access and the view to the river, precluding the formation of riparian habitat, and hindering recreation in river-adjacent lands (LARRMP Final Report, 2007; Figure 9.2.2).

The L.A. basin was formed by 5,486 m of sediment deposited over the last 4 million years on the Miocene siliceous sedimentary rock and diatomaceous shale, siltstone, sandstone, and conglomerate in the San Fernando Valley. Because of its particular geology, the Los Angeles River was one of the few waterways in the region to flow year-round (Harden 2003). Consequently, it was the selected site of native and Spanish colonial settlements that used its water for agricultural and sanitary purposes. In fact, early colonists were attracted to the river, which offered them an oasis in the desert (LARRMP Final Report, 2007), providing a welcome relief from the heat of southern California during the warmer months (Elrick, 2007). Moreover, the availability of water and arable land were important values. The first Spanish settlers who were determined to establish a *pueblo*, chose a low-lying alluvial terrace adjacent to a segment of the L.A. River (Kahrl, 1981).

Figure 9.2.2   The Los Angeles River Bridges and Transport Infrastructures (photo by William Preston Bowling).

The Spanish founded the *Pueblo de Los Angeles* in 1781 and this gradually led to the removal of the Gabrielino Indian original village. The Spanish settlers exploited the river water by creating *zanjas* (irrigation canals) and distributing water to agricultural fields and dwellings. *Zanjas* were used until the nineteenth century, when they were replaced with modern water pipes (Gandy, 2006).

Before the modern era, floods had the beneficial impact of restoring moisture and nutrients to agricultural lands. The River was flowing in a picturesque floodplain typical of the semi-arid landscapes of the American South West. In 1877, William Mulholland, Chief Engineer of the Bureau of Los Angeles Aqueduct, the water conveyance network that would drive Los Angeles to grow into a metropolis, described the river as a "beautiful, limpid little stream with willows on its banks", also calling it the city's "greatest attraction" (Gumprecht, 2001).

Following urban development in the 1880s, although, the city's relationship with the river changed due to the rapid subdivision of agricultural lands into multiple lots and increased building capacity. Moreover, the L.A. River and its underground supply was the city's unique source of water until 1913 (Gumprecht, 2006). In fact, in the 1990s, an explosive growth in Southern California resulted in the pressing need for water. New supplies for the city of Los Angeles were obtained from the Owens Valley on the eastern slope of the Sierra Nevada Mountains (Orlob, 1998). During the 1920s, the city of Los Angeles was attracting an influx of immigrants, as it had acquired an Eden-like image. Many settled along the L.A. River, where factories were concentrated. These areas became known as the "foreign districts" due to the high concentration of newcomers (Gottlieb *et al.*, 2006).

9.2.2   Ecological and environmental issues

The Los Angeles area's topography is naturally flood-prone because its tall mountains that circle the valleys and coastal plain tend to speed stormwater runoff (Elrick, 2007). Moreover, the Los Angeles River has showed a long history of flooding, mostly determined by winter storms. Major floods occurred in 1886, 1914, and 1934. High flows disturbed riverside settlements, creating a hazard that clashed with real estate interests and the needs of existing property owners. From 1935 onwards, the river channel was strengthened with new banks, levees and drainage channels. Following the devastating 1938 flood – when 45 people lost their lives and 1,500 homes were destroyed (Elrick, 2007) – the federal Works Progress Administration and the Corps (U.S. Army Corps of Engineers) tackled this situation. From the 1940s to the 1960s, these public bodies built an 83-km concrete channel (Gandy, 2006). The construction works aimed at draining storm surges twenty thousand times higher than the river's dry season flow (Gumprecht, 2006). The L.A. River became an open flood control channel. Most of the Los Angeles tributaries were also channelised (Figure 9.2.3). The lack of meandering

Figure 9.2.3   The Los Angeles River Artificial Channel in the San Fernando Valley (photo by William Preston Bowling).

caused nearly all of the riverbanks to harden. The river bed concreted for approximately 60 of its 83 km (LARRMP Final Report, 2007). In the 1940s, the freeway system development also worsened the river condition. The river channel was so similar to an empty highway, that in 1948 the Western Asphalt Association suggested to turn the L.A. River into a freeway to enhance the image of the "city's distinctive car-dominated landscape" (Gandy, 2006; Figure 9.2.4).

The Los Angeles area has currently become the most densely populated and industrialised region in California, thus, water quality is low. In the Los Angeles River watershed, impervious surfaces now cover 32% of total lands. Especially in the city, water makes its way to the storm drains and to the river in a short time, also because the upper portions of the watershed are quite steep. Additionally, in the developed areas, most of the streams have been channelised and lined with concrete, increasing the downstream speed of water. Stormwater runoff contributes to worsen the water quality in the watershed, which reaches its poorest standard in the middle and lower portions where human daily activities cause most pollution. Stormwater runoff takes pollutants from streets, lawns, farms, and industrial sites into the river along with fertilisers, dirt, pesticides, and oil. Impervious surfaces, furthermore, do not allow for vegetation and soil to filter contaminants (LARRMP Final Report, 2007).

The process of altering the River for human purposes has created an infrastructure that deprives aquifers, preventing replenishment, and contributes to the need to import massive quantities of drinking water. This artificialisation process has caused the loss of plant and wildlife species, and hinders residents from contact with a natural environment. Furthermore, waste materials and bacteria are often

Figure 9.2.4   The Los Angeles River Concrete Channel Featuring Old Bridges (photo by William Preston Bowling).

found in urban runoff at the confluence with the river. The principal source of nitrogen compounds in the Los Angeles River is from water treatment plants. A variety of actions have been proposed through previous planning efforts to address water quality concerns, but have failed to achieve positive results (LARRMP, 2007).

The Los Angeles River watershed includes three regionally significant ecological areas (SEAs) – Santa Monica Mountains, Verdugo Mountains, and Griffith Park – that are not currently connected to the River corridor (City of Los Angeles, 2016). Moreover, so far, 90% of the riparian habitat surrounding the L.A. River watershed has been artificialised due to its channelisation and urbanisation (State of California, 2016). The L.A. River watershed, until very recently, has also been characterised by a lack of consistent policies addressing ecological and environmental problems. The river, although, is situated on one of the main flyways in the United States. It could become an important destination for migratory birds along the Pacific Flyway, especially if it featured increased wetland. In fact, in its current state, the riverine habitat is not structured and stable enough to allow nesting (City of Los Angeles, 2016).

The Los Angeles River has indeed been a dystopian symbol, "a dried-out dumping ground in the middle of the city" (Wainwright, 2015). It no longer seems a river through much of its course as its channel, bed and banks are encased in concrete. Little water flows in the river except during storms. It can certainly be termed as a degraded urban environment, "the ultimate 'no place' in notorious placeless L.A" (Gottlieb, 2007).

9.2.3   Strategies and techniques

Since the 1980s, the Los Angeles River, which had long been forgotten and had become almost invisible, drew increasing attention. Especially artists and activists rediscovered it. Environmental activist groups as Friends of the Los Angeles River (FoLAR, 2016), Tree People (TreePeople, 2016) and Heal the Bay (Heal the Bay, 2016), have focused on the rehabilitation of the river, watersheds and ocean, declaring their intentions of outlining an alternative to the "single purpose project that is designed strictly to move water as fast as possible out and away" (Desfor and Keil, 2000). As a result, over the past two decades, the City of Los Angeles and the US Army Corps of Engineers of the Los Angeles District (Corps) through various partnerships and agencies – such as Los Angeles County – and activist groups have been actively pursuing the revitalisation of the Los Angeles River.

In 1991, the County of Los Angeles developed the Los Angeles River Master Plan, which was approved in 1996. Since the adoption of the Master Plan, dozens of projects along the River (paths, bikeways, parks) have been completed (Figure 9.2.5). The comprehensive Los Angeles River Revitalization Master Plan (LARRMP) was devised in 2007 (LARRMP Final Report, 2007). The LARRMP focuses on creating a green strip through the City, a network of green areas along the River throughout a continuous 51-kilometre corridor encompassing bikeways, pedestrian paths and public open spaces. This project will extend the River's influence into the city neighbourhoods in order to reconnect communities to the waterway and to each other. Furthermore, regenerating vacant lots, schools,

Figure 9.2.5   River Recreation area at Sepulveda Basin (photo by William Preston Bowling).

campuses and green spaces could help to form a green infrastructure for recreational purposes and stormwater treatment. The long-term vision for the River involves renovating a continuous riparian ecosystem along the River Corridor. Restoring native riparian plant species would support wildlife and would also develop fish passages, fish ladders, and riffle-pool sequences to improve aquifer habitats (LARRMP, 2007).

The main goals of the LARRMP include actions to enhance flood storage and water quality through landscape-based water treatment facilities at major confluences to reduce pollutants carried by tributaries. Maintenance and reestablishment of vegetation as well as urban stormwater runoff treatment will be achieved creating *green strips*, based on the on site characteristics in the riverbanks and in the surrounding linear parkland and streets. Restoring a functional riparian ecosystem and creating a continuous functional riparian corridor providing habitat are also among the key objectives of this project. The plan, furthermore, aims to connect this corridor to other significant habitat and migration routes along the tributaries and into the mountains. Some of the open spaces will incorporate existing and new stormwater outfalls, bio-swales, bio-filtration areas, and surface runoff infiltration strips with the goal of improving runoff water quality in the River Corridor.

There are two main intervention measures to achieve these goals: River Channel Modifications and Open Space Development. River Channel Modifications do not require the reduction of the river flow velocity and are based primarily on vegetation enhancement in the existing river channel. This strategy seeks to

Figure 9.2.6   Los Angeles River Parks, America's Great Outdoors Initiative at North Atwater (photo by William Preston Bowling).

improve the quality of water discharged from stormwater outfalls by developing vegetative bio-swales and bio-filtration areas. River Channel Modifications include flow velocity reduction measures to increase flood protection and to allow the growth of vegetation in and along the river channel. It is also necessary to develop continuous or intermittent channel bottom habitat areas (LARRMP Final Report, 2007). Moreover, these projects provide safe access to the water, ensuring that people can enter-exit the channel without danger and establish a flood warning system in the event of high flow conditions (LARRMP, 2007).

In addition to this range of physical channel modification measures in the River Corridor, the LARRMP encompasses a variety of public space development measures as the creation of small *pocket parks*, natural areas, urban plazas and civic spaces in reclaimed channel areas (Figure 9.2.6). Development features (located in construction areas and existing communities) along the River Corridor would provide local access to the river and would be integrated with community-oriented pedestrian meetings in squares, courtyards, habitat areas, boulevards, *paseos*, and promenades. Riverfront Parks would be established along and adjacent to the river. Portions of the park would also be used as vegetated open space for water quality enhancement. The plan envisages a landscaped buffer zone, which is 10 metres wide, along the river edge. It includes bio-swale, bio-filtration, detention, and infiltration areas, daylighting of existing storm drains, connections to neighbouring communities, and access to the river. Linear Parks featuring landscaped meandering paths, resting areas, and viewpoints can be devised where available land along the river is restricted by other land development projects. In small areas, the River Corridor Pocket Parks can be planned to provide a variety of

Figure 9.2.7   FoLAR Canoeing on Los Angeles River (photo by William Preston Bowling).

Figure 9.2.8   Horse Riding Along the L.A. River (photo by William Preston Bowling).

Part B

passive, limited active, and rest areas. These parks could be promoted as the venue for school educational experiences, joint-use neighbourhood areas, and *"street-end or cul-de-sac parks"* (LARRMP, 2007).

The LARRMP has also implemented the construction of Recreation Fields – spaces available for active sports (such as softball, baseball, soccer, tennis, badminton, and basketball) and associated support facilities – on appropriate locations along the River Corridor; Figures 9.2.7, 9.2.8). The plan aims to develop a network of trails, paths, and bikeways along the 51-kilometre River Corridor that helps to connect the LARRMP greenway to other open spaces (LARRMP, 2007). River Loops, designed as linear features, would support the main LARRMP goal of developing a continuous greenway along the entire Corridor. The main purpose of this open space pathway would be to connect adjacent communities. Gateways would provide river-theme artistic structures at selected access points to the river. The design of pedestrian river crossings and bridge underpasses would enhance personal safety and beautify the area, along with river theme aesthetic treatments to infrastructural elements, lighting, surveillance equipment, interpretive river-theme, and public events (LARRMP Final Report, 2007).

References

City of Los Angeles (2016). [Online]. Available at: www.lariver.org [Accessed 11 May 2016].

Desfor, G. and Keil, R. (2000). Every river tells a story: the Don River (Toronto) and the Los Angeles River (Los Angeles) as articulating landscapes. *Journal of Environmental Policy & Planning* 2:5–23.

Elrick, T. (2007). *Los Angeles River*. Arcadia Publishing.

FoLAR (2016). *FoLAR* [Online]. Available at: http://folar.org/[Accessed 9 April 2016].

Gandy, M. (2006). Riparian anomie: Reflections on the Los Angeles River. *Landscape Research* 31:135–145.

Gottlieb, R. (2007). *Reinventing Los Angeles: Nature and Community in the Global City.* MIT Press.

Gottlieb, R. *et al.* (2006). *The Next Los Angeles: The Struggle for a Livable City.* Berkeley, Calif.: University of California Press.

Gumprecht, B. (2006). *Land of Sunshine: An Environmental History of Metropolitan Los Angeles.* Deverell, W. and Hise, G. eds. Pittsburgh: University of Pittsburgh Press.

Gumprecht, B. (2001). *The Los Angeles River: Its Life, Death, and Possible Rebirth.* JHU Press.

Harden, D. (2003). *California Geology.* Upper Saddle River, NJ: Pearson.

Heal the Bay (2016). *Heal the Bay* [Online]. Available at: http://www.healthebay.org/ [Accessed 12 May 2016].

Kahrl, W.L. ed. (1981). *The California Water Atlas.* Sacramento: Los Altos, Calif: Governor's Office of Planning and Research.

LARRMP (2007). *Los Angeles River Revitalization Master Plan.* City of Los Angeles, Department of Public Works, Bureau of Engineering.

LARRMP Final Report (2007). *Final Programmatic Environmental Impact Report/ Programmatic Environmental Impact Statement.* The City of Los Angeles, Department of Public Works, Bureau of Engineering and US Army Corps of Engineers Los Angeles District Planning Division.

Orlob, G.T. (1998). *Restoration of Degraded Rivers: Challenges, Issues and Experiences.* Loucks, D. ed. Springer Science & Business Media.

State of California (2016). *California State Coastal Conservancy* [Online]. Available at: http://scc.ca.gov/ [Accessed 12 May 2016].

TreePeople (2016). *TreePeople* [Online]. Available at: https://www.treepeople.org/[Accessed 12 May 2016].

Wainwright, O. (2015). Is Frank Gehry really the right person to revitalise the Los Angeles river? *The Guardian* [Online]. Available at: http://www.theguardian.com/cities/2015/oct/23/frank-gehry-revitalise-los-angeles-la-river [Accessed 17 November 2015].

Chapter 9.3
Madrid Río, Spain – Strategies and Techniques

Katia Perini

9.3.1 Context

Madrid Río is the name of the redevelopment project which has interested an important area of Madrid, located on a parallel axis along the Manzanares River, above the former M-30 ring road (Figure 9.3.1). The highway ran along the river for a total 6 kilometres and was relocated underground from 2005 to 2007 through several tunnels. As the motorway was redirected, an extensive urban

Urban Sustainability and River Restoration: Green and Blue Infrastructure, First Edition.
Katia Perini and Paola Sabbion.
© 2017 John Wiley & Sons Ltd. Published 2017 by John Wiley & Sons Ltd.

renovation plan was implemented reusing the space left available (see Chapter 13.3). A vast parkland covering 649 hectares and spreading among six districts was created in its place (Jewell, 2011). The Madrid Río Park – with its average 25-metres width – connects the south-east districts with the city centre (GoMadrid, 2015). It also links several urban parks (Figure 9.3.2): la Casa de Campo (1,500 ha), Parque de Oeste (64 ha), Campo del Moro (21 ha), Cuña Verde de Latina (68 ha), Parque de San Isidro (25 ha), Parque de Manzanares Sur (335 ha), and Parque de Manzanares Norte (865 ha). It creates a green corridor, once completed, stretching from El Pardo to Getafe (Figure 9.3.1), providing the city with a unique environmental infrastructure (Ayuntamiento de Madrid, 2015). This green area features about 25,000 new trees and numerous recreational and cultural facilities. The linear park comprises greenways, pedestrian paths, new footbridges, playgrounds, skate parks, basketball courts and a small urban beach (Jewell, 2011).

Figure 9.3.1   The Madrid Section of the Manzanares River.

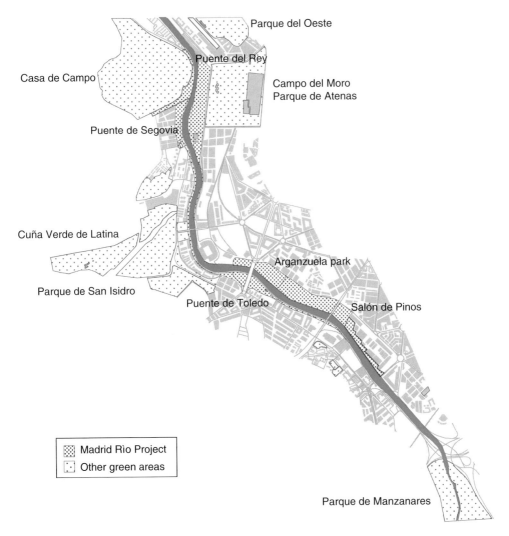

Figure 9.3.2   The Madrid Río Urban Area.

Thanks to the Río Madrid Project, the citizens now have full access to the parkland along the Manzanares river banks above the M-30 highway. In the past, Madrilenians were certainly less aware of the existence of a river flowing in their city and of its surroundings. This project, in fact, has been a crucial step forward for the Spanish capital since the M-30 crossed most of Madrid's centre and cut off some neighbourhoods from the rest of the city (Perrone and Gorelli, 2012). This renovated area has become an integrated and crucial feature within the city centre, while residents would previously ask "what river?" (Jewell, 2011).

The Manzanares River takes its name from the first urban settlement located on its banks, the medieval town of Manzanares el Real. The River source is 2,350 meters above sea level near the Ventisquero de la Condesa (Sierra de Guadarrama) and the waterway runs for 16 kilometres through canyons, pools, waterfalls, springs and other typical mountain environments. It also flows through the Monte del Pardo, an ecologically valuable area on the edge of Madrid (Enguita Puebla, 1999). The River moderates its slope when it connects with urban features and provisioning infrastructures.

Madrid was founded on the banks of the Manzanares River during the time of Muslim invasion in the ninth century, but archaeological sites demonstrate the presence of human settlers along the waterway since the Palaeolithic era. According to the Spanish scholar Fernando Chueca Goitia, Madrid's structure is typical of a coastal city, where the seaside edge (or the growth boundary) is represented by the Manzanares River (Enguita Puebla, 1999). The River has also been an important element for the defence of the City during the Civil War, serving as a protective barrier for the urban residents (Saez Chamorro, 2012). The importance of the River for the urban development is demonstrated by the presence of historical bridges as the Puente de Segovia (1582), which is the oldest in Madrid, the Puente de Toledo (1684), and the Puente del Rey (1816). These crossings have all been recently modernised with railings, wider walkways, and more bike path lanes on the Green Ring (*Anillo Verde*) that loops around the city (Jewell, 2011).

In the last century, urban development has negatively affected the environment of the Manzanares basin due to land use changes around the River to provide urban services (Grupo de Investigadores del Parque Lineal, n.d.). In particular, the M-30 highway was built in the 1970s and this had a major impact on the river ecology and on the surrounding neighbourhoods (País, 2015). This infrastructure created a physical, social and psychological barrier cutting across Madrid's central areas. Moreover, the River became inaccessible to all citizens.

The requalification process has turned the degraded and neglected district surrounding the Manzanares River into an important recreational and meeting area. This transformation has played a key role in the revitalisation of the city as neighbourhoods are now interconnected (Fernández, 2014).

9.3.2 Ecological and environmental issues

Outside the city, the Manzanares River intersects protected areas both in its high basin (from its origin until the El Prado dam) and in its low basin (from Madrid until it empties in the Jarama River). The river flow is naturally low (1,200 l/s) and the waterway is divided into three different stretches: the highest section (*curso alto*), that is, where the source of the river is located, the middle section (*curso medio*), and the lowest section (*curso bajo*). The Manzanares River middle section crosses Madrid and other small urban areas. The lowest section is saturated as it collects the slope's water, working as a drainage system for the surrounding areas (Saez Chamorro, 2012). There is a striking difference between the Madrid section of the Manzanares River and its remaining stages. Ecological and environmental issues occur as soon as the river reaches urbanised settlements (Enguita Puebla, 1999), which are, specifically, low permeability of the river banks, biodiversity loss, and high pollution rates (see Chapter 4; Morley, 2011). Moreover, as in many other cases, during the last century this waterway has been heavily regimented and artificialised to maximise space for urban development. This has determined serious consequences for the hydrogeological, environmental, and landscape systems (Brown *et al.*, 2009).

Land use, urban planning and poor environmental and ecological conditions of the Manzanares River have resulted in an insufficient degree of connectivity between the city linear and cross sections (Enguita Puebla, 1999). The urban districts close to the watershed of the M-30 ring road have been especially isolated and hidden for a long time. In the last decades, several projects have sought to enhance connectivity among the river sections and mitigate environmental problems, inverting the ecological degradation which has occurred in the Manzanares River (Fernández, 2014). In particular, even if the River still flows through a dense urban area, the recent underground relocation of the M-30 highway has allowed for a major ecological restoration of the waterway and its banks.

9.3.3   Strategies, techniques, and results

The Madrid Río Project establishes a physical and conceptual continuity between the city neighbourhoods and the valuable countryside outside the city. As a result, the River Manzanares has been transformed into a connection element (Burgos & Garrido Arquitectos *et al.*, 2011).

The Madrid Río Project is based upon five key elements: the river restoration, Salón de Pinos, green and blue areas, sports and recreation facilities, and urban regeneration. It has totally transformed the life quality of local residents and it has become a first class tourist attraction (Esbjørn, 2013). The new green areas, their connection, the high quality design and planning, and the services and facilities provided are the crucial elements for the success of this outstanding project (Mele, 2014).

According to the designers Burgos & Garrido Arquitectos and West 8 (Burgos & Garrido Arquitectos *et al.*, 2011), vegetation is the main material used in the project. It has been employed to construct a dense and ecologically rich plant structure to create an artificial and urban, yet living, landscape on an inert underground substrate. Following the underground rerouting of a large section of Madrid's inner ring-road, the M-30, half surface area of the Madrid Río Park along the Manzanares River has been created on top of the underground highway tunnels (GoMadrid, 2015). This resulted in complicated technical facilities and large urban infrastructures (Figure 9.3.5; Burgos & Garrido Arquitectos *et al.*, 2011). The Park was designed by using the "3 + 30" method, dividing the project area into a "trilogy of strategic projects". The resulting sub-projects include a large pine tree park, multiple sports areas, 30 km (approximately 30 km) of bicycle paths, more than 10 new playgrounds, six installations for the elderly, and even a sandy beach with humidifiers, parasols, and a kayak-paddling area (Jewell, 2011).

There are several main green areas in the Park, as Huerta de la Partida, a modern interpretation of the original royal orchard boasting a wide variety of fruit trees planted in groups to create an enclosed garden. This section links the Park with the Casa de Campo (former royal hunting ground), and the Arganzuela Park (Figure 9.3.3; Mele, 2014; West 8, 2011), which is based on water attractions

Figure 9.3.3   Arganzuela Park (photo by Jeroen Musch).

and Madrid's Urban Beach. This beach area has three oval-shaped waterside enclosures: a shallow pool of water where people can lie and cool off, an area with jets of water rising to different heights and effects, and a third pool with clouds of spray (Esbjørn, 2013). In addition, more than 5,000 total new trees have been recently planted in this park. Other important features include skating rinks, a concert hall, a new cultural centre and children facilities (GoMadrid, 2015).

All the new and existing green areas in the Madrid Río Park are connected by the *Salón de Pinos*, a green corridor on top of the highway tunnel (Mele, 2014; Ayuntamiento de Madrid, 2015). "The Salón de Pinos was designed as a linear green space along the Manzanares River and features a choreography of 8,000-fold pine trees and a repertoire of cuts" (West 8, 2011). This linear green space is located in a narrow area with only 40 m between buildings and river. In addition, the tunnel below it determines a reduced substrate thickness (Figure 9.3.5). For these reasons, among the *Pinus pinaster*, the *halepensis* and *nigra* species have been selected for the park (País, 2011; Área de Gobierno de Urbanismo y Vivienda, 2009).

Moreover, the Madrid Río Project connects the river banks and the city neighbourhoods thanks to the restoration of the old bridges across the Manzanares River, such as the Puente de Segovia, the Puente del Rey and the Puente de Toledo, and to the construction of 11 new footbridges (GoMadrid, 2015). The new bridges have become urban icons with very different features ranging from the basic three-way "Y"-bridge design to the helicoidal bridge devised by the French

Figure 9.3.4   Salón de Pinos (photo by Jeroen Musch).

architect and designer Perrault. Cascara's twin bridges (Figure 9.3.6) are covered by a thin concrete layer and Daniel Canogar conceived the interior roofing in mosaics. The Spanish artist has paid homage to local flavour by depicting some of the area's most colourful residents (Jewell, 2011). In addition, about thirty crossing paths favour a high degree of permeability between the two sides of the Madrid Río.

The creation of a green corridor is among the most interesting environmental elements of the Project (Área de Gobierno de Urbanismo y Vivienda, 2009). Madrid Río, in fact, comprises about 30,000 new trees, 460,000 shrubs, and 38 species of mainly aromatic plants (País, 2011). Biodiversity is ensured also by the 47 different arboreal species, among these: *Pinus halepensis, Pinus pinea, Populus nigra, Plátanos hispánica, Fraxinus spp., Aesculus hippocastanum, Quercus ilex, Acer spp.* (Ayuntamiento de Madrid, 2015). The plant species were chosen according to riverbanks characteristics. The left side, connected to the riverbed, is more humid and has been planted with deciduous trees. The right side is drier and

Figure 9.3.5 Cross Section of Salon de Pinos (photo credit West 8).

Figure 9.3.6   Cascara's Twin Bridges (photo by Jeroen Musch).

similar to the northern Madrid landscape. For this reason, pines have mostly been integrated in this area (e.g., in the Salón de Pinos; País, 2011).

The Manzanares River is also a corridor for migratory fauna, especially birds and nocturnal animals, which are leaving from the parks located in the north-east area of the city (Casa de Campo, Parque del Oeste, El Pardo) and the large parks in the southeast areas (Manzanares Sur y Parque de Tierno Galván; Ayuntamiento de Madrid, 2015). It is also worth mentioning the strategies developed to favour the movement of aquatic fauna, starting from the Puente de los Franceses (alongside the river and Casa de Campo; Figure 9.3.2) until the Puente de la Princesa. In this tract, a system of water layers – called *escala de peces* (stairs of fishes) – allows underwater fauna to move around the River without the interruption of dams. This strategy increases biologic vitality and, in some specific areas, facilitates game fishing (Ayuntamiento de Madrid, 2015).

These urban regeneration initiatives provide Madrid with new underground and safe infrastructure, improved water quality and a safer hydrological system within the River Manzanares basin, as 13 new km of pipes and storm tanks funnel clean water through the river (with a capability nine times higher compared to the older system), and 110 ha of new green areas (Área de Gobierno de Urbanismo y Vivienda, 2009). The river banks have been transformed into a wonderful park (Morley, 2011). This extensive new green space in the urban centre has successfully renovated a deteriorated environment and the motorway, which was for cars exclusive use, and was a physical and functional barrier within the city. According to the Madrid Municipality, the Madrid Río Park is indeed the most ambitious urban regeneration project developed in the Spanish capital (Área de Gobierno de Urbanismo y Vivienda, 2009).

Part B

References

Área de Gobierno de Urbanismo y Vivienda. (2009). *Proyectos Singulares*. Memoria de gestión. [Online]. Available at: http://www.madrid.es/UnidadWeb/Contenidos/Publicaciones/TemaUrbanismo/MemoGest2009/4ProyectosSingulares/1proyectomadridrio.pdf.

Ayuntamiento de Madrid. (2015). *Madrid Rio*. [Online]. Available at: http://www.madrid.es/portales/munimadrid/es/Inicio/Ayuntamiento/Urbanismo-e-Infraestructuras/Madrid-Rio?vgnextfmt=default&vgnextoid=5acc7f0917afc110VgnVCM2000000c205a0aRCRD&vgnextchannel=8dba171c30036010VgnVCM100000dc0ca8c0RCRD&idCapitulo=5015873 [Accessed 1 December 2015].

Brown, R. R., Keath, N., and Wong, T. H. F. (2009). Urban water management in cities: historical, current and future regimes. *Water Science and Technology*, 59 (5), p. 847–855. *Scopus* [Online]. Available at: doi:10.2166/wst.2009.029.

Burgos & Garrido Arquitectos, Porras la Casta Arquitectos and Rubio & Sala Arquitectos. (2011). *Madrid Río Project 2006–2011*.

Enguita Puebla, A. (1999). Plan especial del tramo norte del río Manzanares. *Revista del Colegio de Ingenieros de Caminos*, Canales y Puertos Nº 46 (1). [Online]. Available at: http://hispagua.cedex.es/sites/default/files/hispagua_articulo/op/46/op46_3.htm [Accessed 28 January 2016].

Esbjørn, A. (2013). *Madrid Río – a project that changed Madrid* | ifhp.org. [Online]. Available at: http://www.ifhp.org/ifhp-blog/madrid-r%C3%ADo-%E2%80%93-project-changed-madrid [Accessed 1 December 2015].

Fernández, D. (2014). Madrid Río: de cicatriz a ribera de unión. *Revista80dias.es*. [Online]. Available at: http://www.revista80dias.es/viajes/madrid-rio-de-cicatriz-a-ribera-de-union/ [Accessed 1 December 2015].

GoMadrid. (2015). *The Madrid Río Project, including the Madrid Beach*. [Online]. Available at: http://www.gomadrid.com/beach/[Accessed 1 December 2015].

Grupo de Investigadores del Parque Lineal. (n.d.). *El Peimansur - Plan Especial de Infraestructuras Manzanares Sur*. [Online]. Available at: http://www.parquelineal.es/proyectos/peimansur.php [Accessed 28 January 2016].

Jewell, N. (2011). *Madrid Rio by West 8 and MRIO*. [Online]. Available at: http://buildipedia.com/aec-pros/urban-planning/madrid-rio-by-west-8-and-mrio [Accessed 1 December 2015].

Mele, F. (2014). Da autostrada a parco sul fiume: il caso felice di Madrid Rìo. *Artwort*. [Online]. Available at: http://www.artwort.com/2014/04/11/architettura/autostrada-parco-fiume-caso-felice-madrid-rio/ [Accessed 1 December 2015].

Morley, R. (2011). *A View of Madrid: Madrid New Riverside Park - Madrid Rio*. [Online]. Available at: http://aviewofmadrid.blogspot.it/2011/06/madrid-new-riverside-park-madrid-rio.html [Accessed 28 January 2016].

País, E. E. (2011). Madrid Río, abierto al completo. *EL PAÍS*. [Online]. Available at: http://elpais.com/elpais/2011/04/15/actualidad/1302855418_850215.html [Accessed 1 December 2015].

País, E. E. (2015). Harvard premia a Madrid Río. *EL PAÍS*. [Online]. Available at: http://ccaa.elpais.com/ccaa/2015/11/05/madrid/1446749671_991345.html [Accessed 1 December 2015].

Perrone, C. and Gorelli, G. (2012). *Governo del consumo di territorio. Metodi, strategie, criteri*. Firenze University Press.

Saez Chamorro, E. (2012). *Características ambientales del Plan Especial Río Manzanares (Estudio de Incidencia Ambiental)*. [Online]. Available at: https://www.eoi.es/blogs/elvirasaez/2012/05/18/caracteristicas-ambientales-del-plan-especial-rio-manzanares-estudio-de-incidencia-ambiental/ [Accessed 28 January 2016].

West 8. (2011). Madrid RIO. *West 8*. [Online]. Available at: http://www.west8.com/projects/madrid_rio [Accessed 1 December 2015].

Chapter 9.4
Paillon River, France – Strategies and Techniques

Paola Sabbion

9.4.1 Context

Nice is the fifth largest French city and has 350,000 inhabitants. It attracts around four million visitors every year and plans are underway to transform it into the "green city of the Mediterranean" (Nice Cote d'Azur Tourisme et Congrès, 2013). The requalification of the Paillon River (*Promenade du Paillon*, 2013), as well as

Urban Sustainability and River Restoration: Green and Blue Infrastructure, First Edition.
Katia Perini and Paola Sabbion.
© 2017 John Wiley & Sons Ltd. Published 2017 by John Wiley & Sons Ltd.

a better management of the urban environment, have been targeted to increase the quality of public spaces and the attractiveness of the city. The renovation of the final section of the Paillon River is part of a wider programme addressing the whole basin (Nice Press Service, 2013).

The Paillon River flows in southestern France, in the Département des Alpes Maritimes, in the region of Provence-Alpes-Cote d'Azur, and is included in the Rhône-Méditerranée drainage basin. The Paillon River has 5 main tributaries, Paillon de Contes, Paillon de l'Escarène, Paillon de Nice, Laghet, Banquière, covering in total 81-kilometre linear streams. Together they form a typical Mediterranean coastal river catchment. The river basin originates in the Nice Prealps and the landscape is characterised by steep and rough slopes and the Nice conurbation (Figure 9.4.1).

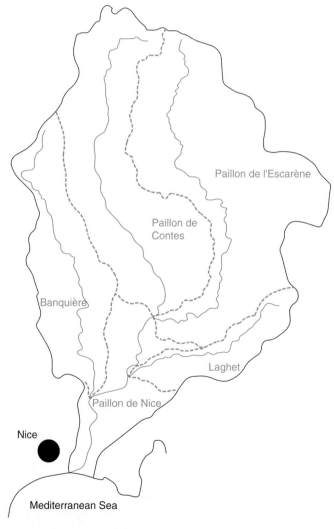

Figure 9.4.1 The Paillon Catchment Area.

The Paillon River and its tributaries flow in a heterogenic territory within rural and urban settlements, alongside artisanal activities, industries including quarries and cement plants, and terminates with the Niçoise agglomeration. The Paillon River was in fact used for centuries as a source of water and energy for the city's industries. The basin also offers some heritage features, especially related to rural life (e.g., production of olive oil). Until the late 1950s, the major agricultural supply of the city of Nice was drawn from the Paillon catchment basin. Agricultural lands, although, have gradually been replaced by urban settlements. Today olive cultivation, tree crops other than olive trees, and market gardening represent minor agricultural activities and livestock farming has also become marginal.

In the Middle Ages, part of the Paillon road network was included in the Road of Salt, which allowed the delivery of salt from Hyères. Salt was then trans-shipped from the port of Nice to the cities of the North of Italy passing trough Sospel, Saorge, Tende and Cuneo. These roads have been improved by the construction of the railway Nice-Cuneo, inaugurated in 1928. The A8 motorway was commissioned in 1976 for the Nice bypass section and, in 1978, for the section between Nice and La Turbie (SIP, 2016).

In the nineteenth century, the river was considered a divisive element separating the medieval town from the modern city, which was expanding westward. Thus, the 1860 development plan approved the coverage of the river to reduce the gap between the left bank, characterised by factories and working-class neighbourhoods and the right bank, inhabited since the eighteenth century by a wealthy elite of residents seeking to spend the winter in the Riviera's mild climate.

The right and left districts were connected with the construction of Place Masséna (Figure 9.4.2). The covering works, begun in 1868 and ended in 1972. This project featured the construction of important structures on the river roof, a development policy that has been pursued until recent decades. In this central area of the city, several entertainment venues were also devised to enhance its animated cultural life, such as the Casino, the Théâtre National de Nice, the Museum of Modern and Contemporary Art, the Louis Nucéra Library, the Acropolis, the Palais des Expositions exhibition centre, the Guillame Apollinaire high school, the Municipal Archives, and the Albert 1st Gardens, which are all easily accessible thanks to the nearby bus station and public parking facilities (Figure 9.4.3).

As a result, the final 11.5 km of the Paillon de Nice are currently completely artificialised. The dykes and edges, which characterise the upstream segment, give way to a complete covering over its last three kilometres. This covering extends from the Palais des Expositions to the sea. The channelised river flows underground into a subterranean tunnel before discharging into the Mediterranean, in the centre of Nice at the Baie des Anges. In this part of the city the river is no longer perceptible (Figure 9.4.4; SIP, 2016).

9.4.2   Ecological and environmental issues

The Paillon River floods are well-known both for their speed and for their intensity. The Paillon is a typical Mediterranean coastal river that drains a catchment area approximately 250 km² wide, which is very compact and highly uneven (SIP,

Figure 9.4.2   Place Masséna Today, After its Redevelopment with the Tram Line Requalification.

2016). In a typical Mediterranean climate, the river alternates between extremely low flows and dry phases and sudden, violent floods. Its flow is typically higher during the autumn rains. Steep slopes and a limestone geological substrate determine the transport of increased solid material loads. This causes a fast runoff time and rare but severe flooding.

The sudden appearance and violence of the river floods have impressed the popular imagination. The victims, in fact, have often been surprised by the flood wave and sometimes witnesses have referred to a full wall of water more than one metre high (Météo-France, 2016). Flood events have been recently reported on 6 and 23 November 2000 (Direction Interrégionales Sud-Est, 2001). As De Saint-Seine describes, citing the French poet Theodore Banville (1860), in the nineteenth and twentieth century, the river was almost dry throughout the year, but when it flooded it became very "fierce, rolling in the mud and pebbles in its muddy waters, [it] covered bridges and stone piers and [it] rushed into the sea with a horrible roar" (Le Gouz De Saint Seine, 1995).

In the upstream segments, the Paillon bed and banks are occupied by riparian woods, which are rich in biological diversity. Dry phases and flooding risks have induced a progressive lack of interest among the residents and the river is no longer perceived as a landscape feature with recreational and ecological purposes, but as a threat. Thus, waste spills and low or no vegetation maintenance can be

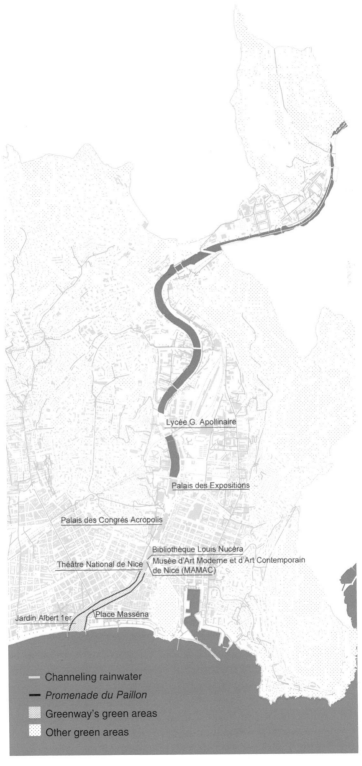

Figure 9.4.3   The Paillon River Area Land Use and the Promenade du Paillon.

Figure 9.4.4   The Rivermouth at the Promenade des Anglais.

observed on most of the territory. This abandonment has an impact on the eco-logical and hydraulic functions of river. In fact, if forests are not well maintained by residents, large woody debris causes jams and extensive damage in case of flooding. For this reason, in order to adopt a conservation approach, a mainte-nance plan has been implemented since 2003 (SIP, 2016).

Along the streams, the Paillon flora consists of riparian herbaceous plants (*Typha spp.*, *Carex spp.* and Gramineae family plants), involved in the water quality maintenance through their pollutant (nitrates, phosphates, pesticides) filtration power. Vegetation protects against flooding by maintaining the banks. The most common trees in the basin are black poplar, white willow, and ash tree. On the hills there are downy oak, Aleppo pine, maritime pine, Scots and Austrian pines. Mimosa is an introduced species that has invaded siliceous substrates and has colonised the acidic soils, eliminating almost all native spe-cies. Brachypodium (*Brachypodium ramosum*) is present on the slopes or on abandoned terraces. In the past, olive tree cultivation was one of the important activities that modified the landscape as it required the creation of terraced slopes on soft terrains (calcareous marl). A large number of olive groves are currently abandoned (SIP, 2016).

There is evidence that the watercourse is partly in good health: for example the eel, which is an endangered species, is present on some Paillon segments, especially in the upper stream. Moreover, Nice is as an axis used by many migratory birds. In particular, random data collected by amateurs in the wet-land habitats of the Paillon area have shown the presence of migratory bird species, although in small numbers due to urbanisation growth (Lemarchand and Frelin, 2016).

9.4.3 Strategies, techniques, and results

The Paillon River restoration project seeks to improve the quality of water to enhance the heritage of the valley, to provide protection against floods, and to promote education and awareness on the need to renovate the aquatic environment and its surrounding area. To attain these goals it is crucial to adopt a series of coordinated actions to preserve natural environments, manage water resources and regain the river landscape as living spaces (Syndicat Intercommunal des Paillons, 2009).

In particular, the Paillons River Contract for Paillon and its tributaries (*Contrat de Rivière des Paillons*) is a technical and financial commitment between national government, local authorities, and local stakeholders, which focuses on the river basin rehabilitation. It supports sustainable management and implementation modalities within the river catchment. It addresses, in particular, five goals: prevention against floods; water quality improvement; restoration of landscape values; wildlife and flora preservation; coordination of measures and information regarding the *river contract* itself (SIP, 2016).

This extensive initiative especially targets the functions of aquatic environments, restoring the banks and the riverbed, as well as mending the relationship between the inhabitants and their river. Current efforts attempt to restore and maintain the vegetation of the river to fight against the weakening of banks in certain sectors; enhance the flow of water; develop the crossing of waterways in villages; increase fish movement patters and habitats and incentivise educational trails.

In the city of Nice the programme highlights the importance of waterway crossings in the city. A 2008 study proposes to recreate continuity across the river through the installation of a vegetation corridor (restoration of the banks by the reconstitution of a lower riparian forest) with pedestrian access to the river and a waterfront path for pedestrian walk and cycling. This initiative is in line with the Paillons River Contract, which advocates ecological continuity while endorsing remarkable sites, fostering the integration of ecological issues and water management policies (Syndicat Intercommunal des Paillons, 2009).

As mentioned, protection against flooding is another major issue undertaken by the Paillons River Contract. Anthropisation has gradually encroached the valleys of the basin and the natural riverbed. To protect people and property from the extremely violent, albeit rare, flooding that characterises this area, some important goals have been devised, such as strengthening the banks and bridges with riprap and restoring thresholds. More space for the water flow also needs to be guaranteed by studying solid transport dynamics and banks recalibration as, also, removing blocks from the riverbed. Flood control is pursued developing a risk culture and implementing and upgrading the flood announcement system.

In 2008, a pedestrian landscaping walk has been realised through the redevelopment of the Paillon banks. The main road now runs below the river banks into a tunnel, along the riverbed. A flooding risk alarm system (SAC) protects the users of this tunnel thanks to a network of measuring stations spread over the catchment, including flow meters and rain gauges. This is an innovative flood warning alarm system to prevent the Paillon river flash floods. The SAC is based on 12 stations measuring rainfall and flow metric; 2 radio relay stations; and 1 management centre (Métropole Nice Cote d'Azur (b), 2016). The station data are located at Cimiez Control Station. A phase of vigilance starts when the effective average cumulative rainfall exceeds the potential absorption capacity of the soil. A pre-alarm phase starts when the water level exceeds 75 cm upstream or when the flow exceeds 200 m³/s at the station located nearest to the tunnel. This phase requires the closing of the tunnel to traffic. In the alert phase, when the level exceeds 180 cm or the flow exceeds 300 m³/s at the station located nearest to the tunnel, the watertight doors of the tunnel are closed (Syndicat Intercommunal des Paillons, 2009).

In 2010, a design competition resulted in a project to rehabilitate the final section of the river roof, which was occupied by the bus station and a large parking lot. This project envisaged a 12-hectare linear park, comprising exotic species typical of the Mediterranean region (Nice-Matin, 2010). This green area, connecting the old town and the new town, built in the late nineteenth century upon the roof river, has been designed by landscape architects Christine and Michael Péna. The *Promenade du Paillon*, inaugurated on October 26, 2013, is intended as a feature boosting both environmental quality and sustainable development in the city, a pole of attraction for many leisure activities, regarding tourism, children's recreation, festivals and events, artistic and cultural programmes (Figure 9.4.5). This linear park built on the roof of the river animates spaces once neglected, improving environmental and urban quality (Figure 9.4.6).

The *Promenade du Paillon* features essentially Mediterranean species, bitter orange trees, palm trees, flowering shrubs and herbaceous plants (Figure 9.4.7; Ville de Nice, 2016). Biodiversity is ensured thanks to the insertion of 6,000 shrubs and 50,000 bushes and plants mainly including Mediterranean or naturalised species and 1,200 new trees planted in 2013 (Meeres, 2013).

This project is sustainable as it employs sustainable or recycled materials and promotes energy saving and limited water consumption. The *promenade* is designed as an ecological corridor. Water elements, devised in various parts of the project, contribute to microclimate improvement and urban heat island decrease as the park

Figure 9.4.5   A Panoramic View of the Promenade du Paillon Park.

Figure 9.4.6   Playground in the Promenade du Paillon (photo by Gian Luca Porcile).

Figure 9.4.7   Landscaping and Herbaceous Borders Along the Park (photo by Gian Luca Porcile).

counts 128 water jets on the mirror of water, as well as 576 water mist nozzles (Figure 9.4.8). Moreover, the vegetation, which is typical of dry climates, and the composition of the absorbent substrate decrease the need for irrigation (Figure 9.4.9). Water management is handled by tensiometric probes, which keep soil moisture and irrigation under control. The impervious surfaces are reduced to the minimum;

Figure 9.4.8   Water Playground: a Main Attraction of the Park (photo by Gian Luca Porcile).

Figure 9.4.9   Vegetation in the Promenade du Paillon Park (photo by Gian Luca Porcile).

the lawn surfaces filter and infiltrate the rainwater that is then collected for irrigation purposes. Water is conveyed toward green surfaces to minimise surface runoff. High luminous efficiency lighting is preferred to respect ecological issues, as it emits only weak UV and infrared radiations, and avoids the emission of light beyond a horizontal line, allowing for intensity variations (Technilum®, 2014).

Due to the great success of the Promenade du Paillon, in a recent interview, mayor Estrosi stated that it will be enhanced to reach the district of Pasteur and Pont-Michel, adding further 2.5 km to the park (Estrosi, 2014). This green corridor is a living space for Nice and has become a symbol to reduce the gap between the city centre and the suburbs (Radio VL, 2015).

Moreover, as explained, major issues in the Paillon basin are represented by chronic dry phases alternated to flash floods which determine significant water speed and sediment transport, compounded by intense urbanisation and the presence of impervious surfaces. Other critical points are water pollution and the use of water resources for industrial and domestic purposes as well as the general disinterest among the residents. The Paillons River Contract is gradually tackling all these aspects, attempting to curb their negative impact.

References

Direction Interrégionales Sud-Est. (2001). *Pluies extrêmes sur le Sud de la France - Période 1958-2000.*

Estrosi, C. (2014). *La Coulée verte se prolongera jusqu'à Pasteur à Nice.* [Online]. Available at: http://archives.nicematin.com/nice/la-coulee-verte-se-prolongera-jusqua-pasteur-a-nice.1999289.html [Accessed 30 January 2016].

Le Gouz De Saint Seine, J. (1995). *Monographie hydrologique et hydraulique du Paillon de Nice en vue de la gestion du risque d'inondation.* Thèse de doctorat, France: INP Grenoble.

Lemarchand, C. and Frelin, C. (2016). Synthèse ornithologique de la ville de Nice. *Faune-PACA Publication 2005–2015*, 55. [Online]. Available at: http://files.biolovision.net/www.faune-paca.org/userfiles/FPPubli/FPP55_2.pdf [Accessed 30 January 2016].

Meeres, S. (2013). The Paillon Promenade. A Central Park for Nice? *Topos*, (85), p. 39–41.

Météo-France. (2016). [Online]. Available at: http://pluiesextremes.meteo.fr/index.php [Accessed 30 January 2016].

Métropole Nice Cote d'Azur (b). (2016). *Systèmes d'Annonce des Crues du Paillon.* [Online]. Available at: http://www.nicecotedazur.org/environnement/assainissement/syst%C3%A8mes-d-annonce-des-crues-du-paillon.

Nice Cote d'Azur Tourisme et Congrès. (2013). *Côte d'Azur - Nice, Green City press kit.* General public information.

Nice-Matin. (2010). *Une coulée verte jusqu'à la mer.* [Online]. Available at: http://archives.nicematin.com/article/nice/une-coulee-verte-jusqua-la-mer.370551.html [Accessed 30 January 2016].

Nice Press Service. (2013). *Nice new plans and ambitions, press kit.* Nice Cote d'Azur Tourisme e Congrès.

Radio VL. (2015). Estrosi: l'ambition du prolongement de la Coulée Verte. http://www.radiovl.fr. [Online]. Available at: http://www.radiovl.fr/estrosi-lambition-du-prolongement-de-la-coulee-verte/[Accessed 30 January 2016].

SIP. (2016). *Rivière Paillons.* [Online]. Available at: http://www.riviere-paillons.fr/index.php [Accessed: 30 January 2016].

Syndicat Intercommunal des Paillons. (2009). *Contrat de rivière des Paillons.* SAFEGE, AP Conseil. [Online]. Available at: http://www.riviere-paillons.fr/index.php/documentation/contrat-de-riviere [Accessed 29 January 2016].

Technilum®. (2014). *Pour tout l'or du Paillon.* [Online]. Available at: http://www.technilum.com/en/node/696 [Accessed 30 January 2016].

Ville de Nice. (2016). *La promenade du Paillon.* [Online]. Available at: http://www.nice.fr/fr/la-promenade-du-paillon?lang=fr [Accessed 31 January 2016].

Chapter 9.5
River Thames, England – Strategies and Technique

Paola Sabbion

9.5.1 Context

The River Thames rises near Cirencester, in Gloucestershire, and flows through Southern England into the North Sea. It is the longest river in England, with a total length of about 346 km, and it has played the most crucial role in the development of London.

The Thames meanders through a heterogeneous landscape. It drains the whole of Greater London, passing through three main sectors: the Thames Valley,

Urban Sustainability and River Restoration: Green and Blue Infrastructure, First Edition.
Katia Perini and Paola Sabbion.
© 2017 John Wiley & Sons Ltd. Published 2017 by John Wiley & Sons Ltd.

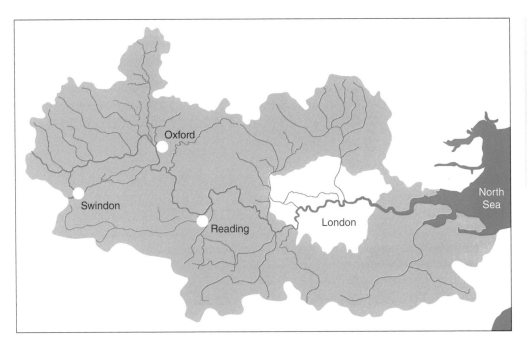

Figure 9.5.1   The Thames River Basin.

between Oxford and West London; the Thames Gateway, from Isle of Dogs to Southend and Isle of Sheppey; and the Thames Estuary, situated around the tidal Thames to the east of London. The Thames river basin covers about 13,000 km^2 and is both rural and heavily urbanised in the eastern and northern areas, and mostly rural in the western parts (Figure 9.5.1).

The industrial character of the river landscape is drawn from its refineries, power stations, factories, goods stations and its street network (Figure 9.5.2). The river basin, although, also includes parks and areas of nature conservation (e.g., Crossness Nature Reserve, Canvey Wick Nature Reserve, Rainham Marshes Nature Reserve, and Lee Valley Special Protection Area). Moreover, agricultural patches are widespread, especially in Essex, Kent, and East London. For centuries, the River Thames and its surroundings have been of great significance to artists and writers, as Turner and Dickens. This environment has inspired designers such as Capability Brown who reorganised the Thorndon parkland in the late eighteenth century and Repton, who designed part of Cobham Park in Kent (DCLG, 2008).

By the eighteenth century, thanks to its large docks, the Thames had become England's most important waterway for commercial transport, setting London as the centre of the British Empire (Figure 9.5.3, 9.5.4). In the nineteenth century, due to discharge of industrial waste and untreated sewage disposal into the river, the water quality declined causing waterborne disease outbreaks. For instance, between 1832 and 1865, tens of thousands of people died of cholera. In 1858, the intolerable level of contamination produced such a bad smell (Faraday, 1855),

Figure 9.5.2   A Panoramic View of Thames Urban Landscape (photo by Colin Pattenden).

Figure 9.5.3   Preserved Cranes Along the Thames (photo by Colin Pattenden).

Figure 9.5.4   Old Pier on the Thames (photo by Colin Pattenden).

that sittings of the House of Commons at Westminster had to be cancelled. This phenomenon went down in history as the *Great Stink*. In the twentieth century, pollutants decreased when heavy industry and tanning processes ceased, while sewage treatment was improved.

9.5.2   Ecological and environmental issues

The River Thames supplies two-thirds of London's drinking water. Most of it comes from the non-tidal river, while groundwater in the catchment area provides less than 40% of the global Thames water supply. Sewer overflow is controlled and thus rare in the non-tidal Thames segment. A combined sewer works along the upper Thames providing an acceptable water quality (Environment Agency, 2009). However, water quality is still a significant issue, particularly because of surface runoff (up to 80% of the floodplain in the Thames area is developed), storm sewage overflows and misconnections. The water quality in the Thames Estuary suffers from the impact of storm discharges from the major main sewage system and from the combined sewer network that frequently empties into the estuary, increasing pollution and degrading habitat quality. Thames Water, the company that is in charge of the public water supply, has planned sewage treatment works along the tidal Thames and the construction of the London Tideway Tunnels, a major new sewer to address point source pollution from the sewerage system and tackle overflows. The Thames Tideway Tunnel is a 25-kilometre tunnel running under the tidal section of Thames, passing through London. It is designed to convey almost all the combined raw sewage and rainwater discharges. The construction of the Thames Tideway Tunnel, scheduled to start in 2016, will be completed in 2023 (Tideway, 2016). This strategy seeks to achieve a good river status, as required by European environmental standards (Environment Agency, 2009).

The progressive artificialisation of the River Thames has led to the loss of habitat diversity. In particular, most of the Thames Gateway is commonly perceived as the wasteland to the east of London (Figure 9.5.5). This landscape is fragmented by overhead power lines, industrial chimneys, landfills, former quarries, derelict land and buildings (Figure 9.5.6, 9.5.7). On the contrary, the Thames River Estuary features extensive wetlands, intertidal salt marshes, mudflats, and many Sites of Special Scientific Interest (SSSI; Environment Agency, 2009). The tidal shore and the estuary marshes provide important habitats for seawater and freshwater fish, such as salmons and sea lampreys. The Thames Estuary has a high level of biodiversity with over 45 species of fish and hundreds of benthic invertebrates and insects. More than 120 species of birds live or overwinter in the Greater Thames, including ducks, geese, wading birds, cormorants, black-headed gulls, and herring gulls. The area hosts a great number of water voles and other small mammals. In certain parts of the estuary, although, the river wildlife is constantly at risk from water pollution events (e.g., CSO; RSPB, 2013).

Figure 9.5.5   Rubbish in the Mud of River Thames (photo by Colin Pattenden).

Figure 9.5.6   Crossness Sewage Treatment Works (photo by Matt Brown).

Figure 9.5.7   North Greenwich (photo by Jørgen K. H. Knudsen).

Figure 9.5.8   Thames Barrier (photo by Jørgen K. H. Knudsen).

The Thames has a low discharge as it flows through one of the driest areas in the UK, where low rainfall occurs compared to the national average. Nevertheless, significant floods have occurred in 1928, 1947, 1953, 1968, and, more recently, in the 1990s and early twenty-first century. Some have been caused by the tidal activity of the North Sea, which has generated consequences in the Thames Estuary. Climate change and sea level rise may also increase the risk of flooding in the Estuary, as predicted by the UK Climate Impacts Programme (UKCIP). Increasingly warm and wet winters, as also hotter and drier summers, are expected in South East England. This could lead to an increased frequency and intensity of extreme weather events such as heat waves, tidal surges, heavy rainfall, and a reduced groundwater recharge period during winter (DCLG, 2008). In 1982, a control device – the Thames Barrier – was devised to prevent East London from being flooded by exceptionally high tides and strong winds from the North Sea, as had occurred in 1953 (Figure 9.5.8). Moreover, in 2002, the 11.6-km Jubilee River channel was opened to re-direct overflow from the River Thames and decrease flooding in Maidenhead, Windsor, Eton, and Cookham. The Jubilee River provides habitat for wildlife and has been defined an excellent pedestrian and sporting infrastructure, even if the efficiency of this system is controversial (BBC, 2014; Figure 9.5.9).

Figure 9.5.9   Across the Jubilee Bridge (photo by Colin Pattenden).

9.5.3   Strategies and techniques

In the last decade, major changes have been achieved in the Thames Gateway. Many strategies have focused on the area stretching 60 km from East London along both sides of the River Thames and Estuary, including Stratford, the Olympic Village, and Canary Wharf. The Thames Gateway has been termed the largest brownfield, ex-industrial land regeneration programme in Europe (Thames Gateway, 2009). It has traditionally been the sub-region where much of London's electrical power has been generated and where much of its waste has been deposited, leaving a significant legacy of degraded environments. Substantial investments are now required to put brownfields back into productive use (Haughton *et al.*, 1997). The planning and development of London's Thames Gateway region is an important strategy for the coastal urbanisation and regeneration, especially when current settlements need to adapt to changing conditions on previously developed lands and face different economic developments. This regeneration programme, described by the UK National Audit Office as the most ambitious in Western Europe (NAO, 2007), aims at creating a new network of public transport, 180,000 new jobs, 120,000 new homes, and 53,000 ha of green space (ODPM, 2005).

The Government recently set some target goals, as the transformation of the Thames Gateway into UK's first eco-region, an international model for sustainable development, low-carbon growth and regeneration. Other objectives include the improvement of the Thames Gateway economy, creating a modern and efficient transport system, developing sustainable dwellings, and enhancing the quality of life for communities throughout the Gateway (DCLG, 2008). According to the London Thames Gateway Development Corporation, this eco-region could tackle climate change and sustain economic growth (Grant in Farrell (ed.), 2009).

A high quality of life, in fact, is likely to attract investments and new residents to the Thames Gateway and encourage employment and a great number of visitors. One of the main goals of the Thames Gateway Delivery Programme is to create remarkable parkland, which can transform the physical aspect and also the perception of this area. According to the promoters, thanks to its high environmental quality, this will become an economic hub, providing tourism and recreational activities (Farrell (ed.), 2009). The focus on environmental restoration could also definitely improve the quality of life for 1,500,000 existing residents and create long-term value by reconnecting communities to the exceptional landscapes of the Estuary (DCLG, 2008).

The Thames Gateway Parklands programme seeks to provide a network of accessible and sustainable landscapes and waterways, which capitalise on existing natural, built, historic and cultural assets. The creation of the Parklands will also support local food production, as also boost biodiversity, strengthen its character and identity, and support the perception of this region as a beautiful place. The large continuous landscapes will help preserve the unique habitats of the Thames Estuary and improve environmental quality. Moreover, the development of this natural area plays an important role in terms of natural drainage provision and flood risk reduction (DCLG, 2008; Figure 9.5.10).

The Parklands vision is built on the special qualities of the Estuary landscape, its environment, its cultural heritage, and its strategic assets. Involving government bodies, landowners, farmers, charities, local actors and establishing partnerships will be a key strategy to extend green spaces to address urban and transport development, flood protection schemes, agricultural improvement, and land regeneration. Water landscapes and green areas constitute a continuous landscape and will become an everyday element in people's lives. This green and blue infrastructure contributes to the enhancement of the Estuary's strategic importance as the centre of the regional economy. The Parklands Programme has established a continuous *green grid* across London, South Essex and North Kent. The Parklands will be connected to adjacent nature areas including the River Roach and River Crouch complex, Thames Chase, Lea Valley Regional Park, the Kent Downs Area and the East London Green Grid, which is part of the Thames Gateway itself (Farrell et al., 2010). Its establishment will enable the Thames Gateway to be more attractive compared to other areas of South East England (DCLG, 2008).

A "functional green infrastructure" was at the heart of the *Greening the Gateway* strategy, aimed at developing a green space network (Defra and ODPM, 2004), responding in particular to the requirements of the Flood and Water Management Bill. This Bill regulates the connections between surface water sewers and Sustainable Drainage Systems (SuDS) included in new settlements (see also Chapter 12). It devises Local authorities as responsible for the maintenance of SuDS serving multiple properties, while highways and road authorities are accountable for the maintenance of SuDs in all adopted roads (Environment Agency, 2009).

Parklands are conceived as a quality network of well-managed, accessible and sustainable landscapes. New nature conservation areas have been planned to

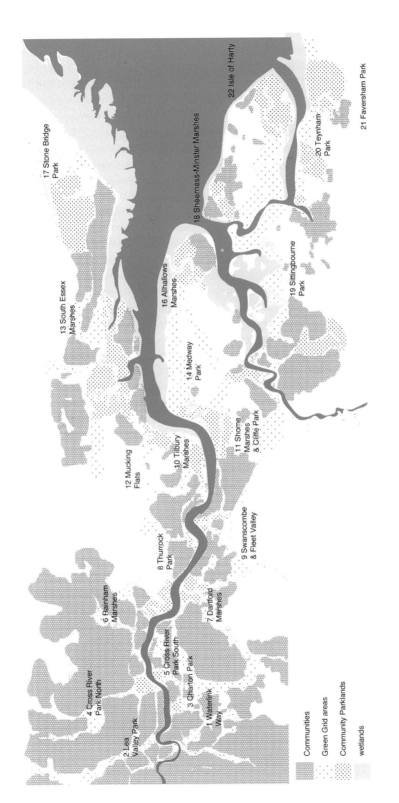

Figure 9.5.10 Parklands Spatial Framework, Based on the Thames Gateway Parklands Vision (DCLG, 2008).

1 Waterlink Way
2 Lea Valley Park
3 Charlton Park
4 Cross River Park North
5 Cross River Park South
6 Rainham Marshes
7 Dartford Marshes
8 Thurrock Park
9 Swanscombe & Fleet Valley
10 Tilbury Marshes
11 Shorne Marshes & Cliffe Park
12 Mucking Flats
13 South Essex Marshes
14 Medway Park
16 Allhallows Marshes
17 Stone Bridge Park
18 Sheerness-Minster Marshes
19 Sittingbourne Park
20 Teynham Park
21 Faversham Park
22 Isle of Harty

Communities

Green Grid areas

Community Parklands

wetlands

provide greater connectivity for wildlife within the Thames Gateway by 2020. This will contribute to counter possible climate change effects in the Thames Basin District (as changes in the rainfall regime and sea level rise; RSPB, 2013). The wetlands, in particular, will become accessible to surrounding communities without compromising their importance as wildlife habitats. Wetlands are indeed important elements that contribute to sustainable water management (including flood water management, water capture, storage, cleansing and distribution).

Thames tributaries should be renaturalised as far as possible to provide green corridors. The River Medway and Cliffe Pools are among the most important landscape resources identified within this programme (DCLG, 2008). The Thames Gateway Parklands project identifies specifically the River Medway as important at national level for leisure activities and cultural heritage offer.

In the last years, several good examples of river restoration projects can be counted within the Thames Basin (e.g., Chinbrook Meadows, Cornmill Gardens in River Ravensbourne, Mayes Brook). These programmes have envisaged retention areas, hence improving flood management. River restoration has been promoted within the Environment Agency's Thames Catchment Flood Management Plan. Most of these projects have incorporated innovative ways to sustain a more natural flood management. For example, during flood events, space for water is provided at Chinbrook Meadows and Sutcliffe Park (2003) at River Quaggy, crucial areas where floodwaters can be stored in case of extreme events.

Finally, the Thames Gateway has large dock complexes that no longer fulfil their original role. These have a great potential and can be reactivated for public use, employing river edges and canals (including the River Lea Navigation and the Thames and Medway Canal). Accessibility can be increased re-establishing former

Figure 9.5.11   A View of a Segment of the Thames Path (photo by Colin Pattenden).

Figure 9.5.12   Tripcock Ness Crossing of Paths and Cycle Routes (photo by Colin Pattenden).

links across the Estuary (DCLG, 2008). The Thames Estuary Path will link the north and south banks of the Estuary from the Isle of Dogs to the coastal path network. It will also connect hinterland areas to the coast with existing paths. Furthermore, it will join important landmarks (O2 Arena, Thames Barrier, Estuary forts, minster churches), passing through urban waterfronts and beaches as well as rural areas (Farrell et al., 2010). A network of pedestrian and cycle routes will be improved, including the National Cycle Network (completed in 2005), Coastal Path (Figure 9.5.11) and the connections to the Great Lines City Park in Medway (Figure 9.5.12).

References

BBC. (2014). Wraysbury residents say Jubilee River is a 'disaster'. *BBC News*. [Online]. Available at: http://www.bbc.com/news/uk-england-berkshire-25727040 [Accessed 16 April 2016].

DCLG. (2008). *Thames Gateway Parklands vision*. London: Department for Communities and Local Government.

Defra and ODPM. (2004). *Creating sustainable communities:Greening the Gateway. A greenspace strategy for Thames Gateway*. [Online]. Available at: http://www.medway.gov.uk/PDF/Creating%20sustainable%20communitie_Greening%20the%20Gateway%20strategy.pdf [Accessed 18 April 2016].

Environment Agency. (2009). *Water for life and livelihoods: River Basin Management Plan, Thames River Basin District*. Environment Agency. [Online]. Available at: https://www.gov.uk/government/uploads/system/uploads/attachment_data/file/289937/geth0910bswa-e-e.pdf [Accessed 16 April 2016].

Faraday, M. (1855). *Observations on the Filth of the Thames*. Letter dated July 7, 1855.

Farrell, T. (ed.). (2009). *The Thames Gateway, where next?* London: The Smith Institute.

Farrell, T., Martin, P., Johnson, B., Lynes, K. and Chambers, R. (2010). *Thames Gateway Parklands:Delivering Environmental Transformation*. London Development Agency.

Haughton, G., Rowe, I. and Hunter, C. (1997). The Thames Gateway and the Re-Emergence of Regional Strategic Planning:The Implications for Water Resource Management. *Town Planning Review*, 68 (4), p. 407–422. [Online]. Available at: doi:doi 10.2307%2F40113468.

NAO. (2007). *The Thames Gateway: Laying the Foundations*. Bourn, J. (ed.). The National Audit Office. [Online]. Available at: www.nao.org.uk.

ODPM. (2005). *Creating sustainable communities. Delivering the Thames Gateway*. [Accessed 18 April 2016].

RSPB. (2013). Details. *The Royal Society for the Protection of Birds*. [Online]. Available at: http://www.rspb.org.uk/news/341010-great-expectations-for-future-of-thames-gateway [Accessed 16 April 2016].

Thames Gateway. (2009). *Thames Gateway Delivery Plan*. [Online]. Available at: http://www.medway.gov.uk/pdf/Thames%20Gateway%20Delivery%20Plan%202009.pdf [Accessed 16 April 2016].

Tideway. (2016). Benefits - Tideway | Reconnecting London with the River Thames. *Tideway*. [Online]. Available at: http://www.tideway.london [Accessed 24 May 2016].

Chapter 9.6
Emscher River, Germany – Strategies and Techniques

Katia Perini

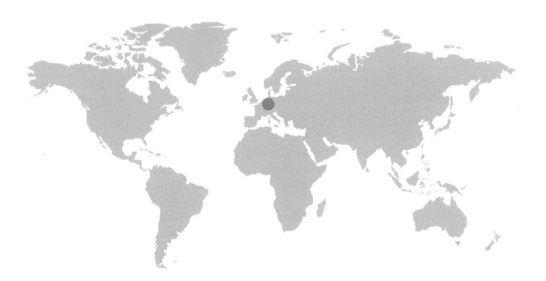

9.6.1 Context

The Emscher River flows in one of the most well-known German industrial regions, the Ruhr area. The Emscher River's natural state was ruined during the age of industrialisation and became heavily polluted, concrete wastewater drains (WIKUE, 2013). Before the era of industrial exploitation, the Emscher originally flowed from its source in Holzwickede through a sparsely populated region characterised by small villages and farms. The River reached the Rhine in the Ruhr

Urban Sustainability and River Restoration: Green and Blue Infrastructure, First Edition.
Katia Perini and Paola Sabbion.

area following a 109-kilometre winding course and a slight drop (Reicher *et al.*, 2011; Emschergenossenschaft *et al.*, 1999).

The Ruhr Valley, situated in western Germany, with its 5 million inhabitants and its high level of urbanisation (more than 40%) once was the country's industrial heartland, the location of steel, chemical and raw materials industries (WIKUE, 2013; Labelle, 2001; Sieker *et al.*, 2006). Since the beginning of the nineteenth century, the industrialisation led to a massive population growth in the region, generating a profound transformation in the valley. The underground coal mining expansion had a major impact on the Emscher River (WIKUE, 2013) as it contributed to increase floods. Furthermore, the industrial wastewater contaminated the river, destroying its ecosystem and increasing the risk of epidemics in the whole Emscher area (especially during floods; WIKUE, 2013). The first hygienic conversion was held from 1906 to 1920 to overcome this emergency: a concrete structure was built along the Emscher and its many tributaries (Figure 9.6.2), the channel was lowered by 9 metres and the river paths were altered (the original 109-km course was reduced to 80 kilometres; WIKUE, 2013; Boon and Raven, 2012).

Industrial production in the Ruhr region played a key role in Germany: the mining and industries based in this region served two world wars, and promoted economic growth during the 1950s and 1960s. In the 1970s, although, the region's output became less competitive, resulting in the ceasing of the mining activities in the 1980s. As a consequence, several areas along the Emscher River became brownfield sites. In this period, the unemployment rate exceeded 15% (Labelle, 2001; Sieker *et al.*, 2006).

The industrial production that characterised this area for almost a century had substantial, long-term effects on the river. In fact, an underground sewage system for industrial and human use was not created mainly due to the mining-induced subsidence risk, which would have damaged pipes. The resulting open wastewater infrastructure is among the main issues considered for the implementation of the river conversion which, nowadays, is under development (Labelle, 2001; Boon and Raven, 2012). The concrete bed elements built along the Emscher River and its catchment were a rational water management solution (also with reference to financial and hygienic aspects) during the most productive years, i.e. during the industrialisation period. This system has currently become unsuitable due to ecological, social and aesthetic reasons (Sieker *et al.*, 2006). Since the 1950s and 1980s, important infrastructures with a higher number of pumping stations were built to process the increasing flow of domestic wastewater (e.g., Europe's biggest sewage treatment plant was created in 1977 at the Emscher estuary in Dinslaken; WIKUE, 2013).

The industrialisation had evident consequences also on the landscape surrounding the Emscher River due to the presence of industrial buildings rising for ten floors or more and slag heaps. According to Labelle (2001), the ecological degradation of the 1980s definitely had a negative impact on the population, causing widespread psychological resignation.

The Emscher River restoration and rehabilitation has focused on water quality and environmental improvement in the whole river catchment (Boon and Raven, 2012). Over the last 20 years, the River has undergone an impressive ecological and socio-economic transformation affecting all aspects of life (WIKUE, 2013).

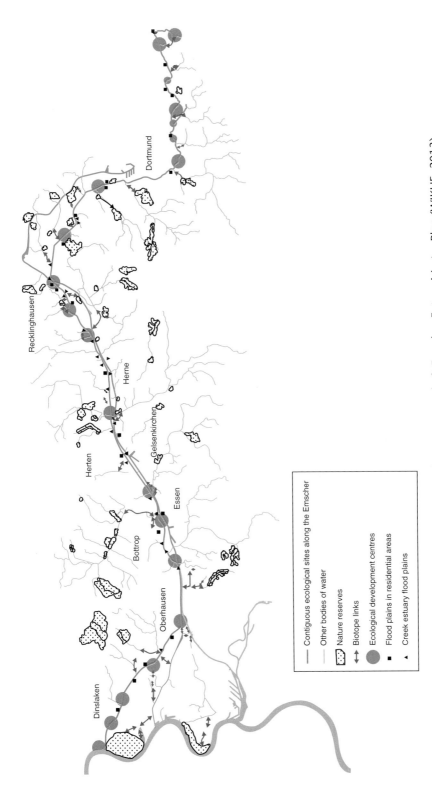

Figure 9.6.1 The Emscher River According to the Emschergenossenschaft Emscher Future Master Plan (WIKUE, 2013).

Figure 9.6.2 One of the Many Tributaries of the Emscher River Transformed Into Open Sewage Channel (photo by Paulina Budryte).

The Emscher's heavily industrialised basin was one of most degraded in Europe. Following the creation of its landscape park and the many actions implemented, it has become a symbol for urban, economic, social, and environmental change (Brown, 2001).

The Ruhr area is still an important industrial centre, even if the delocalisation of most of its intensive production has allowed the Emscher to become a "valuable living space that can contribute to upgrading the region and enhancing its quality of life" (WIKUE, 2013).

9.6.2 Ecological and environmental issues

For decades, the Emscher River has served as a waste water canal for the Ruhr area until the late nineteenth century, gaining the reputation of a biologically dead "open sewer" (Dac&Cities, 2014). The lack of an underground wastewater infrastructure is a major issue that is still posing several problems for the residents, and creates a persistent unpleasant smell (Deutschland, 2014; Schulz, 2012; WIKUE, 2013).

High levels of urbanisation and impervious surfaces, which characterise the area around the river, cause stormwater management problems, inducing flow regime alterations. In addition, combined sewer system overflows (SSO) occur during heavy rainfall, causing poor water quality of the river (Sieker *et al.*, 2006). In the past, local remedial actions have proved insufficient to solve the negative impact of the coal mines on water and wastewater in the whole area, highlighting the need for a comprehensive strategy (Annen, 1990).

From a hydrogeological point of view, the River is sand and clay-dominated and has widely ramified tributaries winding through the landscape, which are defined by low flow velocity. In this highly urbanised area with runoff problems, floods often occur, also due to the changes in the river's course (WIKUE, 2013). Additionally, the waterway's natural conditions have been altered when the riverbed was lowered along most of its length to counteract the effects of mining subsidence (Boon and Raven, 2012). The River is inaccessible along its entire length due to its many transformations. Since industrial areas and traffic routes limit the potential meanders the river could take, the Emscher conversion focuses more on widening its profile to provide a broader flood plain in the areas where there is adequate space (Prominski *et al.*, 2012).

9.6.3   Strategies, techniques, and results

The Emscher and its tributaries can not get back to their original natural condition; however, the ecological development strategy implemented considers the urban waterways in this changed environment and focuses on its damaged ecosystem.

According to the Wuppertal Institut für Klima, Umwelt, Energie GmbH (WIKUE, 2013), the history of the Emscher River can be divided into three different phases, namely Emscher 1.0, Emscher 2.0, Emscher 2.3. Emscher 1.0 - the Emscher's original condition - is lost. Emscher 2.0 can be set during the industrialisation phase. Emscher 3.0 which is still work in progress, regards the improvement of the river's ecological status to create "valuable living spaces". The phase of revitalisation saw relevant efforts to transform the river into a valuable ecological element (see Chapter 13.6). Restoration works have been implemented in the catchment area of the river and its tributaries roughly along 120 kilometres; removing concrete channels to restore natural vegetation. These measures have improved water quality and stormwater management, as well as providing habitats for animals, fostering plant diversity and devising recreational space. In fact, the regional Emscher Landscape Park features green corridors crossing the region from north to south and east to west, also including former industrial sites (Labelle, 2001). Moreover, a functioning aquatic ecosystem is another main objective of the project (WIKUE, 2013).

The restoration of the Emscher River is based on three key areas of innovation, which can be summarised as follows (WIKUE, 2013):

1. Construction (built or under construction) of decentralised wastewater treatment plants and pumping stations to treat wastewater locally. The project also entails an underground canal.
2. Renaturation of rivers and creeks, which is possible in cleaner water, where native species live. Naturalised floodplains also prompt additional urban climate and water supply cycle improvements.
3. Rainwater and wastewater separation that allows reducing the amount of water processed by treatment plants and recharging groundwater and water bodies (with rainwater).

The main purpose of the Emscher's conversion is providing favourable conditions for natural development and, at the same time, developing recreational areas (Figures 9.6.3, 9.6.4, 9.6.5). This is achieved building new infrastructure (treatment plants and large trunk sewer parallel to the rehabilitated rivers; Sieker *et al.*, 2006), clean-up, ecological restoration measures, and renaturalisation. The first step has been the installation of underground sewers to remove waste from the river and plant vegetation, trees and native plants along the riverbank. In addition, re-profiling the river has enhanced flood management. The broadened sections of the waterway, moreover, reduce its flow velocity (Dac&Cities, 2014).

Stormwater runoff is a key issue in terms of water management. The strategy called *Project 15/15* aims at reducing runoff (volume and peak flow) by 15%. This increases the river's ecological potential, improves its environmental conditions and, at the same time, provides for an easier sewer management (Sieker *et al.*, 2006).

As often happens in urban areas, the space for ecological development is limited. For this reason, a network of "ecological hotspots" (a high quality biotope structure), has been created to restore the river's ecological functions, counting on a "ripple effect" (Figure 9.6.1; Jähnig *et al.*, 2011). Connected wetlands (some are included in the Emscher Landscape Park), biotopes, niches and stepping stones (see Chapter 6) can create suitable habitats for flora and fauna, effectively increasing biodiversity (providing space for reproduction and feeding; WIKUE, 2013). This ecological upgrade is proving to be effective in the upper course of the river and has increased the presence of fish species, such as the stickleback (Schulz, 2012).

Figure 9.6.3   The Emscher River in the Bottrop Area (photo by Paulina Budryte).

Figure 9.6.4   The Berne Park in Botro, the Transformation of a Former Waste Water Treatment Plant (Landscape architect: by Piet Oudolf & Gross Max, 2010; photo by Paulina Budryte).

Figure 9.6.5   The Borbecker Mühlenbach in Essen Altendorf (photo by Paulina Budryte).

As mentioned, the renovation strategy envisages a wider river profile to create a broad flood plain, thus providing the river with ecological consistency. This is going to be implemented with a section-by-section work (when possible) to modify the parallelism of the trapezoidal profile to maintain (as a rule) one of the two existing embankments. The revitalisation of large sections of the river will occur thanks to maintenance, the creation of meandering courses, higher hydraulic roughness and reducing the river's flow (Prominski *et al.*, 2012).

Increasing low water flows and favouring natural rainwater management strategies actively contributes to flood protection (up to 20%). In addition, these strategies can reduce the effort and costs of conventional rainwater infrastructure, while improving urban landscapes and microclimates (Prominski *et al.*, 2012; WIKUE, 2013). Besides these strategies, flood retention basins, pumping stations and dykes are needed since the Emscher area has been damaged by the topographical changes related to mining (WIKUE, 2013).

All these strategies play a crucial role, improving the river's performances in terms of ecological and environmental quality. According to WIKUE (2013), the construction or modernisation of the treatment plants is, although, the most important technical part of the Emscher conversion. Along the river, 421 km of underground wastewater canals are under construction to treat the wastewater coming from industries, business facilities and households (involving more than 2.2 million people). This is a complex task based on the construction of a dual lame diameter collector sewer provided with twin tubes to allow inspection and repair, which connect the existing sewer network to a new wastewater treatment plant (Smet, 1996).

The Emscher River canal has required several years of planning and great efforts (Emschergenossenschaft, 2009). Advanced modelling techniques have been essential to evaluate the performance of this project (Pfeiffer and Simon, 1997). It is worth mentioning that, thanks to the new (grey) infrastructure, the river will be able to develop more naturally. The spatial planning approach adopted for the Emscher River, as often occurs with urban waterway conversions, has been based on the available space along the river channel. "Assisted natural recovery" of the Emscher river bed has been possible, only in some areas (Kondolf, 2012).

References

Annen, G. (1990). The Emscher River - a model of integrated water management in an urbanized area: problems and challenges. In: *Hydrological Processes and Water Management in Urban Areas*, 198, 1990, IAHS Publ. [Online]. Available at: http://hydrologie.org/redbooks/a198/iahs_198_0347.pdf [Accessed 18 April 2016].

Boon, P. and Raven, P. (2012). *River Conservation and Management*. John Wiley & Sons.

Brown, B. (2001). *Reconstructing the Ruhrgebiet*. Landscape Architecture.

Dac&Cities. (2014). *Emscher Park: From dereliction to scenic landscapes - Danish Architecture Centre*. [Online]. Available at: http://www.dac.dk/en/dac-cities/sustainable-cities/all-cases/green-city/emscher-park-from-dereliction-to-scenic-landscapes/[Accessed 2 December 2015].

Deutschland. (2014). The renaturation of the Emscher. *Deutschland.de*. [Online]. Available at: https://www.deutschland.de/en/topic/culture/town-country/the-renaturation-of-the-emscher [Accessed 2 December 2015].

Emschergenossenschaft. (2009). *Emscher Sewage Canal*. [Online]. Available at: http://www.abwasserkanal-emscher.de/en/emscher-sewage-canal.html [Accessed 2 December 2015].

Emschergenossenschaft, Peters, R., Stemplewski, J. and Arauner, H. W. (1999). *100 Jahre Wasserwirtschaft im Revier. Die Emschergenossenschaft 1899 - 1999*. Bottrop: Pomp, P.

Jähnig, S., Hering, D. and Sommerhäuser, M. (2011). *Fließgewässer-Renaturierung heute und morgen*. [Online]. Available at: http://www.schweizerbart.de/publications/detail/isbn/9783510530113 [Accessed 18 April 2016].

Kondolf, G. M. (2012). The Espace de Liberté and Restoration of Fluvial Process: When Can the River Restore Itself and When Must we Intervene? In: Boon, P. J. and Raven, P. J. (eds.), *River Conservation and Management*, John Wiley & Sons, Ltd, p. 223–241. [Online]. Available at: http://onlinelibrary.wiley.com/doi/10.1002/9781119961819.ch18/summary [Accessed 18 April 2016].

Labelle, J. M. (2001). *Emscher Park, Germany — expanding the definition of a 'park'*. In: Harmon, D. (ed.), 2001, The George Wright Society. [Online]. Available at: http://www.georgewright.org/37labell.pdf [Accessed 10 April 2016].

Pfeiffer, E. and Simon, M. (1997). Optimization of the rehabilitation of the emscher drainage system using continuous rainfall-runoff-modeling. *Water Science and Technology*, 36 (8–9), p. 33–37. [Online]. Available at: doi:10.1016/S0273-1223(97)00631-8 [Accessed 2 December 2015].

Prominski, M., Stokman, A., Stimberg, D., Voermanek, H. and Zeller, S. (2012). *River. Space.Design: Planning Strategies, Methods and Projects for Urban Rivers*. Walter de Gruyter.

Reicher, C., Kunzmann, K. R., Polívka, J., Roost, F., Utko, Y. and Wegener, M. (2011). *Schichten einer Region: Kartenstücke zur räumlichen Struktur des Ruhrgebiets*. Berlin: Jovis Berlin.

Schulz, M. (2012). Cleaning the Sewer: A Hi-Tech Revival for Europe's Foulest River. *Spiegel Online*, 16 November. [Online]. Available at: http://www.spiegel.de/international/germany/project-rehabilitates-europe-s-largest-open-sewer-in-ruhr-region-a-867406.html [Accessed 2 December 2015].

Sieker, H., Bandermann, S. and Becker, B. (2006). Urban Stormwater Management Demonstration Projects in the Emscher Region. In: *First SWITCH Scientific Meeting University of Birmingham*, 9 January 2006, UK. [Online]. Available at: http://www.switchurbanwater.eu/outputs/pdfs/CEMS_PAP_Urban_stormwater_management_demo_projects_Emscher.pdf [Accessed 18 April 2016].

Smet, W. (1996). Cleaning up the River Emscher: *International Journal of Rock Mechanics and Mining Sciences & Geomechanics Abstracts*, 33 (6), p. pp 19–20. [Online]. Available at: doi:10.1016/0148-9062(96)81972-3 [Accessed 2 December 2015].

WIKUE. (2013). *Emscher 3.0: from grey to blue - or, how the blue sky over the Ruhr region fell into the Emscher - by Wuppertal Institut für Klima, Umwelt, Energie GmbH*. Scheck H and Venjakob (eds.). [Online]. Available at: https://epub.wupperinst.org/frontdoor/index/index/docId/5070 [Accessed 9 April 2016].

Part B

Part C
Opportunities and Policies

Urban Sustainability and River Restoration: Green and Blue Infrastructure, First Edition.
Katia Perini and Paola Sabbion.
© 2017 John Wiley & Sons Ltd. Published 2017 by John Wiley & Sons Ltd.

Chapter 10
Green and Blue Infrastructure Top-Down Policies

Paola Sabbion

10.1 European environmental and water policy

Environmental policies have recently gained attention, becoming one of the primary objectives within the European Union and the United States. Europe is firmly committed to the protection of the environment, as shown by its agenda both at Member State level and on an international scale with regard to the preservation of air and water quality, conservation of resources and biodiversity, waste management, and adverse environmental impacts. European environmental policies aim to support sustainable development through corrective measures relating to specific environmental problems or through cross-cutting measures integrated within other policy areas, such as the *Thematic Strategy on Urban Environment* (Commission of the European Communities, 2006). The latter contributes to the implementation of the priorities of the Sixth Environment Action Programme of the European Community 2002–2012. The Sixth EAP ended in July 2012, but many of its measures and actions continue to be implemented. The Seventh Environment Action Programme, implemented from 2014 to 31 December 2020, defines a long-term vision and the achievement of target goals by 2050 (European Parliament and Council of the European Union, 2013a).

In 2013, the European Union (European Parliament and Council) devised Regulation 1293/2013, establishing a Programme for the Environment and Climate Action (LIFE), and Decision 1386/2013/EU addressing a General Union Environment Action Programme. In these provisions, the EU has agreed to "halt the loss of biodiversity and the degradation of ecosystem services in the Union by 2020, and restore them in so far as feasible, while stepping up the Union contribution to averting global biodiversity loss" (European Parliament and Council of the European Union, 2013a).

In particular, the first priority objective of the Decision 1386/2013 is to protect, conserve and enhance the Union's natural capital: restoring at least 15% of the degraded ecosystems in the Union, and expanding the use of Green Infrastructure to overcome fragmentation of landscape. This action, combined to Birds and Habitats Directives, and supported by Prioritised Action Frameworks "further enhance natural capital and increase ecosystem resilience, and can offer cost-effective options for climate change mitigation and adaptation". It would, in fact, contribute to maintain the existing stock of natural capital at a variety of scales (European Parliament and Council of the European Union, 2013a). In addition, this framework is integrated with other environmental strategies, in particular the 2013 European Commission Communication on Green Infrastructure (see Chapter 1; European Commission, 2013).

The European Union recently highlighted the importance of water policies, stressing the urgency to "ensure that good status of surface water and groundwater is achieved and that deterioration in the status of waters is prevented" (European Parliament, 2000). The EU has established a series of Policies regarding water to achieve these objectives and has devised regulating strategies also to tackle climate change effects. These include the Directive 2013/39/EU of the European Parliament and of the Council, amending the Water Framework Directive 2000/60/EC (European Parliament, 2000) and the Directive on environmental quality standards in the field of water policy (2008/105/EC). Furthermore, water consumption is one of 12 environmental indicators assessed as part of the European Green Capital Award, an initiative undertaken by 15 European cities and launched by the European Commission in 2008. Every year one European Green Capital is granted the Capital Award to promote the role that local authorities play in improving the environment and sustainable development (European Commission, 2016).

Surface and groundwater have to be monitored and the anthropic activities have to be regulated to attain the required *good status* objectives (chemical and ecological status for surface waters and chemical and quantitative status for groundwater; European Parliament, 2000). Every member state should set out objectives of final quality improvement to achieve these goals and implement a series of policies and measures to reduce pollutants, limit exploitation of water resources, and increase the quality of water bodies, defining environmental quality standards, based on the chemical status of surface waters, and a careful balance of ecological aspects.

In particular, the Water Framework Directive (WFD) requires management plans to be developed for each river basin district and all EU Member States to develop effective management systems. The river basin is the focus of this planning approach as it is the most appropriate scale to devise most efforts and political strategies. The EU has adopted a *morphological* approach based on hydrological boundaries rather than administrative boundaries to better address ecological issues (Quevauviller *et al.* (eds.), 2008). This includes the identification of the hydrological systems and processes, the definition of environmental quality standards, the combined control of the forms of alteration, and the integration of management policies on drinking and bathing water, surface water and groundwater (Wilby *et al.*, 2006; Quevauviller, 2014).

These provisions seek to preserve, protect and improve the environmental quality and the rational use of surface water and groundwater resources. Flood risk reduction is not among the Water Framework Directive main objectives, but the European Parliament and the Council assess and manage flood risks according to Flood Directive (2007/60/EC; European Parliament and Council of the European Union, 2007). The latter requires Member States to develop policies referring to water and land uses, considering the potential impact on flood risks and the management of hazards, providing for flood risk management plans. The Member States, according to the Directive, should be focusing on prevention: "Flood risk management plans should take into account the particular characteristics of the areas they cover and provide for tailored solutions according to the needs and priorities of those areas", including "the promotion of sustainable land use practices, improvement of water retention as well as the controlled flooding" (European Parliament and Council of the European Union, 2007).

As described in Chapter 2, climate change is a risk factor for climate-related water threats (floods and droughts; Wilby *et al.*, 2006; Ludwig *et al.*, 2014; Quevauviller, 2014). As a consequence, as part of the EU Strategy on Adaptation to Climate Change, the European Commission has established that river basin management plans to improve Europe's adaptation to climate change and to make it *climate proof* (European Parliament and Council of the European Union, 2013b). In particular, the Flood Directive (European Parliament and Council of the European Union, 2007) and the Communication on the Blueprint to Safeguard Europe's Resources (European Commission, 2012) establish measures to manage flood risk, reducing associated negative effects on natural and human systems and recommending WFD implementation (Quevauviller, 2014). As a precondition, EU Member States are required to increase their knowledge of global/regional water distribution (river systems, groundwater, lakes water levels, soil water content, etc.) and its relative impact to develop an adequate set of strategies. In 2012, the Environment Agency established the Catchment Restoration Fund to curb river pollution. This programme also supports orographic-based catchment recovery by producing guidelines and prioritising projects. It delivers additional ecosystem services while providing good chemical and ecological river status (Gilvear *et al.*, 2013). Awareness on the dynamics and changes in water bodies allows identifying suitable actions to prevent, mitigate, and adapt these trends. Moreover, data collection facilitates the assessment of the impact of climate change on distribution, frequency and severity of floods or drought events and impacts on ecosystems, human activities and infrastructures (such as changes in water demand, different use configurations, effects on water treatment and sewer network operations, etc.). According to Quevauviller, these policy trends are very closely related to the capacity to retrieve supporting scientific information and to bridge knowledge gaps (Quevauviller, 2014). For this reason, the EU is currently planning the future research programme *Horizon2020* (2014–2020) as a way to increase Member States' efforts to map and assess ecosystems and their services, as this will improve data availability.

According to EU Directives, Member States should take into account the economic value of ecosystem services at Union and national level and this would result in better management of the Union's natural capital (European Parliament and Council of the European Union, 2013a). With this aim, the environmental agencies of single EU Member States "are producing guidelines for river rehabilitation planning […] at the catchment scale to prioritise projects that deliver other ecosystem services beyond just good ecological status" (Gilvear *et al.*, 2013).

So far, European environmental policies have achieved important results at both Member State level and internationally. Every Member State is required to integrate EU directives in its specific policies, developing and implementing national strategies of governance to attain the required obligations. Therefore, the normative framework of Member States can vary significantly and can have a great impact on the effectiveness and flexibility of territorial management tools (Giachetta, 2013).

Several national strategies aspire to accomplish the goal of good ecological status through river rehabilitation. Specific, successful restoration projects have been undertaken in Europe as part of a policy approach and agenda-setting based on this new environmental focus. Some European states as Austria, Denmark, Germany and the Netherlands "have already identified significant funds to take forward large scale rehabilitation, often on the back of flood risk reduction" (Gilvear *et al.*, 2013). In the Netherlands, since 2008, the Rotterdam Climate Proof was implemented to create a climate resilient city by 2025 and is now part of the Rotterdam Climate Initiative (RCI; European Commission, 2016).

In the United Kingdom, the economic and social impact of climate change and flooding have been resolutely tackled. A series of strategies, such as *United Kingdom Water Research and Innovation Framework 2011–2030*, have been devised to integrate surface water and drainage system management, and to target flood risk reduction, water quality improvement, and sewer load management (DEFRA, 2008). Since 2004, the Environment Agency (EA) has implemented *Making Space for Water*, the strategy for flood and coastal erosion risk management, which addresses in particular the anthropic impact of urbanisation (Batterbee *et al.*, 2012; Gilvear *et al.*, 2013; DEFRA, 2005). In general, the UK policy agenda is shifting from erecting structural defences to developing resilience to flooding (DEFRA, 2005), implementing permeable capacity and supporting natural channellisation to reduce the impact of containing and culverting. New strategies seek to cater for environmental, aesthetic and socio-economic needs (Everett and Lamond, 2014). The concept that urban environments need to adapt to climate change effects, producing *water sensitive cities*, has lead to the promotion of *Blue-Green Flood Risk Management* approaches and the implementation of green infrastructure to restore the natural water-cycle (Everett and Lamond, 2014). In Scotland, the Flood Risk Management Act (2009) is based on a "holistic approach to flood risk reduction" through land management and river rehabilitation in the upper and middle catchment to reduce downstream flooding (Bracken *et al.*, 2016; Gilvear *et al.*, 2013).

In France, the law of December 16 1964 structured water management for each river drainage basin. In 2006, a comprehensive law on water and aquatic environments was adopted to meet the European WFD requirements taking into account the climate change-related issues. The law sets out some main goals, including the standards required to achieve good chemical and ecological *status*, nondegradation of water bodies, pollution reduction and compliance with the guidelines related to protected areas (Ministère de l'Environnement, de l'Energie et de la Mer, n.d.). Water management and environmental protection has been undertaken with the Grenelle Environment Forum (2007). This project aimed at counteracting biodiversity loss and landscape fragmentation, and restoring ecological corridors, translating into practice the guidelines set by the European Ecological

Figure 10.1   Vegetated Basin to Fulfil French Requirements at La Boiserie, Salle Polyvalente et de Spectacle (Mazan, France).

Figure 10.2   Rain Garden - La Boiserie, Salle Polyvalente et de Spectacle (Mazan, France).

Figure 10.3   GBI Systems at Le Naturoptère, Centre Culturel et Pédagogique (Sérignan-du-Comtat, France).

Network (Ministère de l'Environnement, de l'Energie et de la Mer, 2007). The French law of 12 July 2010 - *Grenelle II* - confirms these provisions by adding goals regarding reduction of pollutant discharge and diffusion, restoration of habitats and ecological corridors, optimisation of water consumption, and risk management, thus improving settlement planning, moving residential areas away from flood-prone areas and reducing the share of population exposed to this hazard.

10.2   American environmental and water policy

In the United States, since 1948, water pollution management has been regulated by the Clean Water Act (CWA), designed to restore and maintain the chemical, physical, and biological integrity of water. The Federal Water Pollution Control Act (FWPCA) was enacted in 1948, and revised with the Federal Water Pollution Control Act Amendments of 1972. The Water Quality Act of 1987 has subsequently introduced major changes via amendatory legislation (Gilvear *et al.*, 2013).

Since 2009, the U.S. Environmental Protection Agency (EPA) under Administrator Lisa Jackson has endorsed the promotion of green infrastructure with the support of the New York State Department of Environmental Conservation (DEC). The EPA, with its mission to protect human health and the environment, writes and enforces regulations based on laws passed by the U.S. Congress, including, among others: the Clean Air Act (CAA; 1963), the comprehensive Federal law that regulates air emissions from stationary and mobile sources, and which authorised EPA to establish National Ambient Air Quality Standards (NAAQS); and the Federal Water Pollution Control Act Amendments, commonly known as the Clean Water Act (CWA), adopted in 1977, which regulates discharges of pollutants into water and sets quality standards for surface waters (U.S. EPA, 2016b; New York City Department of Environmental Protection, 2010). In many cases, the CWA plays an important role supporting the adoption of corrective measures where outdated sewage systems are polluting waterways (see for example the Bronx River Case Study, Chapter 9.1).

The United States has a different approach and a less prescriptive normative framework compared to Europe in this field. The EPA provides local municipal grants and technical support to cities for GI implementation to fulfil CWA requirements (U.S. EPA, 2016c). According to Angotti (2013), the role of the Federal and State Administrations in restoring urban areas is linked to financial backing, even if private funding also plays an important role (Crauderueff *et al.*, 2012). Regulatory aspects at the Federal level are also crucial for the diffusion of GI as, in several cities, stormwater runoff is managed using green infrastructure to advance EPA regulatory requirements. Local municipalities spend great sums to reduce the volume of stormwater runoff in order to meet the regulations of the CWA and to achieve swimmable and fishable waters (Crauderueff *et al.*, 2012).

Top-down policies significantly vary among States and Cities. For example, the State of California is currently experiencing dramatic droughts and a number of State agencies provide planning, design, and construction, grant funding, deliver studies and projects for water bodies management (see the case of Los Angeles River, Chapter 13.2). At federal Level, the Urban Waters Federal Partnership (U.S. Environmental Protection Agency, EPA) established seven Urban Waters Pilot locations in June 2011 with the aim of working closely with local partners to restore urban waterways: "The Urban Waters Federal Partnership reconnects urban communities – particularly those that are overburdened or economically distressed – with their waterways by improving coordination among federal agencies and collaborating with community-led revitalisation efforts to improve [...] water systems and promote their economic, environmental and social benefits" (U.S. EPA, 2016a). A number of Conservancy authorities also have a strong tradition, including the California Coastal Conservancy and the California Department of Water Resources. The California Natural Resources Agency acts to restore, protect, and manage natural, historical, and cultural resources. It delivers the River Parkways Program, and other bond programmes (State of California, 2016).

Many other agencies act to preserve open spaces and habitats, as the California State Parks and Mountains Recreation and Conservation Authority, the San Gabriel and Lower Los Angeles Rivers and Mountains Conservancy. Moreover, the State Water Resources Control Board and the Los Angeles Regional Water Quality Control Board protect ground and surface water quality in the Los Angeles Region (California Environment Protection Agency, 2016). The Los Angeles Regional Board is one of nine Regional Boards in the State, part of the California Environmental Protection Agency. The US Army Corps of Engineers of Los Angeles District deliver a range of LA River related studies and projects as part of the Los Angeles District's program (see Chapter 13.2; U.S. Army Corps of Engineers, 2015).

Another effective model (at city-level) is New York City. The city clearly experiences a tremendous volume of rainwater runoff from rooftops, streets, and other impervious surfaces (New York Department of City Planning, 2011). New York City has 25,900 inhabitants per square kilometre, an urban density higher than figures registered in 40 American states and its population density is 800 times higher than the rest of the United States (Owen, 2010). This means that green and blue infrastructure (GBI) can play a very important role in reducing environmental and ecological imbalances, as well as mitigating the Urban Heat Island (UHI) phenomenon (Susca *et al.*, 2011). The importance of green infrastructure, trees, green roofs and other forms of ecological infrastructure are recognised for their recreational, ecological, and economic function. NYC has invested in a network of green corridors, streets and other dedicated paths that perform multiple functions, including promoting recreation, capturing stormwater, and cleaning the air (New York Department of City Planning, 2011).

In the late 1990s, 14 sewage treatment plants were built in New York City to comply with the Federal Clean Water Act in problematic areas of the city (e.g., West Harlem; Angotti, 2008). In October 2012, the damage caused by Hurricane Sandy left more than 800,000 people without power, damaged tens of thousands of homes and businesses, and killed 43 residents. This demonstrated the importance of green infrastructure systems in complementing traditional *grey infrastructure* and implementing the City's climate resilience efforts. Hurricane Sandy highlighted the need to bolster the City's resiliency and reduce its GHG emissions to help stave off the worst potential impacts of climate change (New York Department of City Planning, 2013). *PlaNYC. A Stronger, More Resilient New York* (New York City Department of Environmental Protection, 2013) was hence developed in 2007 to make the City able to withstand the forces of climate change and react more quickly when extreme weather strikes. The plan recognises the importance of increased green area capacity to absorb flood waters and city-wide expansion of green infrastructure. The PlaNYC Sustainable Stormwater Management Plan (2008) was issued by the Interagency Best Management Practices (BMPs) Task Force that concluded that GBI – including bioswales, green roofs, and subsurface detention systems (see Chapters 6 and 7) – was feasible in many areas in the City and could be more cost effective than certain large infrastructure projects such as CSO storage tunnels or tanks (during heavy storms, these can exceed capacity and are designed to discharge a mix of stormwater and wastewater into New York Harbor to prevent treatment plants from becoming compromised; New York City Department of Environmental Protection, 2012). PlaNYC was a bold agenda to meet challenges related to growing population, ageing infrastructure, a changing climate, and an evolving economy and to build a greener, greater NYC (New York Department of City Planning, 2011). The ambitious goal of PlaNYC is to reduce citywide GHG emissions by 30% below 2005 levels by 2030 (known as 30 by 30).

Several other initiatives have been launched in NYC to increase the resilience of the built environment, including a $ 2.4 billion Green Infrastructure Plan intended to improve rainfall management and reduce the impact of Combined Sewer Overflow (CSO; New York Department of City Planning, 2013). It is worth mentioning that the City government has recognised the importance of GI before Hurricane Sandy (2012), as a cost-effective stormwater management practice.

In fact, The Green Infrastructure Plan was hence launched in 2010 to invest in new and restored green infrastructure for stormwater management in place of traditional grey infrastructure thanks to a $1.5 billion commitment for green infrastructure development over the following 20 years (New York City Department of Environmental Protection, 2010). Furthermore, a set of High Performance Infrastructure Guidelines have been developed to implement sustainable Green Infrastructure practice (New York Department of Design and Construction, 2005).

During the administration of Mayor Michael Bloomberg, several policies were developed to reduce greenhouse gas (GHG) emissions by 30% by 2030, and to improve residents' quality of life, as outlined in PlaNYC. Researches have identified further cost-effective strategies to reduce environmental and ecological imbalances, including a study conducted by Columbia University Center for Climate Systems Research, Hunter College, and SAIC Corporation, which investigates effective programmes to mitigate UHI (Rosenzweig *et al.*, 2006). Results show that a combined strategy that maximises the amount of vegetation by planting trees along streets and in open spaces and building ecological infrastructure can mitigate the phenomenon in NYC and offer more potential cooling than any individual strategy.

Many projects have been developed to demonstrate GBI's effectiveness and its application on a variety of land uses. This has allowed evaluating the potential effects of green roofs, as a means of supporting ecological connectivity. Moreover, these projects have demonstrated that green roofs, can create ecological links between fragmented ecosystems and habitats, reducing UHI effect and energy costs for buildings, and improve stormwater management (New York City Department of Environmental Protection, 2013). The pilot project "living laboratory for innovative green roof design", implemented by New York City Department of Parks and Recreation (NYC Parks), tests different types of green roofs available on the market (Figure 10.4). This project also serves as a way to educate and inspire park staff and patrons, as well as supplying a resource for peers in the field. According to Rollins (2013), green roof investments are effective for NYC with regard to stormwater management. The Department spends small amounts to process water through sewage treatment plants during storms. However, the cost is about $7 to build the sewage treatment plants to process 3.7 litres (one gallon) of water. Since the savings are high, the Department of Environmental Protection is allocating significanat grants every year to private and commercial businesses to install green roofs. Green roofs would be a relevant cost saving initiative. However, high investments are required to manage the large surface areas of green roofs. A greenway system was developed starting with the Greenway Plan for New York City, released in 1993 and intended to double 2007 levels bicycle commuting by 2012 and tripling them by 2017 (New York Department of City Planning, 2013).

Among several widespread smaller initiatives implemented in New York City to increase vegetation, the *Greenstreets* programme is notably transforming unused road space, traffic islands, and industrial areas into green assets (Figure 10.5). The vegetated streets created by this programme capture stormwater and improve water quality, and serve as important ecological respites within the urban landscape. Since 1996, Greenstreets has been implemented throughout the City's five boroughs using specially designed soils and plants (New York City Department of Environmental Protection, 2013).

Part C

Figure 10.4 NYC Park's Green Roof Pilot Project (photo by Artie Rollins).

Figure 10.5 Greenstreet in the Bronx (NYC).

GBI design and planning is a growing practice in the United States to counteract soil erosion and to improve stormwater management, increasing soil water storage potential through runoff reduction and water transpiration (Xiao and McPherson, 2002; Bartens *et al.*, 2008). Green streets and other sustainable design practices, such as pedestrian and cycle paths, traffic moderation and the scenic amelioration of streetscapes, are also part of these scheme (Thompson and Sorvig, 2007). Green street design is especially important in Portland (Podobnik, 2011; Sharifi, 2016), Seattle (City of Seattle, 2008), New York City (New York Department of Design and Construction, 2005), and Chicago (City of Chicago, nd) where increasing permeable pavements and natural drainage projects with a subsoil infiltration system are provided.

A number of programmes implemented by NYC bodies involve or were conceived to increase citizens' participation (with a top-down approach). For example, GreeNYC's aim is to encourage residents to adopt sustainable practices in their daily lives; the programme supports PlaNYC by driving the City's sustainability goals. GreeNYC's campaigns seek to present a compelling case for behavioural change at the individual level using simple, action-oriented messages (City of New York, 2016). With its slogan "I'm counting on you", MillionTreesNYC is one of the 132 PlaNYC initiatives and is a public-private programme intending to plant and care for one million new trees across the City's five boroughs over the next decade (City of New York, 2015).

The important role played by the community with regard to green infrastructure maintenance is recognised in the case of New York City and has also been crucial in the case of the Los Angeles to attract the attention of policy-makers on citizens' daily needs and develop new ideas and actions (see Chapters 13.1, 13.2). As stated in the NYC Green Infrastructure Plan, stakeholder participation is critical to build and maintain green infrastructure, and the New York City Department of Environmental Protection has led the outreach effort to involve community boards, stormwater advocacy and non-profit environmental organisations, Citizens Advisory Committees (CACs), civic organisations, other City agencies, environmental justice organizations, and local communities (New York City Department of Environmental Protection, 2010).

According to Francis and Lorimer (2011), some reconciliation or habitat enhancement techniques may be characterised as top-down approaches, including the creation of habitats in public parks and recreational spaces, and the planting of vegetation along urban infrastructures. Generally, however, reconciliation relies much more heavily on localised and coordinated efforts of a large number of people and organisations with high levels of spatial, social, and economic diversity, which are based on a classic bottom-up structure (see Chapter 11).

References

Angotti, T. (2008). *New York for sale community planning confronts global real estate.* Cambridge, Mass.: MIT Press.

Angotti, T. (2013). *Personal communication in: Katia Perini, 2014. Urban areas and green infrastructure. Research report, published by Urban Design Lab Columbia University ISNB 978-09822174-5-0.* [Online]. Available at: http://urbandesignlab.columbia.edu/files/2015/04/3_Urban_Areas_Green_Infrastructure.pdf.

Bartens, J., Day, S. D., Harris, J. R., Dove, J. E., and Wynn, T. M. (2008). Can Urban Tree Roots Improve Infiltration through Compacted Subsoils for Stormwater Management? *Journal of Environment Quality*, 37 (6), p. 2048. [Online]. Available at: doi:10.2134/jeq2008.0117.

Batterbee, R., Heathwaite, L., Lane, S. N., McDonald, A., Newson, M., Smith, H., Staddon, C., and Wharton, G. (2012). *Water policy in the UK: The challenges*. In: 2012, Royal Geographical Society. [Online]. Available at: http://eprints.lancs.ac.uk/56158/1/RGS_IBG_Policy_Document_Water_7_32pp.pdf [Accessed 8 April 2016].

Bracken, L. J., Oughton, E. A., Donaldson, A., Cook, B., Forrester, J., Spray, C., Cinderby, S., Passmore, D., and Bissett, N. (2016). Flood risk management, an approach to managing cross-border hazards. *Natural Hazards*, 82 (2), p. 217–240. [Online]. Available at: doi:10.1007/s11069-016-2284-2.

California Environment Protection Agency. (2016). *State Water Resources Control Board - Los Angeles*. [Online]. Available at: http://www.waterboards.ca.gov/losangeles/ [Accessed 27 May 2016].

City of Chicago, Daley, R. M.-M., Byrne, T. G., and Attarian, J. L. (nd). *The Chicago Green Alley Handbook. An Action Guide to Create a Greener, Environmentally Sustainable Chicago*. City of Chicago, Streetscape & Urban Design Program, Department of Transportation.

City of New York. (2015). *MillionTrees NYC*. [Online]. Available at: http://www.milliontreesnyc.org/html/about/about.shtml [Accessed 26 May 2016].

City of New York. (2016). *GreeNYC*. [Online]. Available at: http://www1.nyc.gov/site/greenyc/about/about.page [Accessed 26 May 2016].

City of Seattle. (2008). *Seattle's Natural Drainage Systems*. Seattle Public Utilities.

Commission of the European Communities. (2006). *Communication from the commission to the council and the European Parliament on Thematic Strategy on the Urban Environment*. [Online]. Available at: http://ec.europa.eu/environment/urban/pdf/com_2005_0718_en.pdf.

Crauderueff, R., Margolis, S. and Tanikawa, S. (2012). *Greening Vacant Lots: Planning and Implementation Strategies. A report prepared fot The Nature Conservancy as part of the NatLab collaboration*. [Online]. Available at: http://docs.nrdc.org/water/files/wat_13022701a.pdf.

DEFRA. (2005). *Making Space for Water. Developing a new Government strategy for flood and coastal erosion risk management in England*. DEFRA, London.

DEFRA. (2008). *Future Water:The Government's water strategy for England*. Department for Environment Food and Rural Affairs. [Online]. Available at: https://www.gov.uk/government/uploads/system/uploads/attachment_data/file/69346/pb13562-future-water-080204.pdf [Accessed 8 April 2016].

European Commission. (2012). *Communication from the Commission to the European Parliament, the Council, the European Economic and Social Committee and the Committee of the Regions - A Blueprint To Safeguard Europe's Water Resources*.

European Commission. (2013). *Green Infrastructure (GI) — Enhancing Europe's Natural Capital. Communication from the Commission to the European Parliament, the Council, the European Economic and Social Committee and the Committee of the Regions*. [Online]. Available at: http://eur-lex.europa.eu/LexUriServ/LexUriServ.do?uri=COM:2013:0249:FIN:EN:PDF.

European Commission. (2016). *European Green Capital*. [Online]. Available at: http://ec.europa.eu/environment/europeangreencapital/rotterdams-water-square/ [Accessed: 3 May 2016].

European Parliament. (2000). *Directive 2000/60/EC of the European Parliament and of the Council of 23 October 2000 establishing a framework for Community action in the field of water policy*.

European Parliament and Council of the European Union. (2007). *Directive 2007/60/EC of the European Parliament and of the Council of 23 October 2007 on the assessment and management of flood risks*.

European Parliament and Council of the European Union. (2013a). *Decision N. 1386/2013/ EU of the European Parliament and of the Council of 20 November 2013 on a General Union Environment Action Programme to 2020 'Living well, within the limits of our planet'*.

European Parliament and Council of the European Union. (2013b). *Regulation (EU) N. 1293/2013 of the European Parliament and of the Council of 11 December 2013 on the establishment of a Programme for the Environment and Climate Action (LIFE) and repealing Regulation (EC) No 614/2007*.

Everett, G. and Lamond, J. (2014). *A conceptual framework for understanding behaviours and attitudes around 'Blue-Green' approaches to Flood-Risk Management*. In: 18 June 2014, p. 101–112. [Online]. Available at: doi:10.2495/FRIAR140091 [Accessed 15 December 2015].

Francis, R. A. and Lorimer, J. (2011). Urban reconciliation ecology: The potential of living roofs and walls. *Journal of Environmental Management*, 92 (6), p. 1429–1437. [Online]. Available at: doi:10.1016/j.jenvman.2011.01.012 [Accessed 30 January 2014].

Giachetta, A. (2013). Diffusion of Sustainable Construction Practices. A Case of International Cooperation. *Open Journal of Energy Efficiency*, 02 (01), p. 46–52. [Online]. Available at: doi:10.4236/ojee.2013.21008 [Accessed 22 January 2014].

Gilvear, D. J., Spray, C. J., and Casas-Mulet, R. (2013). River rehabilitation for the delivery of multiple ecosystem services at the river network scale. *Journal of Environmental Management*, 126, p. 30–43. [Online]. Available at: doi:10.1016/j.jenvman.2013.03.026.

Ludwig, F., van Slobbe, E., and Cofino, W. (2014). Climate change adaptation and Integrated Water Resource Management in the water sector. *Journal of Hydrology*, 518, Part B, p. 235–242. [Online]. Available at: doi:10.1016/j.jhydrol.2013.08.010.

Ministère de l'Environnement, de l'Energie et de la Mer. (2007). *Le Grenelle de l'environnement de 2007 à 2012*. [Online]. Available at: http://www.developpement-durable.gouv.fr/-Le-Grenelle-de-l-environnement-de-.html.

Ministère de l'Environnement, de l'Energie et de la Mer. (n.d.). Direction générale de l'Aménagement, du Logement et de la Nature. [Online]. Available at: www.developpement-durable.gouv.fr.

New York City Department of Environmental Protection. (2010). *NYC Green Infrastructure Plan*. [Online]. Available at: http://www.nyc.gov/html/dep/pdf/green_infrastructure/gi_annual_report_2012.pdf.

New York City Department of Environmental Protection. (2012). *NYC Green Infrastructure Plan 2011 Update*. [Online]. Available at: http://www.nyc.gov/html/dep/pdf/green_infrastructure/gi_annual_report_2012.pdf.

New York City Department of Environmental Protection. (2013). *PlaNYC. A Stronger, More Resilient New York*. [Online]. Available at: http://www.nyc.gov/html/sirr/downloads/pdf/final_report/001SIRR_cover_for_DoITT.pdf.

New York Department of City Planning. (2011). *PlaNYC. Update*. [Online]. Available at: http://nytelecom.vo.llnwd.net/o15/agencies/planyc2030/pdf/planyc_2011_planyc_full_report.pdf.

New York Department of City Planning. (2013). *PlaNYC. Progress Report 2013*. [Online]. Available at: http://nytelecom.vo.llnwd.net/o15/agencies/planyc2030/pdf/planyc_progress_report_2013.pdf.

New York Department of Design and Construction. (2005). *High performance infrastructure guidelines: best practices for the public right-of-way : New York City, October 2005*. [New York]: New York City Department of Design + Construction : Design Trust for Public Space.

Part C

Owen, D. (2010). *Green metropolis: why living smaller, living closer, and driving less are the keys to sustainability*. New York: Riverhead Books.

Podobnik, B. (2011). Assessing the social and environmental achievements of New Urbanism: Evidence from Portland, Oregon. *Journal of Urbanism*, 4 (2), p. 105–126. *Scopus* [Online]. Available at: doi:10.1080/17549175.2011.596271.

Quevauviller, P. (2014). European water policy and research on water-related topics – An overview. *Journal of Hydrology*, 518, Part B, p. 180–185. [Online]. Available at: doi:10.1016/j.jhydrol.2014.02.007.

Quevauviller, P., Borchers, U., Thompson, K., and Simonart, T. (eds.). (2008). *The Water Framework Directive – Ecological and Chemical Status Monitoring*. John Wiley and Sons, Ltd. *ISBN:978-0-470-51836-6.*

Rollins, A. (2013). *Personal communication in: Katia Perini, 2014. Urban areas and green infrastructure. Research report, published by Urban Design Lab Columbia University ISNB 978-09822174-5-0.* [Online]. Available at: http://urbandesignlab.columbia.edu/files/2015/04/3_Urban_Areas_Green_Infrastructure.pdf.

Rosenzweig, C., Solecki, W. D., and Slosberg, R. B. (2006). *Mitigating New York City's heat island with urban forestry, living roofs, and light surfaces. New York City regional heat island initiative.* [Online]. Available at: http://gis.fs.fed.us/ccrc/topics/urban-forests/docs/NYSERDA_heat_island.pdf [Accessed 21 February 2014].

Sharifi, A. (2016). From Garden City to Eco-urbanism: The quest for sustainable neighborhood development. *Sustainable Cities and Society*, 20, p. 1–16. [Online]. Available at: doi:10.1016/j.scs.2015.09.002.

State of California. (2016). California Natural Resources Agency | Resources Agency. *California Natural Resources Agency.* [Online]. Available at: http://resources.ca.gov/ [Accessed 27 May 2016].

Susca, T., Gaffin, S. R., and Dell'Osso, G. R. (2011). Positive effects of vegetation: Urban heat island and green roofs. *Environmental Pollution*, 159 (8–9), p. 2119–2126. [Online]. Available at: doi:10.1016/j.envpol.2011.03.007 [Accessed 22 January 2014].

Thompson, J. W. and Sorvig, K. (2007). *Sustainable Landscape Construction: A Guide to Green Building Outdoors*, Washington: Island Press.

U.S. Army Corps of Engineers. (2015). LA River ecosystem restoration report available for public review and. *U.S. Army Corps of Engineers Los Angeles District.* [Online]. Available at: http://www.spl.usace.army.mil/Media/NewsReleases/tabid/1319/Article/621504/la-river-ecosystem-restoration-report-available-for-public-review-and-comment.aspx [Accessed 11 May 2016].

U.S. EPA, O. (2016a). *About the Urban Waters Federal Partnership.* Overviews and Factsheets. [Online]. Available at: https://www.epa.gov/urbanwaterspartners/about-urban-waters-federal-partnership [Accessed 27 May 2016].

U.S. EPA, O. (2016b). *Laws & Regulations.* Collections and Lists. [Online]. Available at: https://www.epa.gov/laws-regulations [Accessed 26 May 2016].

U.S. EPA, O. (2016c). *Learn about Water.* Collections and Lists. [Online]. Available at: https://www.epa.gov/learn-issues/learn-about-water [Accessed 26 May 2016].

Wilby, R. L., Orr, H. G., Hedger, M., Forrow, D., and Blackmore, M. (2006). Risks posed by climate change to the delivery of Water Framework Directive objectives in the UK. *Environment International*, 32 (8), p. 1043–1055. [Online]. Available at: doi:10.1016/j.envint.2006.06.017.

Xiao, Q. and McPherson, E. G. (2002). Rainfall interception by Santa Monica's municipal urban forest. *Urban Ecosystems*, 6 (4), p. 291–302.

Chapter 11
Bottom-Up Initiatives for Green and Blue Infrastructure

Katia Perini

11.1   Bottom-up and top-down approaches

Urban planning approaches can be either based on top-down or bottom-up strategies. The former devolves much of the decision-making process, in particular the selection of targets and administration, to national governments (Nemet, 2010). Urban citizens' participation, although, is essential for the effectiveness of top-down approaches, as users' satisfaction is a key element contributing to the success of every new policy (Francis and Lorimer, 2011). The United Nations Framework Convention on Climate Change (UNFCCC) best exemplifies a top-down approach on a world scale aimed at securing a global agreement to reduce greenhouse gas emissions and protect the environment.

Bottom-up strategies are based on community-generated self-managed initiatives advocating new spatial settings that need to be harmonised on a regional or urban scale. Bottom-up initiatives play a key role in restoring environmental and ecological quality in urban areas and are focused on democratic and empowerment evaluations (Krogstrup, 2004). In general, participation is defined as active involvement of people in processes and decisions. The voting system implies a direct form of participation. Active involvement is required ever more so with the organisation of demonstrations, public discussions, and conferences. In some cases, political activism can highly influence the decision-making processes and, on some terms, it can also be semi-legal or illegal as in the case of occupations of residential or industrial buildings (squatting) or traffic clocks as a means of protest (Gabriel and Holtmann, 2005; WIKUE, 2013). Bottom-up approaches are often based on this kind of community involvement and local protests which can sometimes be illegal or semi-legal. Reconciliation ecology focuses on preservation of biodiversity and the integration of social and environmental values (see Chapter 5). According to Francis and Lorimer (2011), it demonstrates that an anthropogenic

Urban Sustainability and River Restoration: Green and Blue Infrastructure, First Edition.
Katia Perini and Paola Sabbion.
© 2017 John Wiley & Sons Ltd. Published 2017 by John Wiley & Sons Ltd.

environment may be modified to encourage non-human use and biodiversity preservation without compromising societal utilisation. It is based on both bottom-up and top-down approaches. It focuses on a bottom-up strategy when it relies on localised and coordinated efforts of a large number of people and organisations with high levels of spatial, social and economic diversity (Francis and Lorimer, 2011). Francis and Lorimer, in fact, highlight that the success of many initiatives depends on the participation of urban citizens.

Reconciliation between different urban planning concepts may also employ top-down processes, as plans for new habitats and vegetation in public parks, recreational spaces and along urban infrastructures.

11.2   Bottom-up initiatives in the United States

In most cases, communities play an important role in restoring environmental conditions in urban areas (see Chapters 13.1 and 13.2). The issue is not only related to their functional contribution (e.g., maintaining or building a green area), but also to the engagement of the community, which is especially relevant for the improvement of environmental conditions in low-income areas, as demonstrated in the case of the Bronx River. The case of the Los Angeles River also reveals a successful bottom-up approach based on a first push from the community, which was later supported by institutional bodies at the City, State, and Federal level.

Local participation in the United States is based on an ingrained tradition, which according to Angotti (2013) is connected to a multicultural society, slavery and the history of exclusion of all black people and indigenous Indians. The past American political system is what Michael Parenti calls "democracy for the few" (Parenti, 2010). The "constitutional foundation explains why, in the United States, there is a tradition of local participation and expectation that everybody has the right to say something" (Angotti, 2013).

The Environmental Justice Movement (EJM) started its national campaigns in the US in the 1980s, among a confluence of events that brought about the terms *environmental racism* – the disproportionate effects of environmental pollution on racial minorities – and *environmental justice*, the social movement that emerged in response to this problem into the public space (Sze, 2008, 2007).

Environmental justice, with its central concern on the disproportionate impact of noxious facilities on communities of low income and of colour, has enriched sustainability with a progressive approach, stressing the importance of social justice in environmental and land use planning. As a result, many of the current community plans arise from the struggles of this movement (Angotti, 2008). The EJM was founded to address the inequity of environmental protection in local communities (U.S. EPA, 2016). It defines environmental justice as: "the fair treatment and meaningful involvement of all people regardless of race, color, national origin, or income, with respect to the development, implementation, and enforcement of environmental laws, regulations, and policies. "Fair treatment means that no group of people should bear a disproportionate share of the negative environmental consequences resulting from industrial, governmental and commercial operations or policies", according to this movement's principles.

In 1990, the EPA created the Environmental Equity Workgroup. Since 1994, the latter has become the Office of Environmental Justice (OEJ) and addresses allegations that "racial minority and low income populations bear a higher environmental risk burden than the general population". In the same year, David Dinkins, New York's first African-American Mayor took office with the support of a broad coalition of social, community and environmental movements. In 1991, the first People of Color Environmental Leadership Summit took place defining and spreading the "Principles of Environmental Justice" (Sze, 2008).

Following the election of Democrat Bill Clinton as President (1993 to 2001), neighbourhood groups became more involved in policy management regarding social and ecological issues (Angotti, 2008). On February 11 1994, Clinton signed Executive Order 12898, "Federal Actions to Address Environmental Justice in Minority Populations and Low-Income Populations". This attempt focused federal attention on the environmental and human health conditions of minority and low-income populations (U.S. EPA, 2016). This is not the first case in which policies at the national level were focused on community involvement. Another example is a Federal programme that funded architects and planners to favour community involvement, which was developed by the Democratic Presidents John F. Kennedy and Lydon Johnson from 1961 onwards (Angotti, 2013).

American architectural and planning theories have also claimed the need of a bottom-up approach. "A Pattern Language: Towns, Buildings, Construction" – one of the most important architecture masterpieces – emphasises the importance of the participation of owners and users in the building design, claiming that all town and city planning should be based on local forms of participation, based entirely on neighbours' participation for neighbourhoods (Saunders, 2002). Interesting examples of bottom-up initiatives that have increased green and blue infrastructure are the community gardens of New York City. These are properties that were in some cases purchased by not-for-profit organisations, which still own them, but are protected by the City and the State of New York through a Memorandum of Agreement (Crauderueff et al., 2012). More than 1,000 community gardens exist in the City (New York Department of City Planning 2011) and play an important role in terms of stormwater capture, even if they are not designed for this purpose, as in NYC more than 70% of the surface is impervious (Figure 11.1). Additionally, in more than 80 community gardens, rainwater harvesting systems are used for irrigation (Crauderueff et al., 2012) and food is grown in approximately 80%, mostly in neighbourhoods with limited open space and inadequate access to fresh and healthy produces (New York Department of City Planning, 2011).

It is worth mentioning the relation between planning policies and bottom-up initiatives in New York City. Some neighbourhoods, in particular, have been the scene of important struggles carried out by local community organisations, especially Sunset Park in Brooklyn, West Harlem in Manhattan, and the South Bronx. Planning policies had an enormous impact on these minority-majority and low-income communities (Sze, 2007). In 1916, New York City Zoning was approved, defining three different type of zoning districts related to use (residence, business, and "unrestricted" - in practice, mostly industrial), building height and area. In 1961, the City was divided by a zoning resolution into residential (R), commercial (C), and manufacturing (M) areas. According to Maantay (2000), "The re-zoning

Figure 11.1   Community Garden, Brooklyn, New York City.

Figure 11.2   Community Race at Barretto Point Park.

pattern corresponds to policy trends regarding privatization, gentrification, the importance of industry, and the roles of governmental and community-led planning". Although zoning regulations were not explicitly racial or discriminatory, they contributed to discrimination through the application of land-use policies (Sze, 2007). For example, in Sunset Park in Brooklyn, zoning changes accelerated trends of abandonment and housing decline (Winnick, 1990). Manufacturing increased in the Bronx, the borough with very high levels of minority and low income populations, while decreasing in Manhattan.

Sunset Park, West Harlem, and the South Bronx are all mixed-use districts with heavy manufacturing zones on the industrial waterfront, and these areas have the lowest levels of safety protections related to residential and commercial zones (Maantay, 2000). Since 1963, during the administration of Mayor Robert Wagner, community planning boards were authorised to advise the Borough President and City Planning Commission on local matters. This process started by Robert F. Wagner Jr., chairman of the City Planning Commission, who established 12 community planning boards in xxx that became a model for the City (Viteritti, 2009).

In the late 1980s, renowned local community organisations were formed to fight against poor environmental and social conditions in NYC neighbourhoods, often starting from a specific project or situation. This is the case of the West Harlem Environmental Action (WE ACT), founded in 1988 by community activists to monitor and campaign against the operations of the North River Sewage Treatment Plant, located near a densely populated housing development (Angotti, 2008; Sze, 2007). The wastewater disposal facility had been built to comply with the Federal Clean Water Act, but drew citizen protests and lawsuits. Partially in response to the community discontent, the City compelled the State of New York to build the Riverbank State Park on a platform above the treatment plant (Angotti, 2008). WE ACT, with the Natural Resources Defence Council (NRDC, a major national environmental group), won a $1.1 million settlement from the City of New York and the Department of Environmental Protection in State Court in response to numerous water quality and air pollution violations. Eventually, the City was required to deliver a $ 55 million programme to reduce odours, and funds were provided to WEACT and NRDC towards the establishment of the North River Fund to address community, environmental and public health issues (Sze, 2007).

In addition to its advocacy regarding the North River Plant, WE ACT also participated in planning decisions in West Harlem, steering the public policy agenda to include environmental justice as a major political issue (Shepard, 1994). WE ACT currently describes itself as one of the first environmental organisations in New York State to be run by people of colour, and the first environmental justice organisation in New York City. The Northern Manhattan community-based organisation's mission is to build healthy communities by ensuring that people of colour and/or of low-income participate meaningfully in the creation of sound and fair environmental health and protection policies and practices. It was founded as the result of local communities' struggles against environmental threats and the resulting health disparities, "institutionalised racism", and the lack of social and political capital. Peggy M. Shepard, WE ACT's Executive Director and Co-founder, described the group's work in Harlem (Bullard *et al.*, 2007) as an attempt to achieve a safe and sustainable environment for science, technology and research on environmental safety standards in West Harlem. The lack of scientific literacy, information, and data in this context – according to Shepard – has been a serious void contributing to the systemic exclusion of communities of colour from decision making. For this reason, WE ACT, as well as other local community organisations, conducts outreach programmes, and education and communication campaigns (WE ACT for Environmental Justice, 2004).

The community efforts based in Sunset Park on the Brooklyn waterfront are another interesting example. This area was chosen as the site for two of the eight sludge plants where the City administration planned to convert waste into fertiliser pellets. The United Puerto Rican Organization of Sunset Park (UPROSE) played a fundamental role in coordinating opposition from the neighbourhood's Latino, Asian-American, and Italian-American communities, arguing that the proposal was a classic example of environmental injustice. After developing an alternative masterplan for the Sunset Park waterfront that included a mix of industrial preservation, public space, and residential blocks, UPROSE became one of the neighbourhood's most vocal advocates for community planning (Angotti, 2008). Formerly known as United Puerto Rican Organization, UPROSE was founded in 1966 as the first Latino social service agency in Brooklyn and, in the 1990s, was reorganised to focus on environmental justice issues (Sze, 2007).

UPROSE's efforts include those aimed at reducing vehicular traffic, planting trees, teaching young people empowerment, testifying at public hearings, organising meetings and protests, delivering research, and developing strategies for community engagement, such as training youth to measure toxic carbon monoxide (CO) and particulate matter that contribute to respiratory distress (Bader, 2013). As an environmental justice organisation, UPROSE is dedicated to planning processes that are inclusive and allow local residents to have a voice in making decisions. Waterfront development, land use, brownfield regeneration, transportation improvement, air quality, creation of open spaces, alternative energy use, and environmental health are primary concerns of this organisation. UPROSE, in particular, has worked on the design of a community *Greenway-Blueway* for Sunset Park, a plan that coordinates the construction of an extended green space path (Greenway) within the community alongside a planned waterfront park. UPROSE is committed against climate change as well, since it believes young people of colour should be trained to become environmental "change makers" (Bader, 2013).

Many grassroots environmental justice campaigns targeting the development of community plans also started in the Bronx, a low-income area in northern New York City. "As a neighborhood, the South Bronx has struggled for nearly three decades under the negative connotations of its name as a flash point for violent crime, drugs, and unchecked urban decay" (Loria, 2009). This area also houses 15 waste transfer stations and four power plants. Sustainable South Bronx (SSBx) was funded by activists who merged environmental issues with cultural development and community planning priorities. It was launched in 2001, following the successful campaign against the proposal to locate a new waste facility in the South Bronx, which would have handled 40% of the City's garbage (Cohen, 2008). It has since become one of the strongest advocates for community planning in the South Bronx, along with the POINT Community Development Corporation, which since 1994 creates plans for the Bronx waterfront, public spaces, and housing (Angotti, 2008).

SSBx is actively involved in the restoration of the Bronx River (see Chapter 13.1). This organisation seeks environmental justice solutions addressing land use, energy, transportation, water and waste policies, and education to advance the environmental and economic rebirth of the South Bronx (Loria, 2009). The Bronx Environmental Stewardship Training (BEST) programme stands out as a so-called "green collar" job training, addressing environmental, health, poverty, and quality of life issues by equipping urban residents to work in green collar positions, such as those offered in the fields of ecological restoration, hazardous waste cleanup, green roof installation, and landscaping.

SSBx devises policies to increase the use of GI, such as incentives to plant trees and install green roofs (Loria, 2009). With its aim to "green" the community, Sustainable South Bronx is planting hundreds of trees along the South Bronx greenway and throughout the Hunts Point peninsula (Cohen, 2008) and has provided spaces for urban agriculture as part of its green roofs programme, thus producing fresh, healthy food, and providing educational opportunities for children and adults (Loria, 2009). According to Wyse, Community Greening Coordinator, Sustainable South Bronx works to enhance people's awareness and community consciousness, not only to maintain green areas but also to create a "green" network so that other projects can engage especially school students: "Sustainable South Bronx helps people realize that they can fight for themselves, that they can do something more" (Wyse, 2013).

In Los Angeles, (FoLAR) Friends of the Los Angeles River (a non-profit organisation founded in 1986) played a central role in rediscovery, protection and restoration of the natural, social and historic heritage of the Los Angeles River (see Chapter 13.2). Since the 1980s, FoLAR has made a great effort to counteract intense paving of the river, and has led, especially, to the river re-discovery. The waterway, in fact, had disappeared from collective imagination and from physical space. With technical knowledge and tenacity, this community organisation started natural habitat restoration, developing recreational public activities and educational programmes. While working on community engagement, FoLAR has developed strong political actions aimed at achieving a democratic management of the river, including the foundation of the L.A. River Conservancy "to coordinate public management of the River, to enact land-use ordinances and zoning laws and to manage development in the riparian corridor", as also to include the L.A. River bridges on the National Historic Registry and enhance their cultural value (see Chapters 9.2 and 13.2; FoLAR, 2016). Since its foundation, this organisation has counteracted the building of high walls along the last twelve miles of the River (proposed by the Los Angeles County Drainage Area), modifying original plans. It has driven the creation of the Los Angeles and San Gabriel Rivers Watershed Council. It has successfully created a community park at the Cornfield Yards, a land which had been slated for warehouse development and a State Park at Taylor Yard.

These efforts demonstrate how California and the Los Angeles area are the location of many important activist, environmental and no-profit organisations (i.e., the Sierra Club, Concerned Citizens of South Central L.A., Mothers of East Los Angeles, Latino Urban Forum) fighting for environmental and social justice. Some non-profit organisations, such as Tree People (TreePeople, 2016) and Heal the Bay (Heal the Bay, 2016), have especially focused on the renaturalisation of

Part C

Figure 11.3   Friend of Los Angeles River, During Fishing Activities (photo by William Preston Bowling).

Figure 11.4   LA River Photo Tour (photo by William Preston Bowling).

the river environment and ocean waters and coasts. Several of these organisations have managed to capture citizens' attention, providing information on environmental issues and carrying out decisive battles through the engagement of communities and government bodies.

11.3   Bottom-up initiatives in the European Union

A question arises. Would community involvement work as well in Europe if correctly supported? When asked about the community involvement in the United States and in Europe, Angotti, Professor of Urban Affairs and Planning at Hunter College and the Graduate Center of City University of New York, stated that there is a fundamental historical difference in the constitutional approaches that influence the relative political agendas. Europe's policies, especially in France and Italy, are structured by the Napoleonic tradition: "Individual actions and individual liberty is part of the institution of the United States; the States began with a structural weakness. The United States were not supposed to be powerful because everything had started from the federation of 13 colonies to protect individual freedom. This makes the United States very different from Italy and France, where local governments, especially historically, have depended on the national government" (Angotti, 2013).

According to Kenyon (2005), participatory environmental governance is growing within Europe (i.e., through citizens' juries), especially in the management of water resources. In fact, the EU Water Framework Directive (Article 14) requires multiple forms of citizens' involvement, from public information on planning phases, to community consultations and stakeholders' involvement. Nevertheless, "critical questions arise over the implementation and achievements of participatory water planning on the ground" (Benson *et al.*, 2014). Many scholars have considered the different outcomes of public participation in the European Water Framework Directive (WFD) implementation following its adoption in 2000. In countries such as Norway, Germany, Estonia and Finland the WFD has been applied within different basin districts. In some cases, this has resulted in conflict between different levels of governance.

In Sweden, for example, a country with a traditional strong governance at the local level, the implementation of the WFD has increased water management at a regional level (Andersson *et al.*, 2012). In fact, Sweden has been divided into five river basin districts (RBDs), each of which comprises several river basins, with a River Basin District Authority (RBDA) governed by a Water District Board appointed by the government. Therefore, the implementation of the WFD has led to the shift from the municipal level to regional level in order to consider the natural river basin in the planning process (Andersson *et al.*, 2012). This can result in possible tension between levels of governance due to a strictly top-down EU perspective that does not consider the traditional role of municipalities in Swedish water governance (Lundqvist, 2004). According to Carter (2007), water planning and land-use strategies are traditionally implemented at the municipal level, but they are now threatened by the WFD. As a result, in Sweden, the implementation of the WFD may result in a process of shifting from the municipal level to the supraregional level and conflicts can arise in a phase of managing land use and water planning at the local level (Andersson *et al.*, 2012).

In other EU Member States, the situation is similar. For example, in the United Kingdom, which is characterised by a traditional top-down agencies-oriented water management approach (Fritsch and Benson, 2013), public participation has increased as a result of WFD implementation, albeit with regional differences. Even if the UK has met the basic WFD participatory requirements (Benson *et al.*, 2014), participation is certainly not equally solid in all regions of the United Kingdom. In particular, Scotland and Wales seem to be more public engagement-oriented at local level than England and Wales (Woods, 2008). Public debates in Northern Ireland and local focus groups in Scotland have provided an excellent public education about water and the environment within WFD provisions. On the contrary, public consultations and engagement have not been so effective in England and Wales (Woods, 2008). According to Benson *et al.* (2014), residents' involvement was "technocratic and centrally determined, at times lacked representativeness, and resulted in only limited instrumental learning". Community-led catchment management in England and Wales has actually only limited connectivity to the WFD process (Cook *et al.*, 2012). Non-profit and voluntary organisation engagement is complicated and sometimes these organisations are distrusted in some 'official' bodies (Cook *et al.*, 2012; Benson *et al.*, 2014). As a result, EU governance oriented at sustainable development, as stated by the Water Framework Directive prescriptions, meets some difficulties due to multiple reasons. Above all, voluntary groups are usually focused at catchment, not at the region scale and there is little consistent data for England and Wales regarding constitution and distribution of the third sector (charities, community groups, and non-governmental bodies; Cook *et al.*, 2012).

In Italy, bottom-up actions do not actually have a strong tradition due to a traditional top-down oriented planning practice. The experience of Amici di Pontecarrega (Friends of Pontecarrega), in the city of Genoa, is one of the few successful examples in this field. This non-profit group is formed by citizens who claim "the right to express their opinions about the planning strategies of their territory" (amicidipontecarrega, 2016). In 2013, they founded an organisation in a heavily urbanised area on the banks of the river Bisagno, badly affected by the 1970 flood and then by the 2011 and 2014 river overflows. Amici di Pontecarrega (that take its name from the main ancient bridge on the River Bisagno) enquires about the development in this area and informs citizens. During the past flooding events, most residents had to leave their homes, but "a spirit of cooperation and solidarity arose". It was shared by a community that was, despite all, "alive and pulsating, proud and full of ideas" (amicidipontecarrega, 2016). The common objective of creating a more liveable neighbourhood in complex and heavily urbanised surroundings developed after the first flood clean-up works. This local community association works with the support of some national heritage and environmental bodies and universities (in particular FAI, WWF, Polytechnic University of Milan, Figure 11.5), fighting against real estate projects, as the construction of a new shopping centre in a river basin holding a high hydrological risk. The partnership with WWF has result in an ongoing environmental education programme. Among the latest projects, the *Rise Up* project involves several environmental and municipal associations, and engages young volunteers in

Figure 11.5   An Event on the Carrega Bridge on the River Bisagno (Genova, Italy) Seeking to Include the Bridge in the Italian Heritage Sites (photo by Fabrizio Spiniello).

environmental restoration projects. It seeks to create new public green spaces in the neighbourhood where they are now non-existent.

This overview shows that in the European context, the cooperation between different levels and institutions is characterised by a growing complexity. This, although, is implicit in a phase of supranational directive implementation. Every Member State needs to adapt and organise planning in its particular national context, and this leads to more or less successful outcomes (Andersson *et al.*, 2012). The several noteworthy North American bottom-up initiatives could probably be an example to inspire similar actions in the European context. This would strengthen communities and citizen participation, and could be planned with particular attention to each peculiar national context.

References

Amicidipontecarrega. (2016). Amici di Ponte Carrega. *Amici di Ponte Carrega*. [Online]. Available at: http://www.amicidipontecarrega.it [Accessed 30 May 2016].

Andersson, I., Petersson, M., and Jarsjö, J. (2012). Impact of the European Water Framework Directive on local-level water management: Case study Oxunda Catchment, Sweden. *Land Use Policy*, 29 (1), p. 73–82. [Online]. Available at: doi:10.1016/j.landusepol.2011.05.006.

Angotti, T. (2008). *New York for sale community planning confronts global real estate.* Cambridge, Mass.: MIT Press.

Angotti, T. (2013). *Personal communication in: Katia Perini, 2014. Urban areas and green infrastructure. Research report, published by Urban Design Lab Columbia University ISNB 978-09822174-5-0.* [Online]. Available at: http://urbandesignlab.columbia.edu/files/2015/04/3_Urban_Areas_Green_Infrastructure.pdf.

Bader, E. J. (2013). *UPROSE Uplifts Sunset Park.* [Online]. Available at: http://www.brooklynrail.org/2013/04/local/uprose-uplifts-sunset-park-1 [Accessed 1 April 2014].

Benson, D., Fritsch, O., Cook, H., and Schmid, M. (2014). Evaluating participation in WFD river basin management in England and Wales: Processes, communities, outputs and outcomes. *Land Use Policy,* 38, p. 213–222. [Online]. Available at: doi:10.1016/j.landusepol.2013.11.004.

Bullard, R. D., Mohai, P., Saha, R., and Wright, B. (2007). *Toxic Wastes and Race at Twenty 1987–2007.* United Church of Christ.

Carter, J. G. (2007). Spatial planning, water and the Water Framework Directive: insights from theory and practice. *Geographical Journal,* 173 (4), p. 330–342. [Online]. Available at: doi:10.1111/j.1475-4959.2007.00257.x.

Cohen, S. (2008). Sustainable South Bronx: Helping the Bronx Become a Sustainable Community. *New York Observer.* [Online]. Available at: http://observer.com/2008/06/sustainable-south-bronx-helping-the-bronx-become-a-sustainable-community/ [Accessed 2 April 2014].

Cook, H., Benson, D., Inman, A., Jordan, A., and Smith, L. (2012). Catchment management groups in England and Wales: extent, roles and influences. *Water and Environment Journal,* 26 (1), p. 47–55. [Online]. Available at: doi:10.1111/j.1747-6593.2011.00262.x.

Crauderueff, R., Margolis, S., and Tanikawa, S. (2012). *Greening Vacant Lots: Planning and Implementation Strategies. A report prepared fot The Nature Conservancy as part of the NatLab collaboration.* [Online]. Available at: http://docs.nrdc.org/water/files/wat_13022701a.pdf.

FoLAR. (2016). FoLAR. *Friends of the Los Angeles River.* [Online]. Available at: http://folar.org/ [Accessed 9 April 2016].

Francis, R. A. and Lorimer, J. (2011). Urban reconciliation ecology: The potential of living roofs and walls. *Journal of Environmental Management,* 92 (6), p. 1429–1437. [Online]. Available at: doi:10.1016/j.jenvman.2011.01.012 [Accessed 30 January 2014].

Fritsch, O. and Benson, D. (2013). Integrating the Principles of Integrated Water Resources Management? River Basin Planning in England and Wales. *International Journal of Water Governance,* 1 (3), p. 265–284. [Online]. Available at: doi:10.7564/13-IJWG7.

Gabriel, O. W. and Holtmann, E. (2005). *Handbuch Politisches System der Bundesrepublik Deutschland.* Oldenbourg Verlag.

Heal the Bay. (2016). Heal the Bay. *healthebay.org.* [Online]. Available at: http://www.healthebay.org/ [Accessed 2 May 2016].

Kenyon, W. (2005). A Critical Review of Citizens' Juries: How Useful are they in Facilitating Public Participation in the EU Water Framework Directive? *Journal of Environmental Planning and Management,* 48 (3), p. 431–443. [Online]. Available at: doi:10.1080/09640560500067558.

Krogstrup, H. K. (2004). User Participation in Evaluation-Top-down and Bottom-up Perspectives. *Nordic Journal of Studies in Educational Policy,* 2003 (1). [Online]. Available at: http://nordstep.net/index.php/nstep/article/download/26788/37176 [Accessed 30 May 2016].

Loria, K. (2009). *Sustainable South Bronx.* [Online]. Available at: http://cooperator.com/articles/1916/1/Sustainable-South-Bronx/Page1.html [Accessed 2 April 2014].

Lundqvist, L. (2004). Integrating Swedish water resource management: a multi-level governance trilemma. *Local Environment,* 9 (5), p. 413–424. [Online]. Available at: doi:10.1080/1354983042000255324.

Maantay, J. (2000). *Industrial Zoning Changes and Environmental Justice in New York City: An Historical, Geographical and Cultural Analysis*. Doctoral dissertation, Rutgers University, New Brunswick.

Nemet, G. F. (2010). Robust incentives and the design of a climate change governance regime. *Energy Policy*, 38 (11), p. 7216–7225. [Online]. Available at: doi:10.1016/j.enpol.2010.07.052 [Accessed: 23 January 2014].

New York Department of City Planning. (2011). *PlaNYC. Update*. [Online]. Available at: http://nytelecom.vo.llnwd.net/o15/agencies/planyc2030/pdf/planyc_2011_planyc_full_report.pdf.

Parenti, M. (2010). *Democracy for the Few*. Boston: Cengage Learning.

Saunders, W. S. (2002). Book Reviews. A Pattern Language, by Christopher Alexander, Sara Ishikawa, and Murray Silverstein, with Max Jacobson, Ingrid Fiksdahl-King, and Shlomo Angel New York: Oxford University Press, 197. *Harvard Design Magazine*, Hard/Soft, Cool/Warm (16). [Online]. Available at: http://www.townofchapelhill.org/Modules/ShowDocument.aspx?documentid=7783.

Shepard, P. (1994). Issues of Community Empowerment. *Fordham Urban Law Journal*, 21 (3), p. 739.

Sze, J. (2007). *Noxious New York: the racial politics of urban health and environmental justice*. Cambridge, Mass.: MIT Press.

Sze, J. (2008). The question of Environmental Justice. In: Plunz, R. and Sutto, M. P. (eds.), *Urban climate change crossroads*, New York: Urban Design Lab of the Earth Institute, Columbia University.

TreePeople. (2016). TreePeople. *TreePeople*. [Online]. Available at: https://www.treepeople.org/ [Accessed 12 May 2016].

U.S. EPA. (2016). *Environmental Justice*. Collections and Lists. [Online]. Available at: https://www.epa.gov/environmentaljustice [Accessed 30 May 2016].

Viteritti, J.P. (2009). *When Mayors Take Charge: School Governance in the City*. Brookings Institution Press.

WE ACT for Environmental Justice. (2004). *Harlem on the River-Making a Community Vision Real*. [Online]. Available at: http://www.weact.org/Portals/7/Harlem%20on%20the%20River-Making%20a%20Community%20Vision%20Real.pdf.

WIKUE. (2013). *Emscher 3.0 : from grey to blue - or, how the blue sky over the Ruhr region fell into the Emscher - by Wuppertal Institut für Klima, Umwelt, Energie GmbH*. Scheck H and Venjakob (eds.). [Online]. Available at: https://epub.wupperinst.org/frontdoor/index/index/docId/5070 [Accessed 9 April 2016].

Winnick, L. (1990). *New People in Old Neighborhoods : The Role of New Immigrants in Rejuvenating New York's Communities*. New York : Russell Sage Foundation.

Woods, D. (2008). Stakeholder involvement and public participation: a critique of Water Framework Directive arrangements in the United Kingdom. *Water and Environment Journal*, 22 (4), p. 258–264. [Online]. Available at: doi:10.1111/j.1747-6593.2008.00136.x.

Wyse, C. (2013). *Personal communication in: Katia Perini, 2014. Urban areas and green infrastructure. Research report, published by Urban Design Lab Columbia University ISNB 978-09822174-5-0*. [Online]. Available at: http://urbandesignlab.columbia.edu/files/2015/04/3_Urban_Areas_Green_Infrastructure.pdf.

Chapter 12
Selection of Management Practices and Guidelines
Paola Sabbion

12.1 Sustainable urban development

In recent years, sustainable development in urban neighbourhoods has gained increasing attention. In a review of the guiding principles for sustainable urban neighbourhood development, Luederitz *et al.* (2013) note fundamental social, ecological, cultural, and economic aspects related to this process. In the United States and in Europe, several initiatives have been undertaken to promote sustainable neighbourhoods, and a variety of tools have been developed to assess the sustainability and the performance of planning practices (Sharifi and Murayama, 2012).

These attempts have recognised the importance of neighbourhoods for the sustainability of whole cities (Choguill, 2008). Sharifi and Muruyama (2012) identify two main categories of Neighborhood Sustainability Assessment (NSA) tools. The first comprises third-party building assessment tools, which can be useful also to evaluate sustainability beyond the single building level, as the LEED for Neighborhood Development (LEED-ND), the first American rating system for planning and developing new green neighbourhoods. LEED-ND demonstrates that compact and mixed-use neighbourhoods with pedestrian and sustainable connections among communities should be encouraged to promote Neighbourhood Development. Moreover, according to LEED-ND plans, "green neighborhood developments will play an integral role in reducing greenhouse gas emissions and improving quality of life" (USGBC, 2009).

The second category encompasses tools that are embedded into neighbourhood-scale plans and sustainability initiatives to assess their performance, including the *Ecocity* and *HQE²R* initiatives in Europe and the *EcoDistricts Toolkit* in the United States.

Urban Sustainability and River Restoration: Green and Blue Infrastructure, First Edition.
Katia Perini and Paola Sabbion.
© 2017 John Wiley & Sons Ltd. Published 2017 by John Wiley & Sons Ltd.

HQE²R and Ecocity are both European-funded projects aimed at identifying strategies for sustainable urban development. An Ecocity includes compact, pedestrian-oriented, mixed-use neighbourhoods integrated into an efficient public transport system. Ecocities are also provided with attractive public and green spaces, and cultural heritage sites contributing to the "health, safety and well-being of the inhabitants", curbing biodiversity and habitat loss (Ecocity, 2005; Schubert, 2005).

According to the HQE²R Project sustainable neighbourhoods and buildings preserve and enhance natural and cultural heritage and resources related to energy, water and landscape. This model of neighbourhood project, moreover, improves the quality of the local environment with regard to comfort, health, safety, air quality, pollution, and waste (Sustainable Urban Development European Network, 2004).

In the United States, a similar approach has been adopted with EcoDistricts, an integrated set of programmes originated in Portland (Oregon) that focuses on urban regeneration to obtain higher performances in terms of air quality, green energy, access and mobility, water control, community vitality, habitat and ecosystem functions (EcoDistricts, 2016).

Moreover, a worldwide programme, called *C40 Cities Climate Leadership Group*, established 10 years ago, is implemented in more than 80 of the world's megacities. C40 is focused on tackling climate change and driving urban action to reduce greenhouse gas emissions and climate risks. Policies and programmes in 40 world megacities are, hence, coordinated and implemented thanks to C40 Cities (C40 Cities, 2016). Both Ecocity and C40 Cities are initiatives working on climate change adaptation to tackle global challenges through actions triggered within the single cities.

In this framework, green and blue infrastructure (GBI) can join management practices to increase the quality of the urban environment and prevent the risk of flooding. GBI can, in fact, reduce stormwater runoff at the catchment and neighbourhood scales (as described in Chapters 6,7, and 8). GBI is among the main strategies implemented for urban sustainability, as highlighted through several Neighborhood Sustainability Assessment tools.

In this context, special attention is given to the so-called Water Sensitive Design, a series of strategies developing innovative solutions for the management of rainwater and surface runoff water in urban areas. Water Sensitive Design strategies include the use of GBI and natural elements to improve the relationship between the water system and urbanised areas. The following are the most widespread guidelines for GBI implementation: Best Management Practices (BMPs, especially in US), Low Impact Development (LID, especially in the US and Canada), Sustainable Drainage System (SuDS, especially in Europe), and Water Sensitive Urban Design (WSUD, especially in Australia and England).

12.2   Best Management Practices (BMPs)

Best Management Practices (BMPs) include a series of stormwater approaches, which are widespread especially in the United States. BMPs are based on the application of a number of techniques, or control tools targeting interventions on the quantity and quality of stormwater runoff. BMPs also aim to improve the water quality in the final receptor, facilitate water collection and reuse, ensuring the hydraulic invariance of surface runoff and increasing infiltration into the soil (IOWA Department of Natural Resources, 2009).

In the United States, each State has its own specific manual containing information and observations pertaining to the environment, particularly climate, soil type and characteristics of the urban development. It is possible to distinguish two categories of BMPs: Nonstructural BMPs and Structural BMPs. Nonstructural BMPs include normative, regulatory, and educational guidelines for land-use planning to limit the conversion of rain in runoff, with subsequent impacts on the territory. These solutions are identified with Stormwater Better Site Design Practices, precisely because they are applied at a planning phase, in particular for new developments. Structural BMPs, instead, are focused on strategies and techniques for stormwater treatment at the beginning of the drainage system to intercept the rainfall on the ground. The main purposes of BMPs include: surface flow speed control; reduction of runoff volume from urbanised areas; and reduction of pollutant and contaminant sources. Water quality control is of particular importance, and it is a common element in all the Northamerican BMP manuals. Manuals recommend a joint use of the various components composing a treatment train (see Chapter 7). An important distinction of the structural components of rainwater management depends on their applicability according to site and function. General Application Structural Stormwater Controls are structural measures that can be used in a wide variety of situations, without strictly depending from the context. The latter are able to satisfy all the qualitative and quantitative management objectives and include: ponds, wetlands, bioretention areas, sand filters, infiltration trenches, and swales (see Chapers 6 and 7). Differently, Limited Application Structural Stormwater Controls are structural measures recommended only for specific sites or with special design conditions (i.e. commercial, industrial or institutional areas). They mainly operate on rainwater quality and include, among others: filter strips, grass channels, and porous paver systems (Atlanta Regional Commission, 2014).

Three main actions drive the design of structural components in terms of both quality and quantity associated to the flow of rainwater due to urban development. First of all, maximising the use of best practices for site planning and nonstructural methods can reduce the generation of surface runoff and pollution derived from the runoff. Secondly, managing and treating runoff is achieved through the use of structural controls. Finally, applying pollution prevention practices to rainwater can limit potential contaminants. Minimum standards are set to help local governments to comply with regulatory requirements imposed by national and federal programmes that deal with water issues. These include the National Pollutant Discharge Elimination System (NPDES) and the National Flood Insurance Program (NFIP) established by the Federal Emergency Management Agency (FEMA). BMPs also provide Unified Sizing Criteria for the design of structural control systems in order to achieve an integrated approach to rainwater management, specifically focusing on four quality and quantity performances. These relate to pollutant removal from stormwater runoff and water quality improvement; prevention of downstream erosion on the river banks and riverbeds; reducing downstream flooding; and decreasing runoff resulting from exceptional rain or ensuring its safe flow (Atlanta Regional Commission, 2014).

12.3 Water Sensitive Urban Design (WSUD) strategies

Water Sensitive Urban Design is an approach developed in the 1990s in Australia (Department of the Environment, 2009) and then implemented in England to protect water resources. It aims to integrate the urban hydrological cycle management with the planning process. As the other guidelines analysed in this Chapter, its main goal is to minimise the negative impact on both the water cycle, water bodies, and the sea, simulating the natural drainage system. It offers an alternative to the traditional rainwater management approach by acting at the level of the surface runoff source, then intervening in the instant in which the rain meets the ground, thereby enabling to reduce the size of structural stormwater conveyance systems (Department of the Environment, 2009).

Each initiative under this programme is guided by the key principles of sustainability, such as limiting water consumption, recycling, minimising waste and enhancing environmental protection. In addition, the joint planning and stormwater management has additional benefits regarding urban value increase, as it reduces pollutant transportation caused by runoff, it delays runoff and reduces the need of irrigation water. The WSUD planning and design approach is focused on the following potential opportunities. First of all, the use of water-efficient appliances and rainwater, stormwater, wastewater, groundwater and greywater reuse. Along with water-efficient landscaping these alternative sources can reduce the consumption of potable water. WSUD Stormwater management strategies, in addition, provide for water detention, storage and infiltration (Figure 12.1). Vegetation is especially useful to filter stormwater. The preservation of water-related environmental, recreational and cultural values is a further objective, achieved by minimising the ecological footprint of water-related projects. Long-term planning and localised strategies, ongoing monitoring, evaluation and review should be pursued

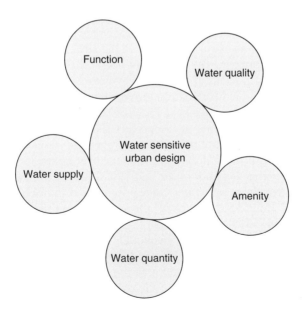

Figure 12.1 WSUD Objectives (based on Department of the Environment, 2009).

as well as flexible institutional arrangements. In Australia, as in the US for BMPs, each region has developed its own system of WSUD, which is managed by different government agencies. Designers can thus refer to local authorities. Each region, moreover, provides its own manual containing the necessary documentation for the design and development of WSUD. Regional manuals, although, provide a certain uniformity of content thanks to the national reference guide *Evaluating Options for Water Sensitive Urban Design* (Department of the Environment, 2009). Its key principles regard the reduction of potable water demand (for non-drinking purposes), maximum reduction of wastewater generation, water quality improvement for reuse and/or discharge, and the restoration of catchments' natural hydrological regime. Other principles focus on the improvement of quality, health and aesthetics of waterways and their connections. An interesting aspect of the Australian approach is the need to address stormwater management from different points of view. Citizens' projects are integrated in its general framework. Furthermore, different types of manuals have been created for every category of users. *Urban Stormwater* provides WSUD guidance for less technical approaches, focusing on motivations and objectives. *WSUD Stormwater Engineering Procedures* contains specific instructions on the size of each control component (therefore, it caters mainly for designers and constructors). This model of design approach and the dissemination of stormwater management practices is aimed at integrating different levels of planning, from the smallest neighbourhood scale to the regional one. Great importance is also given to the maintenance of the new systems, dedicating specialised manuals for maintenance and technical inspection specifications for each component (Greater Sydney Local Land Services, 2014).

The objectives of WSUD strategies depend on the priorities of urban environment issues set by the impact of rainwater on the ground. The choice of the goals is also guided by the key principles of the *sensitive* method of stormwater management, which allow focusing in general on the qualitative or quantitative control. The Best Practices Planning (BPP) is a preliminary phase that provides the basis for subsequent rainwater management measures. It includes the analysis of the physical and natural features of the sites to assess the feasibility of locating WSUD components. BPP can be applied at the strategic level, thus including land-management policies, for example by acting on the guidelines of urban plans. It can also be implemented at the project level, thus constituting a particular design approach. Best Management Practices (BMPs) refer to the phase of selection of the structural elements of the project that perform the functions of prevention, collection, treatment, transport, storage and re-use within a WSUD system. In addition to the runoff water management strategies, techniques to reduce the potable water demand within individual private houses are also provided. The latter range from rainwater collection tanks to household items that limit waste, such as flow accelerators in the taps or dual-flush toilets (Mazzarello and Raimondo, 2015).

Differently to the American model, in the Australian approach, the structural control features are not grouped according to their application (in general or limited to their ability to adapt to the context), but by the degree of guaranteed purification, e.g. by the size of the pollutants that are retained. Primary treatment provides a physical selection or rapid sedimentation that allows removing floating materials, coarse sediments, oils and fats contained in water. These include gross pollutant traps, grassed swales and sediment basins. Secondary treatment includes sedimentation techniques for finer particles and filtration techniques to dissolve organic pollutants (e.g., permeable pavements, vegetated filter strips, vegetated swales, infiltration systems, and bioretention systems). Finally, the tertiary treatment provides the most advanced biological absorption thanks to sedimentation and filtration techniques for retaining nutrients, heavy metals and bacteria, i.e. wetlands and ponds (Department of the Environment, 2009).

Following the choice of BMPs and their possible location on the site, three WSUD steps define a Stormwater Management Plan. The Option Evaluation involves designers to verify the achievement of project objectives. The Option Assessment defines whether a WSUD system is appropriate. Public authorities, such as Local Government, assess the feasibility of available WSUD options with respect to the impact on the ground. The assessment process addresses a range of site-specific objectives, including general outcomes. In particular, it deals with the integration of the whole water cycle; management and minimisation of hydrologic impacts; protection and enhancement of the ecological functions; reduction of potable water use; maintenance and/or enhancement of visual and social amenity values; and minimisation of life asset costs. Once the plan for stormwater management is developed, it is necessary to select the various control instruments or treatments that have to be provided. To this end, similarly to the US experience, the Australian manuals provide detailed design directions and instructions, calculation modules and technical drawings (Department of the Environment, 2009).

12.4   Low Impact Development (LID)

Since the 1990s, in the United States, Low Impact Development (LID) was implemented along with Best Management Practices, as an alternative to traditional stormwater management systems. "It is based on the conveyance of runoff into the receiving water" (Department of Environmental Resource *et al.*, 1999). LID is also used in Canada (Toronto and Region Conservation Authority *et al.*, 2010). The LID approach includes a number of techniques capable of acting on the control of pollutants, volume reduction, runoff speed, and flood control. This "stormwater management strategy seeks to mitigate the impacts of increased runoff and stormwater pollution by managing runoff as close to its source as possible". LID includes a set of site design strategies to "minimise runoff and distribute small-scale structural practices that mimic natural or predevelopment hydrology through the processes of infiltration, evapotranspiration, harvesting, filtration and detention of stormwater. These practices can effectively remove nutrients, pathogens and metals from runoff, and they reduce the volume and intensity of stormwater flows" (United States Environmental Protection Agency, 2007).

The issue of stormwater management in the US arose due to the high levels of pollution. The Clean Water Act of 1972, then updated in 2001, established the quality requirements. The latter feature in the *National Pollution Discharge Elimination System* (NPDES), which claims that water runoff should be treated before it can be discharged into water bodies (Country of San Diego - Department of Public Works, 2014). Each State requires all property owners to outline a

Stormwater Management Plan (SWMP) to meet these requirements. BMPs have been indicated as measures to contain the pollutants resulting from runoff waters. Moreover, this scheme highlights the need to tackle the issues related to the increase of impervious surfaces due to urban development. Noting the consequences of surface runoff on such transformation processes, BMPs have been added to create low-impact design practices, precisely in order to drive the development process focusing on runoff control as a fundamental design criteria (Country of San Diego - Department of Public Works, 2014).

Manual LID practices integrated with BMPs introduce a new stormwater management approach. A set of strategies and techniques integrate the control of rainwater in the planning and design processes, reducing the overall flow, managing rainwater as a resource and focusing on source control. The Low Impact Development approach, therefore, mimics the natural cycle, controlling runoff at the source, using micro-scale checks distributed throughout the catchment. In fact, LID structures rainwater management not only as a mere disposal process. Instead of piping the runoff resulting from small and frequent weather events directly in the underground sewer system or drainage systems away from the site, the components dissipate LID and infiltrate rainwater using the characteristics of the soil and permeable surfaces, thus reducing runoff volumes and filtering the water before it moves away from the place where it was produced. Since LID practices are environmentally friendly structural controls, they can be considered part of the BMPs. Initially, BMPs were devised to control pollutants contained in the water resulting from runoff, while the LID approach was developed to guide the inevitable territorial transformations on permeable surfaces in order to contain runoff volume surface. However, in the current integrated approach of qualitative and quantitative stormwater control, the two methods tend to coincide (Mazzarello and Raimondo, 2015).

Traditionally, stormwater management systems were designed according to specific site conditions. This determined the risk that such practices were not equal in different scenarios. For example, the relative sizing for events with a 100-year return period, implies an over-drained system for all frequent weather phenomena, degradation of natural streams and downstream water quality problems linked to the transport of pollutants through urban areas and watershed receptors. The standards for the control of superficial outflows were formulated for public safety and for property damage reduction, but have nothing to do with the protection of the ecosystem. Experience has shown the importance of a stormwater management system specifically designed over regular time occurrences on a weekly or monthly schedule, and not on exceptional events to preserve the integrity of rivers. Using the controls of decentralised sources, the LID method is based on frequent weather events and is therefore more effective. LID, moreover, automatically control events with a return period of 10 or 100 years, thanks to the restoration of the natural inflows/outflows relationships. More control techniques are used, and the more the system will be similar to the natural water cycle. In flood prone areas, however, it is recommended to use a hybrid system for higher security. In fact, the LID system does not require to be separated from conventional technologies (Mazzarello and Raimondo, 2015).

The LID approach developed initially in Maryland where its first manual was created (Department of Environmental Resource *et al.*, 1999) and then became the benchmark for all others. Its basic principles include the use of site hydrology as a reference framework for the integration of the project, aiming to preserve the existing natural hydrological functions. This approach hence deploys micro-management techniques around the site, providing smooth control of meteoric water and helping to preserve the existing natural water system. This guarantees additional benefits such as the great ability to adapt the system to the conditions of the site, the maintenance of the natural functions of recharge aquifers, the reduction of long-term maintenance costs thanks to the use of low-cost components and optimal design, as well as citizens' involvement in the management tasks (Figure 12.2). Other principles include source control, mitigation of the impacts of hydrological land-use activities, and the use of non-structural methods to preserve the natural water cycle. The LID approach offers an alternative stormwater management that evenly and strategically integrates control elements within multi-functional characteristics of the landscape, where runoff can be micro-managed and controlled at the source. With the LID method every urban environment or infrastructure component can be designed to perform several functions (Low Impact Development Center, Inc., 2007).

LID can be distinguished from other strategies as it is based on the built environment as an integral part of the ecosystem. In addition, the LID system does not

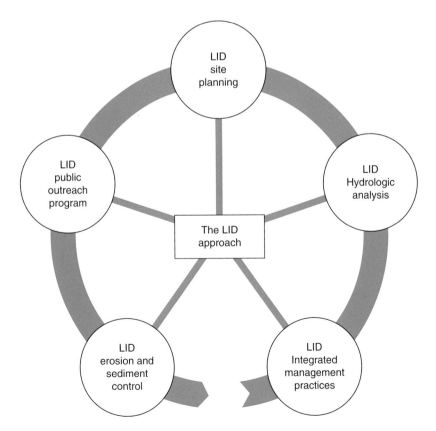

Figure 12.2   Main Components of Low Impact Development Approach (based on Department of Environmental Resource *et al.*, 1999).

rely on technical conservation or growth control, but uses the most advanced technology to support its development. It provides the tools that planners need to implement the transformation of the territory, preserving the existing hydrological and ecological functions. In a certain sense, other sustainable design methods can rely on LID tools to implement their conservation and restoration objectives. The LID approach should not replace local planning practices that govern land use, but can be a completion or enrichment to better manage rainwater in new developments (Mazzarello and Raimondo, 2015).

American and Australian approaches have very similar objectives. Both distinguish between structural and non-structural components, that is, Best Planning Practices (BPP) and Best Management Practices (BMPs). Ferrier and Jenkins (2009) show how an integrated land-use and appropriate hydrological cycle can solve most of the problems related to water management policies. They claim BMPs were developed in the United States to address the issues arising from more or less frequent and small-scale events, considering all ecological benefits or enjoyment as an added value. The LID approach, on the other hand, was created to manage the outflows arising from events of any size and quality characteristic that can be encountered in an urban context (Ferrier and Jenkins, 2009).

12.5   Sustainable Drainage System (SuDS)

Among all water management methods, the SuDS approach has been the most disseminated in Europe, starting from England. The Water Management Act of 2010 confirmed UK's concern in the field of sustainable water control. It determined that SuDS would become the main management practice in this country, fully replacing conventional systems. The *National Standards for Sustainable Drainage (DEFRA-Department for Environment, Food and Rural Affairs, 2011)* support this profound change, and helps involved companies, designers and authorities to respect the legislative requirements. In particular, Robert Bray Associates have developed a pioneering approach that has been crucial for the creation of SuDS (Robert Bray Associates, 2016). The founder Robert Bray, in fact, has been operating in the field of sustainable drainage in England since 1996. He has made an essential contribution to the definition of design layouts of different SuDS components, which are now also promoted by the non-profit Construction Industry Research and Information Association (CIRIA; Ballard *et al.*, 2007).

Sustainable Drainage System (SuDS) guidelines (Dickie *et al.*, 2010; Ballard *et al.*, 2007) have been developed to curb the negative impact of urbanisation on the natural water cycle and the inability of traditional methods to cope with increasing impervious surfaces due to continuous land transformation processes. Sustainability is central to this approach, as suggested by its name. In particular, the advocates of this approach argue that sustainable development is only possible if human activities are delivered in relation to the environment where they are performed. The drainage management of urban areas are part of the human activities that should respect natural processes. The concept of sustainable drainage, in addition, is not limited to comprise a series of rainwater management strategies to prevent them from causing damage to the environment. The traditional methods of runoff control, in fact, only focus on the physical aspect of the problem. A sustainable approach, on the contrary, elects water as a tool to achieve other benefits that embrace even seemingly distant fields, which may include technical, environmental, social and economic aspects. For this reason, stormwater management involves different actors, becoming an interdisciplinary element considering all parts of the hydrological cycle (Mazzarello and Raimondo, 2015; Dickie *et al.*, 2010; Ballard *et al.*, 2007).

In particular, the SuDS method considers three aspects: water quality, water quantity, and amenity/biodiversity (the so-called "SuDS triangle"). The components for the SuDS system must be chosen and fitted following a series of evaluations and analyses, which should start with the site planning stages. The performance and proper functioning of SuDS depend on a number of specific considerations that need to be added to conventional building practices to avoid errors. The use of inappropriate plants, lack of attention in protecting the system from debris or by external agents and the lack of care in the integration with the surrounding landscape can determine a lower performance (Ballard *et al.*, 2007).

SuDS strategies intend to simulate the natural drainage occurring in pristine water or in pre-development conditions. This is achieved through the following actions: storing runoff and releasing it slowly (attenuation); allowing water to seep into the ground (infiltration); filtering pollutants; allowing the sediments to settle by controlling the flow of water; and creating attractive environments for communities. The main objective is to control the environmental risk resulting from runoff in urbanised areas, while contributing – where possible – to an improvement of the same ecosystem conditions. Alongside the "SuDS traingle", its several other benefits are pursued (Figure 12.3). SuDS systems can be designed to manage stormwater considering climate change effects, as also to control water quality, and reduce flood risks. In this way, traditional sewer systems and waterways can be relieved from rainfall burden and flooding can be limited. SuDs, moreover, can guarantee the complete recharge of underground water sources. Quality of life, attractiveness and biodiversity can be increased by SuDS vegetated systems and the integration of SuDS can provide educational amenities and economic benefits (see Chapter 4).

Treatment trains are among the most important SuDs strategies. These are a set of drainage techniques arranged in series to increment the reduction of pollutants and the speed of runoff volumes (see Chapter 7). They are fundamental to simulate the natural water cycle. The hierarchy of processing techniques that should be employed in a treatment train includes several steps. The first is prevention in terms of house site design to reduce runoff and pollution, and collection/stormwater reuse techniques. The second step regards source control, managing runoff components (with porous paving, green roofs, etc.). The third step involves local control (infiltration or detention), and includes the use of several local sources as swales, detention basis, etc. The fourth and last step refers to regional control, typically considering flow from its source including ponds and wetlands (see Chapters 6 and 7; Dickie *et al.*, 2010).

In general, the SuDS approach prioritises prevention and source control techniques (Mazzarello and Raimondo, 2015), however, when the upstream control opportunities are limited, other strategies that are less preferable such as water conveyance, are required. This occurs only if it is impossible perform an on-site treatment. Moreover, the purpose of a series of control techniques is effective both

Part C

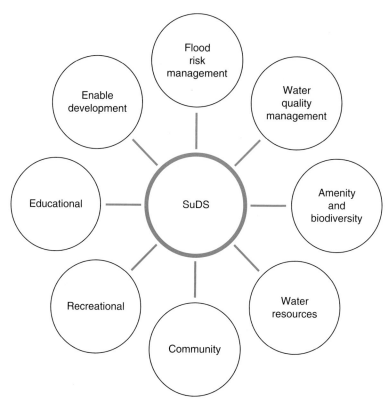

Figure 12.3   SuDS Benefits (based on Dickie *et al.*, 2010).

on rainwater runoff and on the concentration of pollutants resulting from leaching. The connections between the individual parts of a treatment train must be guaranteed by the use of natural conveying components, such as the depressions in the ground or filter trenches.

References

Atlanta Regional Commission. (2014). *Georgia Stormwater Management Manual*. [Online]. Available at: http://www.atlantaregional.com/environment/georgia-stormwater-manual [Accessed 6 June 2016].

Ballard, B. W., Kellagher, R., Martin, P., Jefferies, C., Bray, R., and Shaffer, P. (2007). *Site Handbook for the Construction of SUDS*. CIRIA. [Online]. Available at: http://www.orkneywind.co.uk/advice/SEPA%20Pollution%20Advice/ciria%20c698.pdf [Accessed 7 June 2016].

C40 Cities. (2016). *C40 Cities*. [Online]. Available at: http://www.c40.org/ [Accessed 7 June 2016].

Choguill, C. L. (2008). Developing sustainable neighbourhoods. *Habitat International*, 32 (1), p. 41–48. [Online]. Available at: doi:10.1016/j.habitatint.2007.06.007 [Accessed 6 February 2014].

Country of San Diego - Department of Public Works. (2014). *Low Impact Development Handbook Stormwater Management Strategies*. [Online]. Available at: http://www.sandiegocounty.gov/content/dam/sdc/dplu/docs/LID_Handbook_2014.pdf [Accessed 7 June 2016].

DEFRA-Department for Environment, Food and Rural Affairs. (2011). *National Standards for sustainable drainage systems Designing, constructing, operating and maintaining drainage for surface runoff.* [Online]. Available at: https://www.gov.uk/government/uploads/system/uploads/attachment_data/file/82421/suds-consult-annexa-national-standards-111221.pdf [Accessed 7 June 2016].

Department of Environmental Resource, Department of Resources and Programs and Planning Division. (1999). *Prince George's County, Maryland, Low Impact Development Design Strategies. An integrate design approach.* [Online]. Available at: http://www.lowimpactdevelopment.org/pubs/LID_National_Manual.pdf [Accessed 7 June 2016].

Department of the Environment. (2009). *Evaluating options for water sensitive urban design – a national guide.* Text. [Online]. Available at: https://www.environment.gov.au/resource/evaluating-options-water-sensitive-urban-design-%E2%80%93-national-guide [Accessed 6 June 2016].

Dickie, S., McKay, G., Ions, L., and Shaffer, P. (2010). *Planning for SuDS - making it happen.* CIRIA. [Online]. Available at: http://www.eastcambs.gov.uk/sites/default/files/C687%20Planning%20for%20suds.pdf.pdf [Accessed 7 June 2016].

Ecocity. (2005). *Urban Development Towards Appropriate Structures for Sustainable Transport.* [Online]. Available at: http://www.rma.at/sites/new.rma.at/files/ECOCITY%20%20_%20Final%20Report.pdf.

EcoDistricts. (2016). *EcoDistricts.* [Online]. Available at: https://ecodistricts.org [Accessed 24 June 2016].

Ferrier, R. C. and Jenkins, A. (2009). *Handbook of Catchment Management.* John Wiley & Sons.

Greater Sydney Local Land Services. (2014). *Water Sensitive Urban Design.* [Online]. Available at: http://www.wsud.org/.

IOWA Department of Natural Resources. (2009). *Iowa Stormwater Management Manual.* IOWA DNR. [Online]. Available at: http://www.iowadnr.gov/Environmental-Protection/Water-Quality/NPDES-Storm-Water/Storm-Water-Manual [Accessed 6 June 2016].

Low Impact Development Center, Inc. (2007). *LID Urban Design Tools - Background.* [Online]. Available at: http://www.lid-stormwater.net/background.htm [Accessed 7 June 2016].

Luederitz, C., Lang, D. J., and Von Wehrden, H. (2013). A systematic review of guiding principles for sustainable urban neighborhood development. *Landscape and Urban Planning*, 118, p. 40–52. [Online]. Available at: doi:10.1016/j.landurbplan.2013.06.002 [Accessed 23 January 2014].

Mazzarello, M. and Raimondo, M. (2015). *Infrastrutture verdi: una gestione alternativa delle acque meteoriche. Genova, verso una 'Water Sensitive City'.* Università degli Studi di Genova Scuola Politecnica: Dipartimento di Scienze per l'Architettura.

Robert Bray Associates. (2016). *Sustainable Drainage Systems (SuDS) Design Experts: Robert Bray Associates.* [Online]. Available at: http://robertbrayassociates.co.uk/ [Accessed 8 June 2016].

Schubert, U. (2005). *Ecocity. Urban Development towards Appropriate Structures for Sustainable Transport.* [Online]. Available at: http://www.rma.at/sites/new.rma.at/files/ECOCITY%20%20_%20Final%20Report.pdf.

Sharifi, A. and Murayama, A. (2012). A critical review of seven selected neighborhood sustainability assessment tools. *Environmental Impact Assessment Review.* [Online]. Available at: http://www.sciencedirect.com/science/article/pii/S0195925512000558 [Accessed 23 January 2014].

Sustainable Urban Development European Network. (2004). *HQE2R.* [Online]. Available at: http://www.suden.org/.

Toronto and Region Conservation Authority, Credit Valley Conservation Authority, Sustainable Technologies Evaluation Program, Aquafor Beech Limited, Schollen & Company, Dougan and Associates, Kidd Consulting, Center for Watershed Protection

Part C

and Chesapeake Stormwater Network. (2010). *Low impact development stormwater management planning and design guide. Version 1.0.* [Online]. Available at: http://www.creditvalleyca.ca/wp-content/uploads/2014/04/LID-SWM-Guide-v1.0_2010_1_no-appendices.pdf [Accessed 7 June 2016].

United States Environmental Protection Agency. (2007). *Reducing Stormwater Costs through Low Impact Development (LID) Strategies and Practices*. Report No. EPA 841-F-07-006. Washington, D.C. [Online]. Available at: http://www.creditvalleyca.ca/wp-content/uploads/2012/02/lid-swm-guide-chapter1.pdf.

USGBC. (2009). *LEED for Neighborhood Development*.

Chapter 13.1
The Bronx River, USA – Opportunities and Policies

Katia Perini

13.1.1 Project development

The Bronx River and its surrounding area have undergone an eye-catching makeover in recent years, as this industrial no-man's land has turned into an increasingly people-friendly waterfront (Wall, 2012). The successful restoration of the Bronx River is the result of a long and productive collaboration between local community organisations and public bodies, which have both played a fundamental role. On the one hand, the main credit for the renovation must be granted to the strong interest of the Bronx community. On the other hand, the City, State and Federal bureaucracies have provided support, especially in terms of funding and this has allowed several crucial initiatives to be implemented.

In the last few years, improving New York City waterways became among the major objectives held by policies at a local level. As stated in the PlaNYC (New York Department of City Planning, 2011, 2007): "We must remove historical pollution that has had a prolonged and damaging effect on our waterways. We must also address the present day pollution that comes from CSOs [Combined Sewer Overflow] and continue finding ways to restore natural systems". In PlanNYC, it was claimed that this programme will have high costs, but that it is necessary to address the problems affecting public health. At the same time, this project should enable citizens to have free access to their waterfront, as it has been "off limits for recreational use for decades", and as it is crucial to entrust the next generation with "a clean and healthy harbour ecosystem" (New York Department of City Planning, 2011).

Federal policies are also concerned with polluted waterways, as the State requires New York City to regulate pollutant discharge into rivers and improve water quality, as stated by the EPA Clean Water Act of 1977 and its successive amendments (see Chapter 10). According to Robin Kriesberg, Ecology Director of

Urban Sustainability and River Restoration: Green and Blue Infrastructure, First Edition.
Katia Perini and Paola Sabbion.

the Bronx River Alliance, New York City would spend millions of dollars to fix the existing grey infrastructure (Kriesberg, 2013). A more cost-effective approach would be to combine the amelioration of grey infrastructures with green infrastructure techniques to reduce stormwater runoff (resulting in a lower load for grey infrastructure; see Chapter 4).

The recent history (from 1970s to the present) of the main projects and initiatives regarding the Bronx watershed is represented in this timeline, which also mentions the most important actors involved in this project. The timeline seeks to convey the role played by bottom-up initiatives and top-down policies (Figure 13.1.1) and is based on a broad survey of local newspapers dating back to the 1970s. It is also focused on a bibliographic analysis and research on the plans released by local community organisations and NYC Departments over the past 40 years.

The ecological restoration of the Bronx River started in the mid-1970s, before the famous campaigns for environmental justice staged in the 1980s. The interest and commitment of local communities drew attention to the ecological restoration of the Bronx River conditions as a means to improve the neighbourhood rundown characteristics. Local community residents started to clean up the river without any funds, fighting to obtain land for community recreation along the river (as stated in the newspaper Bronx Press Review, Anderberg, 1975). In 1974, local residents formed the Bronx River Restoration Project, Inc. and removed debris from the shoreline of the Bronx River, reversing the trend of deferred maintenance and negligence established over the previous decades (New York City Department of Environmental Protection, 2010; See Chapter 9.1). It is striking to notice that the involvement of the Bronx community started during a period of economic crisis, as New York City was close to bankruptcy in 1975. This coincided with the very end of President Richard Nixon's Administration, when neighbourhoods as the South Bronx were written off by local and national policies as declining areas (Angotti, 2008).

In this period, simple communication and community outreach initiatives implemented to restore the Bronx River were among the most important and effective. Seminars conducted by a team of ecological experts from the City University of New York examined the causes which had engendered the poor state of the Bronx River and set long range plans for its restoration. The latter were implemented soon after, in 1974, by the Bronx Community College (Bronx Press Review, VV.AA., 1974). Fairs, exhibitions, and festivals were also organised (Bronx Press Review, VV.AA., 1975), as the Bronx River Rehabilitation Exhibit (Bronx Press Review, VV.AA., 1975). These initiatives played an important role in raising awareness about the Bronx River conditions.

The Bronx River Restoration Project (BXRR) released the Bronx River Restoration Plan (Bronx River Restoration Project, 1977). This first renovation project was sent to the White House to the attention of the Democratic President Jimmy Carter [1977–1981] to obtain assistance for the master plan, which was aimed at revitalising the physical environment of the Bronx area, addressing a number of strongly felt needs (economic, social, cultural, educational and recreational), as also identifying the adequate channels to receive federal funding (Horn, 1977).

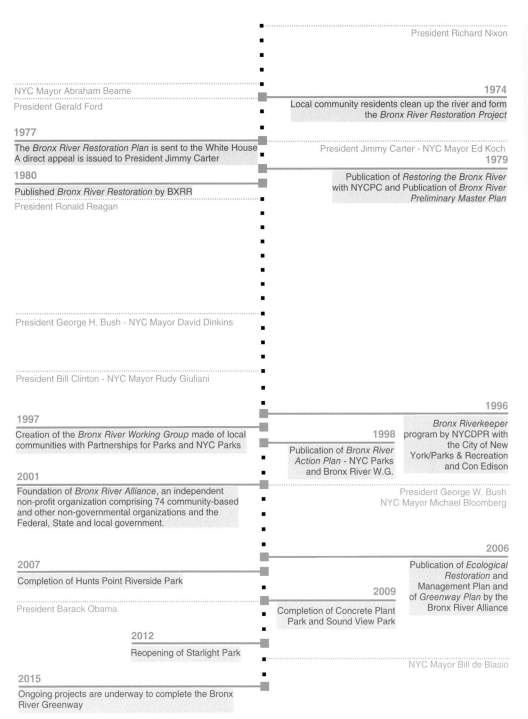

Figure 13.1.1   The Bronx River Timeline.

In 1979, just a few years after the community started its work to restore the Bronx River, the New York City municipality formalised its involvement with the release of Restoring the Bronx River. This project was devised by the Department of City Planning to allocate the land use along the eight miles and a half comprising the Bronx river banks between Westchester and the East River. As noted by the City Planning Commission Chairman Robert Wagner: "With little government money, volunteers have already cleaned a portion of the river and have drawn plans for creating a variety of riverfront recreational activities. Now it is our job to open the way for people to reach the water [...] and to control raw sewage discharges [...] and protect the river water quality" (Wagner, 1979).

In the same year, as the efforts made by the Bronx River Restoration Project were underway, the State Legislature funded the Bronx River Preliminary Master Plan, to implement a joyous programme to clean, revitalise, and beautify the Bronx River (Bronx Press Review, VV.AA., 1979). Interest for new renovation measures continued to mount and the BXRR released the Bronx River Restoration report (1980), documenting group work and comments made by participants in individual interviews.

The activities implemented to improve the River and the neighbourhood registered an interruption in the 1980s, however, but regained momentum at the end of the century. According to Angotti (2013), this trend can be related to federal and local politics: "Most political scientists would agree that [the administration of President Ronald] Reagan (1981–1989) was a real turning point in government policies away from welfare state to neoliberal state", while President Bill Clinton's Administration (1993–2001) and Mayor Rudolph Giuliani's Administration (1994–2001) both played an important role with regard to the Bronx River restoration initiatives (Angotti, 2013).

In the 1990s, the dynamic trend for the Bronx River started with the 1992 Bronx River Trailway Plan to create a comprehensive greenway following the full length of the River, as described in The New York Times. (Howe Verhovek, 1992). The greenway was conceived not only as a pedestrian and bicycle route, but as a linear park that would serve a population which had long been deprived of green open spaces and waterfront access (Bronx River Alliance, 2006b; Figure 13.1.2). In this period, several groups and programmes were created, involving both local community groups and NYC Departments. Among these, was the Partnerships for Parks, a joint programme founded in 1995 by local activists, the City Parks Foundation and NYC Parks. The Bronx Riverkeeper Program was also developed in 1996 by the Parks Department in partnership with Con Edison (NYC energy provider). Grassroots organisations, formed by local activists, created the Bronx River Working Group in 1997. The founders reclaimed their right to renovate and restore at the River and joined with Partnerships for Parks and other units of NYC Parks to draft the Bronx River Action Plan (Bronx River Alliance, 2006b; New York City Department of Environmental Protection, 2010).

The Bronx River restoration project was made possible by grants and funds from NYC Parks and the Federal Government, which also funded a reconnaissance study examining flood control and the potential to restore the damaged

Figure 13.1.2   The Bronx River Greenway.

ecosystem of the Bronx River, as stated in the newspaper Norwood News (Minners, 1999). Efforts to restore the river further increased when City Parks Commissioner Henry Stern declared 1999 would be the "Year of the Bronx River", pledging $60 million to restore this waterway (Johnson, 2000).

In 2001, the Bronx River Working Group formed the Bronx River Alliance, an independent non-profit organisation working in close partnership with NYC Parks. This organisation has maintained a community-based structure to protect and improve the Bronx River corridor and transform it into a healthy ecological, recreational, educational, and economic resource. The Bronx River Alliance is in charge of the coordination of the initiatives regarding the Bronx River Greenway and the creation of new tracks (New York City Department of Environmental Protection, 2010). It currently comprises 74 community-based organisations and other non-governmental organisations as well as the Federal Government (i.e., the Environmental Protection Agency – EPA); the State and local government; Community Boards; the Department of Environmental Protection, NYC Parks, and several schools among its partners and supporters (Bronx River Alliance, 2016).

13.1.2 The greenway

Especially since 2006, the Alliance's work has led to important results as the restoration and creation of several green areas, which have been connected through the Greenway project. The Alliance has released several plans that emphasise priorities and steps to create the greenway path, and target the ecological restoration of the River. The Ecological Restoration and Management Plan was drawn by 22 organisations (public bodies, local community organisations, non-profit organisations) to develop policy solutions for the stormwater management in the Bronx River watershed in 2006. This plan assesses the Rivers environmental conditions, sets goals for its improvement, and defines the scope of projects (Bronx River Alliance, 2006a). The Greenway Plan (2006) presented a comprehensive vision of the Bronx River Greenway and stemmed from the close collaboration between the Bronx River Alliance and NYC Parks, which sought to develop the greenway as a new flagship park within the City parks system (Bronx River Alliance, 2006b). The Waterbody/Watershed Facility Plan Bronx River was drawn in 2010 to comply with the existing water quality standards (New York City Department of Environmental Protection, 2010).

Despite the success of the restoration activities, some areas around the Bronx River were still affected by serious problems, which were tackled through some useful and valid projects for the community. This occurred, specifically, in the Hunts Point Peninsula (Bronx River Estuary section), where industrial activities continue to this day to pose an environmental threat and constitute a health hazard as high asthma rates can be registered in this area. Some noticeable problems are related to the traffic connected to the Hunts Point Food Distribution Centre, one of the world's largest food distribution hubs. Every weekday, 10,000 trucks pass through the neighbourhood, producing toxic air and polluting nearby residential areas, as defined in the newspaper Bronx Beat (Korengel and Lubick, 2000). The local community, though, has been actively promoting renovation initiatives, as the inauguration of the Hunts Point Riverside Park in 2007. This is the first waterfront park in the South Bronx created over the past 60 years (Figure 13.1.3) and, since its foundation, this small green area has been at the heart of community involvement and has been the location for the Environmental Stewardship Program (ESP), boating and fishing programmes, scientific monitoring projects, and community events (New York City Department of Environmental Protection, 2010).

Figure 13.1.3   Mural Painting in the Hunts Point Peninsula.

The Concrete Plant Park constitutes another interesting and successful project promoted by a partnership of community organisations and public agencies. The land of its setting was acquired by NYC Parks in 2000 to promote a revitalisation programme. Since then, it has been used as a public park, also thanks to the temporary pathway constructed by volunteers. This is the result of a participative process involving institutions and citizens alike, as Bronx residents guided the final design for the park grounds. Half of the existing structures of the cement manufacturing facility, which closed in 1987, were maintained as relics of the site's industrial history (Bronx River Alliance, 2006b; Figure 13.1.4). According to Catherine Nagel, Executive Director of City Parks Alliance, the Concrete Plant Park "exemplifies the power of public-private partnerships to create and maintain urban parks that make our cities sustainable and vibrant" (Milosheff, 2011). In recent years, the Bronx River Alliance has given a noteworthy contribution based on a community involvement strategy to solve the environmental problems, which are still currently affecting the Bronx watershed. In fact, it has devised several programmes managed by teams that meet four times a year to discuss the best way to manage partnership work. These programmes targeting citizens' participation are crucial since volunteers are in charge of maintenance in green areas (Figure 13.1.5). The collaborative approach adopted by the Alliance ensures that Bronx residents liaise with designers and agency staff when discussing design concepts and implementation priorities for the Greenway.

River clean up and restoration efforts are driven by the Ecology Team, a committee formed by scientists, City, State, and Federal agency representatives, and local community spokesmen who work to manage stormwater infiltration and reduce runoff, CSOs and pollution. The Greenway Team – comprising community

Figure 13.1.4   The Concrete Park Plant.

Part C

Figure 13.1.5   Volunteers at a Tree Planting Event Along the Bronx River.

and agency planners, designers, and advocates – guides the planning and implementation of the Bronx River Greenway. The Education Program involves teachers,
community-based educators, and scientists in a common effort to use the Bronx
River as a classroom setting for ecological initiatives, and to educate the public
about this waterway and train volunteers to monitor its conditions (Figure 13.1.5).
The Bronx River Stewards Program engages individuals and groups in monitoring
water quality. The Outreach Program is a joint initiative featuring community, civic,
and business representatives to promote the work undertaken by the Alliance, raise
interest on the Bronx River, and organise events that draw people to the river,
including the Bronx River Flotilla (Figure 13.1.6). The Recreation Program sponsors
recreational bike and canoe trips in this area (Bronx River Alliance, 2016).

13.1.3   Policies and local community

The case of the Bronx River demonstrates how effective collaboration between
local community organisations and public bodies can have an impact within a
low income community, and in a neighbourhood concerned with many social
and environmental issues. This entire project was launched by few residents
cleaning up the river 40 years ago and was engendered by the protests of local
community organisations staged over the years, but has now become a better
organised endeavour, acting as a lever to urge the City and the State to take action.
This project shows a long history of work, fights, plans, and efforts to involve the

Figure 13.1.6   Canoeing on the Bronx River Greenway.

New York City administration to deploy funds and grants and sought-after teaching and outreach activities. The Bronx River Alliance has become a leading actor in this process thanks to its community-based approach and support from 74 different organisations ranging from community and non-governmental organisations to public bodies. Its success is primarily based on addressing community priorities and funding by State and City resources. This proves that the community still plays a fundamental role in the Bronx River district, since the New York City municipality cannot effectively cater for the maintenance of all its green areas and requires the cooperation of volunteers. This also illustrates how local community organisations work to involve residents and how this is an incredibly effective bottom-up approach, because it is responsive to citizens' interests (Figure 13.1.3). The community-based efforts to improve and restore housing and green spaces have also created a viable Bronx, which is attracting new investments, resulting in a gentrification process (Angotti, 2013).

Another important improvement of the quality of New York City waterways and stormwater management has been heralded by the commitment of the City to meet the swimmable and fishable water quality standards fixed by the Federal Government through the Clean Water Act. The use of green infrastructure to reduce stormwater runoff and to improve water quality is a cost-effective measure for NYC, and this is one of the reasons why the City is investing in the Bronx River Greenway. Among the initiatives launched by PlaNYC (New York Department of City Planning, 2007) green areas received much attention for recreational amenities, ecological function, and economic development.

Recent history indicates that also the Federal Government has played an important role for the environmental development of the Bronx watershed. When federal funding ceased, as during the Reagan Administration, its effects were strongly felt in this area which has benefited from the increased attention later granted by the Clinton and Giuliani Administrations (1993–2001). According to Angotti (2013), the City government funding follows economic trends and does not have a constant flow. This proves that community efforts have been incredibly effective in the past and continue to be so to this day even when economic support is low.

References

Anderberg, R. (1975). Official Vandalism? Myron Garfinkle. *Bronx Press-Review*, New York.

Angotti, T. (2008). *New York for sale community planning confronts global real estate.* Cambridge, Mass.: MIT Press.

Angotti, T. (2013). *Personal communication in: Katia Perini, 2014. Urban areas and green infrastructure. Research report, published by Urban Design Lab Columbia University ISNB 978-09822174-5-0.* [Online]. Available at: http://urbandesignlab.columbia.edu/files/2015/04/3_Urban_Areas_Green_Infrastructure.pdf.

Bronx River Alliance. (2006a). *Bronx River Ecological Restoration and Management Plan.* [Online]. Available at: http://www.bronxriver.org/puma/images/usersubmitted/greenway_plan/FULLwEcoPlan.pdf.

Bronx River Alliance. (2006b). *Bronx River Greenway Plan.* [Online]. Available at: http://www.bronxriver.org/puma/images/usersubmitted/greenway_plan/BronxRiverGreenwayPlan.pdf.

Bronx River Alliance. (2016). *Bronx River Alliance - homepage.* [Online]. Available at: http://www.bronxriver.org/ [Accessed 24 November 2015].

Bronx River Restoration Project. (1977). *Bronx River Restoration Plan.*

Horn, A. (1977). Bronx River Restoration Plea Sent to White House. Myron Garfinkle. *Bronx Press-Review*, New York.

Howe Verhovek, S. (1992). A Plant to Conserve New York's Wilderness. *The New York Times.*

Johnson, O. (2000). Bronx River's path grows greener. Columbia University Graduate School of Journalism. *Bronx Beat.*

Korengel, K. and Lubick, N. (2000). Trash recycles an old debate. Columbia University Graduate School of Journalism. *Bronx Beat.*

Kriesberg, R. (2013). *Personal communication in: Katia Perini, 2014. Urban areas and green infrastructure. Research report, published by Urban Design Lab Columbia University ISNB 978-09822174-5-0.* [Online]. Available at: http://urbandesignlab.columbia.edu/files/2015/04/3_Urban_Areas_Green_Infrastructure.pdf.

Milosheff, P. (2011). Concrete Plant Park. *The Bronx Times.* [Online]. Available at: http://www.bronx.com/.

Minners, J. (1999). New Guide Charts Comeback. *Norwood News.* [Online]. Available at: http://www.bronxmall.com/norwoodnews/past/31199/news/page1.html.

New York City Department of Environmental Protection. (2010). *Waterbody/Watershed Facility Plan Bronx River.* [Online]. Available at: http://www.hydroqual.com/projects/ltcp/wbws/bronx_river/bronx_river_cover.pdf.

New York Department of City Planning. (2007). *PlaNYC.* [Online]. Available at: http://nytelecom.vo.llnwd.net/o15/agencies/planyc2030/pdf/planyc_2011_planyc_full_report.pdf.

New York Department of City Planning. (2011). *PlaNYC. Update.* [Online]. Available at: http://nytelecom.vo.llnwd.net/o15/agencies/planyc2030/pdf/planyc_2011_planyc_full_report.pdf.

VV.AA. (1974). Bronx River Seminar Series Set by BCC. Myron Garfinkle. *Bronx Press-Review*, New York.

VV.AA. (1975). Environmental Committe Plans Fifth Ecology Fair. Myron Garfinkle. *Bronx Press-Review*, New York.

VV.AA. (1979). Plan for Bronx River. Myron Garfinkle. *Bronx Press-Review*, New York.

Wagner, R. (1979). Bronx River access asked. Myron Garfinkle. *Bronx Press-Review*, New York.

Wall, P. (2012). New Bronx River Parks Are Beautiful But Dangerous to Reach, Advocates Say - Claremont Village - DNAinfo.com New York. *DNAinfo New York*. [Online]. Available at: http://www.dnainfo.com/new-york/20120926/claremont-village/new-bronx-river-parks-are-beautiful-but-dangerous-reach-advocates-say [Accessed 4 April 2014].

Part C

Chapter 13.2
Los Angeles River, USA – Opportunities and Policies

Paola Sabbion

13.2.1 River revitalization plans

Over the past two decades, several stakeholders – the City of Los Angeles, the US Army Corps of Engineers of the Los Angeles District (Corps), Los Angeles County, partnerships, agencies, and activist groups – have participated in the revitalisation of the Los Angeles River.

Since the 1930s, due to continuous flooding, the Corps has played an increasingly important role. In 1935, the Corps began the channelisation and dam construction, which continued to the late 1990s. The Flood Control Act (1936) established that the Corps would supervise the Los Angeles County Drainage Area (LACDA) in coordination with Los Angeles County. In the 1980s, floods in the lower Rio Hondo and in the Los Angeles River increased. Task forces were established in 1989 and in 1990 (County of Los Angeles River Task Force) to increase the flood control capacity. This was also addressed thanks to the LACDA Project (1990), which devised 33 km of levee modifications, 24 bridge crossings, and important landscape changes (DPW, 2016). This project was furthered and improved with the The County of Los Angeles River Master Plan (1996), coordinated by the Los Angeles County, and approved by the Board of Supervisors. This Plan recognised the importance of the River as a natural and strategic resource and the need to renovate and renaturalise it. Both projects, although, have been under continuous criticism. In fact, environmental activist groups and local state agencies (e.g., the City of Los Angeles Planning Commission) have stressed that the LACDA had negative ecological, economic and aesthetic consequences, especially for "the total subordination of water and environmental issues to the logic of engineered flood control" (Desfor and Keil, 2000). They have also called for a greater participatory role in the LACDA and Master Plan planning on the basis of "an open consensus building project".

Urban Sustainability and River Restoration: Green and Blue Infrastructure, First Edition.
Katia Perini and Paola Sabbion.
© 2017 John Wiley & Sons Ltd. Published 2017 by John Wiley & Sons Ltd.

Since the 1980s, the Los Angeles River specifically became the focus of an environmental battle in Southern California. In 1985, during a performance, the poet and activist Lewis MacAdams cut through the river's fence north of downtown Los Angeles and declared that the River was alive below the concrete (Linton, 2005). Friends of the L.A. River (FoLAR) – which is a non-profit organization aiming to protect and restore the natural and historic heritage of the river and its habitat through inclusive planning, education and stewardship – was founded after this event (FoLAR, 2016). The Great L.A. River CleanUp (1989) has also marked the foundation of a new environmental strategy. This initiative has since been held every spring and gathers one of the highest turnouts and multiethnic volunteer participation in California. On its twenty-seventh anniversary, in 2016, it has attracted a record 9,000 volunteers featuring as the biggest American river cleanup initiative (Figure 13.2.1; FoLAR, 2016). Moreover, FoLAR in coordination with the L.A. Coalition of Essential Skills and University of California has devised a range of educational activities and water quality management practices. The River School, in particular, is one of the main activities for school children (Elrick, 2007; Figure 13.2.2, 13.2.3, 13.2.4). The main environmental goal is encouraging community involvement (Figure 13.2.2, 13.2.3) to trigger an

Figure 13.2.1   The 2015 Los Angeles River Cleanup (photo by William Preston Bowling).

Figure 13.2.2   FoLAR Monitoring the State of the Water (photo by William Preston Bowling).

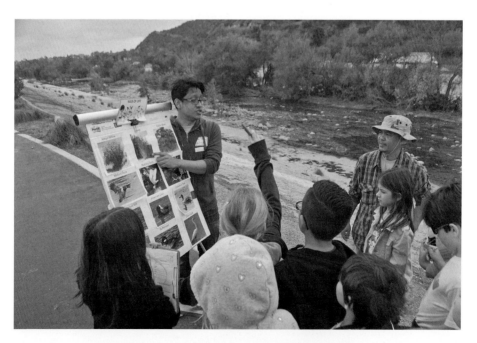

Figure 13.2.3   Educational Activities Engaging Children (photo by William Preston Bowling).

Part C

Figure 13.2.4   FoLAR River Rover at Crossroads School (photo by William Preston Bowling).

ecological redevelopment in the areas surrounding the River and revitalise poor, segregated neighbourhoods (Desfor and Keil, 2000; Figure 13.2.3).

In 2000, in California, the claim for the river renaturalisation led to the approval of a referendum on parks (Gandy, 2006). The new ecological approach is regulated by the Safe Neighborhood Parks, Clean Water, Clean Air and Costal Protection Bond Act, that pioneers an ecologically-oriented flood control strategy. In June 2002, the Los Angeles City Council set the Ad Hoc Committee on the Los Angeles River to coordinate actions with stakeholders on issues and goals concerning revitalisation, urban ecology, neighbourhood redevelopment, neglected space re-evaluation, and sense of place retrieval (LARRMP, 2007).

In 2007, the City Council adopted the Los Angeles River Revitalization Master Plan (LARRMP), which is overseen by L.A. County's Department of Public Works. It is developed according to the California Environmental Quality Act lead agency and the National Environmental Policy Act lead agency, historically responsible for overseeing the various functional aspects of this latest Master Plan (LARRMP, 2007). So far, the team has reviewed and evaluated about 115 previous relevant reports (LARRMP Final Report, 2007), including: Los Angeles River Master Plan (1996); Watershed and Open Space Plan (2001); Los Angeles Citywide General Plan System (2002); Los Angeles State Historic Park (*Cornfields*; 2005); Arroyo Seco Watershed Management and Restoration Plan (2005); City of Los Angeles, Department of Water and Power, Urban Water Management Plan (2005); State of California Global Warming Solutions Act (2006); and Integrated Regional Water Management Plan (2006).

The 2007 Master Plan is seeking to overcome the engineering approach to improve the river ecology and the quality of life along the waterway. It lacks, although, both financial resources and jurisdictional capacity when compared to the well-funded and supported 1996 LACDA Master Plan (Desfor and Keil, 2000). However, it provides appropriate proposals for revitalising the river's ecological functions while providing parks and green space, connecting communities and reducing private car mobility (LARRMP Final Report, 2007). As a result, dozens of parks, extensive bike trails, and public art installations have been developed, involving more than 100 communities (Linton, 2005).

The Master Plan, moreover, focuses on Opportunity Areas where different spatial transformation and river revitalisation opportunities can be devised. Twenty areas were selected in the initial stage and then reduced to nine focus projects. These Opportunity Areas provide the chance to measure and experiment water quality, flood protection and neighbourhood connection (LARRMP Final Report 2007). Wildlife habitat, management of parks and open recreational spaces, community benefits and economic opportunities are also considered. These Areas represent the range of different approaches to common issues and conditions recurring along the river (LARRMP, 2007). Following community discussions and ongoing research, five of these Opportunity Areas have been selected as showcase projects for in-detail testing (including economic analyses). The latter are not the first implementation projects but the first to assess the potential success of the river renaturalisation (Figure 13.2.5; LARRMP, 2007).

Ongoing research and community discussions have led to concentrate on five showcase projects to address a more detailed development (including economic analysis). The areas concerned allow testing the potential success of the river renaturalisation, even if they are not the first ones where revitalisation projects will be implemented (LARRMP, 2007). The selected Five Opportunity Areas include: the Canoga Park Area (a densely populated, largely single-family neighbourhood); the River Glen Area (highly industrialised, needing water quality treatment and ecological and habitat improvement); the Taylor Yard Area (characterised by concrete channel walls, needing ecosystem and hydro-ecological restoration); the Chinatown-Cornfields Area (needing ecosystem restoration, habitat expansion, and the implementation of water-based recreation); the Downtown Industrial Area (needing a reconnection to the River and within communities as access to the River is strictly constrained by rail lines).

The Plan recognises that the revitalisation process will require a phased, adaptive approach. The achievement of near-term opportunities, including access improvement, recreational value enhancement, water quality treatment, and non-motorised transportation, could take up to 10–15 years. Longer-term changes to restore the river's natural functions could take 25 to 40 years or more (LARRMP, 2007).

All river modifications have to be designed considering the necessity to maintain the existing flood capacity. Adding vegetation to create habitat or providing access to the waterfront, would reduce flood capacity. This is why the project has to incorporate the idea that current channels have to be widened or deepened, also considering that different types of vegetation have different impacts on flood capacity. Grasses, for instance, have less impact than willows or trees because they do not impede flood flows. Less compensation measures are hence required if only grass is used to vegetate the riverbed and banks (LARRMP, 2007; Figure 13.2.6).

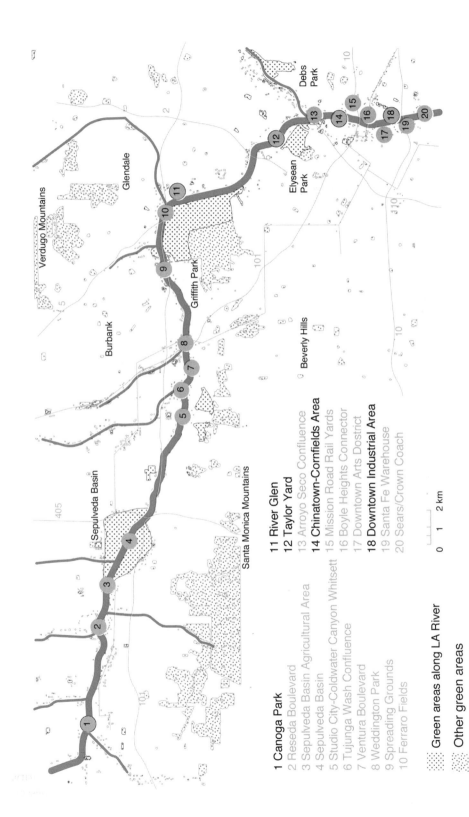

1 Canoga Park
2 Reseda Boulevard
3 Sepulveda Basin Agricultural Area
4 Sepulveda Basin
5 Studio City-Coldwater Canyon Whitsett
6 Tujunga Wash Confluence
7 Ventura Boulevard
8 Weddington Park
9 Spreading Grounds
10 Ferraro Fields

11 River Glen
12 Taylor Yard
13 Arroyo Seco Confluence
14 Chinatown-Cornfields Area
15 Mission Road Rail Yards
16 Boyle Heights Connector
17 Downtown Arts Dsitrict
18 Downtown Industrial Area
19 Santa Fe Warehouse
20 Sears/Crown Coach

Green areas along LA River

Other green areas

0   1   2 km

Figure 13.2.5 The Proposed Twenty Opportunity Areas and the Selected Final Five Opportunity Areas, Based on (LARRMP, 2007).

Part C

Figure 13.2.6   Concrete Banks with Spontaneous Vegetation Grown on the Left Riverside (photo by William Preston Bowling).

In 2006, the County of Los Angeles, the Flood Control District and the Watershed Management Division, have developed the Integrated Regional Water Management Plan (IRWMP), which includes specific recommendations for the Los Angeles River. It seeks, in particular, to reduce and reuse stormwater runoff from developed areas. According to the Plan, the stormwater runoff volumes have to be decreased through onsite measures, such as reducing impervious surfaces, or using BMPs to capture, treat, and infiltrate storm runoff. Performance targets range from a 50% to a 90% storm runoff reduction or reuse in developed areas. Treating and reusing runoff water can be achieved by adopting multi-purpose solutions and a systematic approach that supports functional habitats, provides for recreation and groundwater recharge, and enhances water quality throughout the watershed. Runoff treatment should occur on both public and private sites, employing public properties such as parks, school yards, and civic sites as treatment facilities. This systematic approach has been successful, even if it has only been partially implemented with the Sun Valley Watershed Management Plan (LARRMP, 2007).

13.2.2   Costs and benefits

This project has positive effects on different levels. Communities gain several assets. Ecological balance in the riverfronts and green connections within neighbourhoods provide recreational opportunities and a greater sense of identity. Another successful outcome is the increased value of both properties and businesses.

Part C

Figure 13.2.7   Graffiti Street Art Along the River Channel as a Space Appropriation Strategy (photo by William Preston Bowling).

Los Angeles has become a more attractive city as its waterfront stands for a better water quality and well-being, reduced sprawl and less isolated communities (Figure 13.2.7). From an economic point of view, the Plan can help to achieve environmental justice, development and growth. Further flood-damage reduction, ecosystem restoration, and environmental improvements can be implemented at the federal level (LARRMP, 2007).

Accrued estimated economic benefits in five out of the total Opportunity Areas would range from $2.7 to $5.4 billion and result in 11,000 to 18,000 new jobs. The annual tax revenue would increase from $47 to $81 million (ASLA, 2009). Policy actors should balance the Plan's economic development goals in light of their economic and non-economic side effects. Investments, in fact, may have a collateral impact which should be carefully evaluated and anticipated, as the Plan intends to encourage the public approval process and community achievements (LARRMP, 2007).

The Ad Hoc Committee's most significant funding activity has been the $500-million 2004 Proposition "Measure O for Clean Water, Ocean, River, Beach, Bay, and Storm Water Cleanup" (League of Women Voters of California Education Fund, 2004). The City obtained $25 million for the region and has continued to pursue state-level funding through California State Proposition 50 (Water Security, Clean Drinking Water, Coastal and Beach Protection Act) of 2002 and federal legislation introduced by Lucille Roybal-Allard and Barbara Boxer. The City budget includes a list of over 50 proposals for parks, transportation, and water quality projects along the river, valued at over $650 million (LARRMP, 2007).

Figure 13.2.8   L.A. River Banks Featuring Vegetation that has Grown to Cover the Concrete Channel (photo by William Preston Bowling).

A century of concreting, urbanising and channelling has built a technocratic vision of the U.S. Army Corps of Engineers and urban landscapes which are thought to be a "[compelling] problem because they reveal the materiality of the city as a functional metropolis" (Gandy, 2006). Notwithstanding this, a partial return to nature has been represented by extensive grasses, rushes and other plants spreading on the concrete levees and on the muddy water strips (Figure 13.2.8). The reiteration of the 1930s technical paradigm has been challenged by a more inclusive ecological vision for the whole metropolitan region, embodied by the Southern California Institute of Architecture's call for the creation of a democratically controlled Los Angeles River Valley Authority (Gandy, 2006). Hence, the US Army Corps of Engineers of the Los Angeles District, in conjunction with the City of Los Angeles, have released the Los Angeles River Ecosystem Restoration Study Final Integrated Feasibility Report (U.S. Army Corps of Engineers, 2015). In 2014, the "Alternative 20 of the Los Angeles River Ecosystem Feasibility Study" has been recommended for approval by the Corps and has been pushed through by Mayor Eric Garcetti. The Mayor also addressed President Obama at the White House on this topic. Garcetti's efforts for the

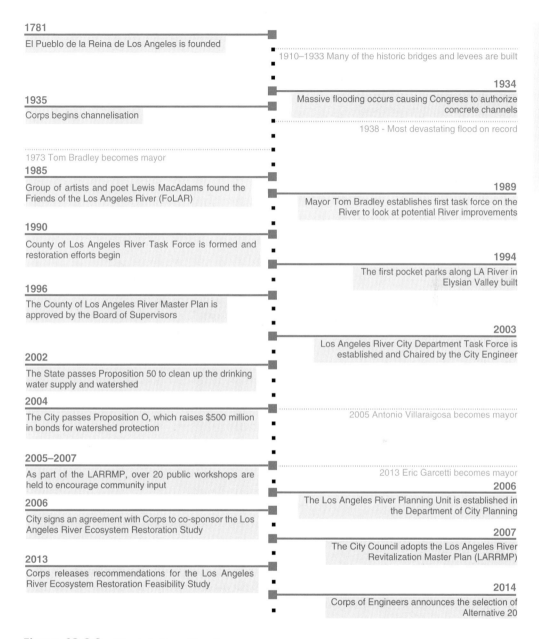

Figure 13.2.9   The L.A. River Timeline.

river have been also praised and recognised by MacAdams, president of the Friends of the Los Angeles River association (Sahagun, 2014). The $9.71-million Feasibility Study was initiated in 2006 at the behest of the US Congress. Alternative 20 – selected in 2014 by Army Corps of Engineers – also defined RIVER (Riparian Integration via Varied Ecological Introduction), is the most comprehensive option devised so far and is aimed at restoring approximately 290 ha of habitat, including tributary restoration on the east side of the Arroyo

Seco watershed, the restoration of the Verdugo Wash and the wetlands of the Los Angeles State Historic Park, leading to a 119% habitat increase (KCETLink, 2015). In July 2015, after an intense lobbying campaign, the $1.3 billion funding marked the starting point for this project. This new plan will contribute to revitalise a 17-km segment of the river and transform the concrete channel into "something resembling the river's natural state" (Sahagun, 2014). The project regards the L.A. River from the San Fernando Valley to Long Beach, as approved by the Civil Works Review Board of the U.S. Army Corps of Engineers in Washington D.C. (KCETLink, 2015).

13.2.3 Community involvement

The local community has been engaged at multiple levels during the LARRMP planning thanks to a 50-member City Department Task Force; a 40-member Advisory Committee with representatives from the community and its leaders (homeowner neighbourhood associations, business groups, etc.); a Stakeholder Committee counting on more than 50 representatives of advocacy organisations (environmental groups, environmental justice and River advocacy organisations); and a Peer Review Committee comprising six leading experts in urban river revitalisation and restoration. All these bodies have participated in 20 community meetings/public workshops, held in various neighbourhoods along the River as well as community event neighbourhood council meetings, an urban watershed forum, meetings on a wide variety of River projects; and a youth summit conference with over 500 participants (LARRMP, 2007).

Community involvement and public support are critical components to the success of all Los Angeles River planning efforts. The process, in fact, has to be neighbourhood-focused, transparent and shared. In particular, the City has developed a formal public participation process that is called Community Plan. The Los Angeles River website (City of Los Angeles, 2016) also provides updates on Committee activities and the Revitalization Master Plan and it currently receives over 50,000 visits every year. Moreover, the Los Angeles River Committee has sponsored five design workshops called "Great Outburst Of Design Initiatives" (GOODIs), involving communities to share and create new design projects along the river. Every year, on the Los Angeles River Day, communities can celebrate past works, present new projects, and support future efforts to increase public awareness on the River. More than 20 community partners have coordinated their support to the 2005 "The Future is Now" Los Angeles River campaign. The Bureau of Sanitation, moreover, has created "Linking Us Together", a short video promoting the vision for the revitalisation of Los Angeles River and anti-litter and plastic recycling programmes.

The role played by activists in L.A. River has also been crucial. They have changed the image of the river with their capacity to attract cultural stakeholders and community-based organisations (Gottlieb, 2007) and marginalised communities, successfully integrating them into the planning process and engaging them in all participation phases (Gandy, 2006; Figure 13.2.10).

Part C

Figure 13.2.10   L.A. River Community Event Organised by FoLAR (photo by William Preston Bowling).

References

ASLA (2009). *Honor Award Los Angeles River Revitalization Master Plan, Los Angeles, CA* [Online]. Available at: https://www.asla.org/2009awards/064.html [Accessed 11 May 2016].

City of Los Angeles (2016). [Online]. Available at: www.lariver.org [Accessed 11 May 2016].

Desfor, G. and Keil, R. (2000). Every river tells a story: the Don River (Toronto) and the Los Angeles River (Los Angeles) as articulating landscapes. *Journal of Environmental Policy & Planning* 2:5–23.

DPW (2016). *Los Angeles County Drainage Area (LACDA) Project* [Online]. Available at: http://ladpw.org/wmd/watershed/LA/LACDA_Drainage.cfm [Accessed 22 May 2016].

Elrick, T. (2007). *Los Angeles River*. Arcadia Publishing.

FoLAR (2016). *FoLAR* [Online]. Available at: http://folar.org/ [Accessed 9 April 2016].

Gandy, M. (2006). Riparian anomie: Reflections on the Los Angeles River. *Landscape Research* 31:135–145.

Gottlieb, R. (2007). *Reinventing Los Angeles: Nature and Community in the Global City*. MIT Press.

KCETLink (2015). *$1.3 Billion L.A. River Habitat Restoration Plan Unanimously Approved in D.C.* [Online]. Available at: https://www.kcet.org/confluence/13-billion-la-river-habitat-restoration-plan-unanimously-approved-in-dc [Accessed 17 November 2015].

LARRMP (2007). Los Angeles River Revitalization Master Plan.

LARRMP Final Report (2007). Final Programmatic Environmental Impact Report/ Programmatic Environmental Impact Statement.

League of Women Voters of California Education Fund (2004). *Measure O: Clean Water, Ocean, River, Beach, Bay Storm Water Cleanup Measure - Los Angeles County, CA* [Online]. Available at: http://www.smartvoter.org/2004/11/02/ca/la/meas/O/ [Accessed 11 May 2016].

Linton, J. (2005). *Down By the Los Angeles River: Friends of the Los Angeles Rivers Official Guide*. Wilderness Press.

Sahagun, L. (2014). *Army Corps to Recommend $1-Billion L.A. River Project* [Online]. Available at: http://www.latimes.com/science/la-me-la-river-approval-20140529-story.html [Accessed 11 May 2016].

U.S. Army Corps of Engineers (2015). *LA River Ecosystem Restoration Report Available for Public Review and* [Online]. Available at: http://www.spl.usace.army.mil/Media/NewsReleases/tabid/1319/Article/621504/la-river-ecosystem-restoration-report-available-for-public-review-and-comment.aspx [Accessed 11 May 2016].

Chapter 13.3
Madrid Río, Spain – Opportunities and Policies
Katia Perini

13.3.1 Project development

The Madrid Río Project devised the transformation of one of the most degraded and neglected zones of the city into one of the most beautiful and vital. Moreover, this project planned to convert the Manzanares River from an urban barrier into a meeting place for citizens, serving as a connection between neighbourhoods and facilities (Sharif, 2012). To pursue these objectives, the M-30 – which is the main ring road surrounding the city – was relocated underground, providing the space for the linear Madrid Río Park. An underground parking suitable for 1,000 vehicles was also created to enhance public transport and curb pollution and congestion.

The Manzanares River benefited from these urban changes and residents can currently enjoy the recreational zone along the river banks (West 8, 2011; Jewell, 2011). This area has thus been the spotlight of important renovation plans, which started in 2003, with the Publication of the Plan de Rehabilitación del Entorno del Río Manzanares, and regarded in particular the construction of the M-30 tunnel and the Madrid Río project. The Plan de Rehabilitación del Entorno del Río Manzanares, published in 2015, is the last restoration initiative, which is going to be implemented in the near future. Thanks to the projects devised over the last 12 years, the Manzanares River has become the pivot of requalification strategies which involve building renovation and economic and social activities (Arquitectos Urbanistas Ingenieros Asociados S.L.P., 2010).

Since its construction in the 1970s, the M-30, has caused the disappearance of the links between the city and its River, which has become isolated, inaccessible and invisible (Burgos & Garrido Arquitectos *et al.*, 2011). To reduce the negative impact of this highway on the Manzanares River and on the surrounding neighbourhoods, the Madrid 2003–2007 legislature under President Esperanza Aguirre (President of the Autonomous Community of Madrid, PP) released its most

Urban Sustainability and River Restoration: Green and Blue Infrastructure, First Edition.
Katia Perini and Paola Sabbion.
© 2017 John Wiley & Sons Ltd. Published 2017 by John Wiley & Sons Ltd.

emblematic project, called Calle 30. This urban renewal plan was undertaken through the Plan de Reforma y Gestión Integral de la M-30 (Ayuntamiento de Madrid, 2015). It sought to reduce air and water pollution, drastically decreasing the estimated thousands of vehicles which were circulating at the time on the urban roads (Esbjørn, 2013).

The Madrid Municipality decided to cover part of the M-30 highway, building an 8-km tunnel on the road stretch affecting the banks of the Manzanares River (Burgos & Garrido Arquitectos *et al.*, 2011). According to Madrid's Alcalde Alberto Ruiz-Gallardón and to his advisors, until this moment the motorway was "a barrier to movement in the urban areas it ran through". The project was sub-divided into two phases due to its technical complexity and the high amount of investment required to complete it (Sharif, 2012). The first phase regarded the tunnel construction for the M-30 underground redirection, the second phase involved the creation of the Madrid Río linear park on the area previously occupied by the highway. It is worth mentioning, in fact, that this has been one of the largest projects employing tunnel boring machines (TBM) in the world (Morley, 2011). After the publication of the *Plan de Rehabilitación del Entorno del Río Manzanares*, in 2003, and of the Plan de Reforma y Gestión Integral de la M-30, in 2005, the first phase of construction began and the tunnel was opened to traffic in February 2007. In the meantime, several predictable congestion problems arose in this area.

Notwithstanding many criticisms, these extensive reform plans proved to be highly successful and a vast network of tunnels – 43-km long – was dug from 2005 to 2007 underneath the city of Madrid to reroute the highway, running parallel to the Manzanares River. An ambitious planning effort, judged by many as utopian, has hence become an integral part of the city centre, offering Madrilenians unique recreational facilities and a higher quality of life (Esbjørn, 2013; Área de Gobierno de Urbanismo y Vivienda, 2009).

The second phase of the renovation project was launched, in 2005, when the Madrid Municipality announced an international ideas competition, seeking to involve the most renowned professionals to redesign an area surrounding the Manzanares River, which encompassed more than 40 ha. On this land the munici-pal administration planned to build parks, playgrounds, infrastructures, and other facilities. Among the participants featured Dominique Perrault, Peter Eisenman, Herzog & de Meuron, and Navarro Baldeweg. The panel of judges awarded the M-Rio Arquitectos with the West 8 landscape architecture design team – which was formed by Burgos & Garrido, Porras & La Casta, Rubio & Álvarez-Sala – in partnership with the West 8 landscape architecture. This winning team of archi-tects, landscape architects, urban designers and engineers signed the draft con-tract for the Plan Especial, under the coordination of the Madrid Municipality. Their plan concentrated specifically on environmental quality management, func-tional aspects, creation of new green areas and connections within the city (Área de Gobierno de Urbanismo y Vivienda, 2009; Sharif, 2012). It would completely transform a deserted area into a family-friendly public park, now known as the Madrid Río (Jewell, 2011). The M-Rio Arquitectos and West 8 design team devised the master plan to renovate this urban area. The team also designed sev-eral urban features comprised in this territory such as: Salón de Pinos, Avenida de Portugal, Huerta de la Partida, Jardines del Puente de Segovia, Jardines del Puente

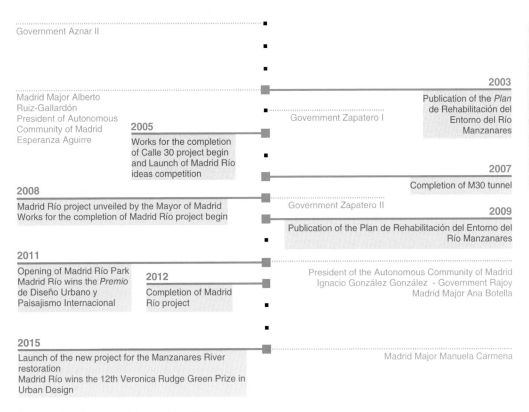

Government Aznar II

Madrid Major Alberto
Ruiz-Gallardón
President of Autonomous
Community of Madrid
Esperanza Aguirre

2005

Works for the completion
of Calle 30 project begin
and Launch of Madrid Río
ideas competition

Government Zapatero I

2003

Publication of the *Plan
de Rehabilitación del
Entorno del Río
Manzanares*

2007

Completion of M30 tunnel

2008

Madrid Río project unveiled by the Mayor of Madrid
Works for the completion of Madrid Río project begin

Government Zapatero II

2009

Publication of the Plan de Rehabilitación del Entorno del
Río Manzanares

2011

Opening of Madrid Río Park
Madrid Río wins the *Premio
de Diseño Urbano y
Paisajismo Internacional*

2012

Completion of Madrid
Río project

President of the Autonomous Community of Madrid
Ignacio González González - Government Rajoy
Madrid Major Ana Botella

2015

Launch of the new project for the Manzanares River
restoration
Madrid Río wins the 12th Veronica Rudge Green Prize in
Urban Design

Madrid Major Manuela Carmena

Part C

Figure 13.3.1   Madrid Río Timeline.

de Toledo, Jardines de la Virgen del Puerto and Arganzuela Park (West 8, 2011). Given the size of the project, the objectives were met step-by-step through smaller projects that focused on specific areas (Sharif, 2012).

The project was presented by the Lord Mayor of Madrid, Alberto Ruíz Gallardón, following a communication campaign targeting citizens' involvement (Área de Gobierno de Urbanismo y Vivienda, 2009; GoMadrid, 2015). According to the municipal government, in fact, awareness and participation among the urban residents would prove a key factor for the success of the project. For this reason, in 2009, the Municipality organised public meetings and opened several communication channels, including specific websites with all the information related to the project. It planned several meetings with the local community and associations (especially with the Federación Regional de Asociaciones Vecinales de Madrid, FRAVM), mailbox and phone call services for individual requests, and information centres. Therefore, even if this was a top-down project, since its beginning the community was engaged. The younger generations were also encouraged to participate. The Madrid Río Children and Young People contest was held in 2005. Following the children's proposals expressed in this competition, the Madrid beach was built and now counts as one of the main water attractions of the Arganzuela Park (Ayuntamiento de Madrid, 2015; Mele, 2014).

The upgrading construction works of the 40-hectares area surrounding the Manzanares River began in 2008 (after the Calle 30 Project and M-30 relocation

Figure 13.3.2   Arganzuela Park (photo credit West 8).

completion) and it was defined by El País (País, 2008b) as the *iniciativa estrella* (star initiative) supported by Mayor Alberto Ruiz-Gallardón. According to the Spanish newspaper (País, 2008a), moreover, the renovation process suffered from the economic crisis which slowed its pace. The project indeed started when the country registered a period of notable economic growth and important economic investments in several fields.

Nevertheless, in 2009, the ambitious transformation of the area on top of the new M-30 motorway along the Manzanares River proceeded and, by the end of the year, the riverbanks were renovated. Decisive steps forward were also underway to conclude one of the most important components of the Madrid Río Project, the Salón de Pinos, a greenway with bike and pedestrian paths shaded by pines, located on the right bank of the river (Área de Gobierno de Urbanismo y Vivienda, 2009). In addition, the efforts to complete other sections of the project were also unabated as the continuous pedestrian and bike path which crosses Madrid along the Manzanares River (Área de Gobierno de Urbanismo y Vivienda, 2009). The Plan de Rehabilitación del Entorno del Río Manzanares was released in 2010 and regards the strategies for the urban requalification of the area left from the two projects Madrid Calle 30 and Madrid Río that still needs to be renovated. This Plan addresses private buildings as well as infrastructure for social and economic activities (Arquitectos Urbanistas Ingenieros Asociados S.L.P., 2010).

The Madrid Río Project was completed during the 2007–2011 legislature and ended exactly on April 15 2011. It covered a total surface area of 1,210,881 m², with 33,623 new trees planted featuring 47 different species, 470,844 shrubs comprising 38 species and 210,898 m² of lawn (Ayuntamiento de Madrid, 2015).

The whole project, which includes the Arganzuela, Matadero, and Puente de Toledo Parks (see Chapter 9.3) was finished a month before the elections. It was completed on time, since the general timeline of the project shows that the planning for the Madrid Río park was scheduled to take place between 2007 and 2008, while the entire project execution had to run from 2008 until 2010 (Sharif, 2012).

It is interesting to notice that, although formally the legislature changed in 2007, the President of the Autonomous Community of Madrid Esperanza Aguirre of the People's Party was elected for the second time. When the Madrid Río project was implemented, Mayor Alberto Ruiz-Gallardón was also elected for the second time. The mayor and the president were hence from the same party. This is why the urban administration saw a certain continuity. In 2015, Manuela Carmela of the PSOE (the Spanish Socialist Workers' Party) was elected mayor but the project was and (still is) supported transversally by both main Spanish parties, as demonstrated by the objectives of the current administrations. The Mayor of Madrid and Mayor of Getafe (south of Madrid) have declared they are going to proceed with the restoration of the area near the Manzanares River that still needs to be upgraded, building a new section of the park stretching from Madrid Río to the Getafe municipality (EcoDiario, 2015a). So far, the urban requalification of this remaining area, which was initially comprised in the Madrid Calle 30 and Madrid Río projects, has been addressed in January 2010 with the Plan de Rehabilitación del Entorno del Río Manzanares. This project supports initiatives such as the renovation of private buildings and boosts local social and economic activities (Arquitectos Urbanistas Ingenieros Asociados S.L.P., 2010).

13.3.2   Project costs and benefits

The Madrid Río and the Calle 30 projects have concerned a massive infrastructure redesign. The first phase, which required submerging the Madrid traffic through 43 km of new underground tunnels, was the most difficult. This was part of a structured technological effort that often infuriated residents despite promises of improved quality of life and higher property values (Jewell, 2011).

The cost of the project was €3.9 billion for the Calle 30 Project - the tunnel work - and €485 million for the Madrid Río Project, an enormous recreational space opened up in the heart of Madrid (Sharif, 2012). The project was mostly funded by the Spanish government via Plan E, the stimulus package pushed through by Spain's Socialist Prime Minister, José Luis Rodríguez Zapatero (The Economist, 2009). The high costs were due to the bulk of works implemented. In fact, in addition to restoring historic monuments along the river, two new bridges were built. The Arganzuela Footbridge, designed by Dominique Perrault (with a cost of approximately €13 million), was covered by interlocking curved metallic strips. This spiralling silver bridge is a large walkway that provides an expansive view over the river and park areas below (Jewell, 2011).

The Madrid Río project demonstrates that the Spanish government was able to invest in renovation projects targeted on public spaces (Mele, 2014). Therefore, while at local level, the Project was conceived and managed by the People's Party, at national level, it was funded by the Spanish Socialist Workers' Party government.

This is a further demonstration of the wide political approval granted to the restoration project.

Despite the many and important environmental, economic, and social improvements deriving from the Madrid Río Project (see Chapter 9.3), criticisms arose over the high costs and some implementation aspects. For example, recently (Lòpez Garro, 2015), some citizens have argued that the greenway is too small (for bikes, skates, pedestrians, etc). Another concern regards the substrate thickness needed to plant trees on top of the tunnel (which is not adequate for big trees) and the magnitude of paved surfaces (Figure 13.3.3; Esetena, 2010). The most successful outcome, although, is that thousands of people use the park on the Manzanares River, especially at weekends (Sànchez, 2013). In the first steps, the project was hindered by the lack of comprehensive and reliable communication between the Administration and the citizens. The residents' participation was low, as the Foro por la Movilidad Sostenible Forum for Sustainable Mobility Platform denounced, pushing the Madrid Municipality to increase information activities starting from 2009 (Área de Gobierno de Urbanismo y Vivienda 2009). Thanks to these efforts, the citizens are now fully supporting the project and giving it the recognition it deserves.

The Manzanares River, in fact, has been a major landmark for Madrid's urban development due to its central role in the profound transformation related to the

Figure 13.3.3   Plataforma del Rey (photo by Jeroen Musch).

M-30 and its environment. The Madrid River project has created a new frame-work for urban renovation, encompassing the urban highway burial and the development of public open spaces. This transformation has played a key role in favouring an overall improvement of the urban scene and has increased private real estate value (Área de Gobierno de Urbanismo y Vivienda, 2009).

In 2015, the Harvard Graduate School of Design awarded the Madrid Río Development Plan with the 12th Veronica Rudge Green Prize in Urban Design defining it the best city space on a world scale. This prize followed the Premio de Diseño Urbano y Paisajismo Internacional, assigned in 2011 by the Comité Internacional de Críticos de Arquitectura (CICA, international panel of critics of architecture; País, 2011). The Madrid Río linear park is, first of all, a great success for the city and has created a friendly and inclusive urban environment, connect-ing the city neighbourhoods and providing green areas. It has certainly improved the citizens' quality of life, as stated by the Harvard Graduate School committee (EcoDiario, 2015b).

References

Área de Gobierno de Urbanismo y Vivienda. (2009). *Proyectos Singulares*. Memoria de gestión. [Online]. Available at: http://www.madrid.es/UnidadWeb/Contenidos/Publicaciones/Tema Urbanismo/MemoGest2009/4ProyectosSingulares/1proyectomadridrio.pdf.

Arquitectos Urbanistas Ingenieros Asociados S.L.P. (2010). *Plan Director de rehabilitación del entorno del río Manzanares*. Ayuntamiento de Madrid Área de Gobierno de Urbanismo y Vivienda Coordinación General de Urbanismo Dirección Gral. de Planeamiento Urbanístico. [Online]. Available at: http://www.upv.es/contenidos/CAMUNISO/info/U0643712.pdf.

Ayuntamiento de Madrid. (2015). *Madrid Rio*. [Online]. Available at: http://www.madrid.es/portales/munimadrid/es/Inicio/Ayuntamiento/Urbanismo-e-Infraestructuras/Madrid-Rio? vgnextfmt=default&vgnextoid=5acc7f0917afc110VgnVCM2000000c205a0aRCRD& vgnextchannel=8dba171c30036010VgnVCM100000dc0ca8c0RCRD&idCapitulo=5015873 [Accessed 1 December 2015].

Burgos & Garrido Arquitectos, Porras la Casta Arquitectos and Rubio & Sala Arquitectos. (2011). *Madrid Río Project 2006–2011*.

EcoDiario. (2015a). *Carmena y Sara Hernández aprueban prolongar el parque de Madrid Río hasta Getafe*. [Online]. Available at: http://ecodiario.eleconomista.es/espana/noticias/7139693/11/15/Manuela-Carmena-y-Sara-Hernandez-aprueban-prolongar-Madrid-Rio-hasta-Getafe.html [Accessed 1 December 2015].

EcoDiario. (2015b). *Harvard distingue a Madrid Río con su primer premio de diseño urbano - EcoDiario.es*. [Online]. Available at: http://ecodiario.eleconomista.es/espana/noticias/7136442/11/15/Harvard-distingue-a-Madrid-Rio-con-su-primer-premio-de-diseno-urbano.html [Accessed 1 December 2015].

Esbjørn, A. (2013). *Madrid Río – a project that changed Madrid | ifhp.org*. [Online]. Available at: http://www.ifhp.org/ifhp-blog/madrid-r%C3%ADo-%E2%80%93-project-changed-madrid [Accessed 1 December 2015].

Esetena, J. (2010). *Pasión por Madrid: Proyecto Madrid Río, una mirada crítica*. [Online]. Available at: http://pasionpormadrid.blogspot.it/2010/01/una-mirada-critica-del-proyecto-madrid.html [Accessed 21 January 2016].

GoMadrid. (2015). *The Madrid Río Project, including the Madrid Beach*. [Online]. Available at: http://www.gomadrid.com/beach/ [Accessed 1 December 2015].

Jewell, N. (2011). *Madrid Rio by West 8 and MRIO*. [Online]. Available at: http://buildipe dia.com/aec-pros/urban-planning/madrid-rio-by-west-8-and-mrio [Accessed 1 December 2015].

Lòpez Garro, J. M. (2015). Madrid Río. *El País*. [Online]. Available at: http://elpais.com/elpais/2015/06/27/opinion/1435420262_421753.html [Accessed: 1 December 2015].

Mele, F. (2014). Da autostrada a parco sul fiume: il caso felice di Madrid Rìo. *Artwort*. [Online]. Available at: http://www.artwort.com/2014/04/11/architettura/autostrada-parco-fiume-caso-felice-madrid-rio/ [Accessed 1 December 2015].

Morley, R. (2011). *A View of Madrid: Madrid New Riverside Park - Madrid Rio*. [Online]. Available at: http://aviewofmadrid.blogspot.it/2011/06/madrid-new-riverside-park-madrid-rio.html [Accessed 28 January 2016].

País, E. E. (2008a). El proyecto 'Madrid Río' avanza a pesar de la crisis. *EL PAÍS*. [Online]. Available at: http://elpais.com/elpais/2008/12/03/actualidad/1228295824_850215.html [Accessed 1 December 2015].

País, E. E. (2008b). La pasarela Y, la bóveda y la tirabuzón. *EL PAÍS*. [Online]. Available at: http://elpais.com/elpais/2008/06/13/actualidad/1213345036_850215.html [Accessed 1 December 2015].

País, E. E. (2011). Madrid Río gana un galardón internacional de arquitectura. *El País*. [Online]. Available at: http://sociedad.elpais.com/sociedad/2011/10/31/actualidad/1320015601_850215.html [Accessed 1 December 2015].

Sànchez, E. (2013). La ciudad redescubre su río. *El País*. [Online]. Available at: http://ccaa.elpais.com/ccaa/2013/09/20/madrid/1379705209_396226.html [Accessed 1 December 2015].

Sharif, S. (2012). *Project Management: Rio Madrid Project*. [Online]. Available at: https://www.eoi.es/blogs/imsd/project-management-rio-madrid-project/ [Accessed 3 February 2016].

The Economist. (2009). Not working. *The Economist*. [Online]. Available at: http://www.economist.com/node/13611650 [Accessed 4 February 2016].

West 8. (2011). Madrid RIO. *West 8*. [Online]. Available at: http://www.west8.com/projects/madrid_rio [Accessed 1 December 2015].

Part C

Chapter 13.4
Paillon River, France – Opportunities and Policies

Paola Sabbion

Part C

13.4.1 Framework of French water policies

In France, the fundamental water policy principles derive from the law of December 16 1964, which structures water management within each drainage basin. The water policy is developed consulting water users, environmental protection associations, industrialists, farmers, and consumers within each basin. These actors are represented in committees, which define objectives and actions every 6 years within a master-scheme regarding water management, known as SDAGE (*Schéma Directeur d'Aménagement et de Gestion des Eaux*). SDAGE objectives apply to all aquatic environments and to all water bodies, surface waters and groundwater. The main goal of French water management policies is addressing environmental protection linking green and blue infrastructure. Moreover, in France, a comprehensive law on water and aquatic environments was adopted on 30 December 2006. This provision enables the country to meet European requirements (European Parliament, 2000), considering the adaptations to climate change. The law sets 4 main objectives: attaining a good chemical and ecological *status*, nondegradation of water bodies, pollution reduction and compliance with the guidelines related to protected areas (Ministère de l'Environnement, de l'Energie et de la Mer, 2007).

The Grenelle Environment Forum (2007) is another provision regulating water management and environmental protection. This project seeks to reduce biodiversity loss and landscape fragmentation, enabling and facilitating the genetic exchange necessary for the survival and movement of wild species. In particular, it addresses the valorisation and restoration of ecological corridors. It officially designates the green and blue network (*trame verte et bleue, TVB*), translating into practice the guidelines set by the European Ecological Network (Ministère de l'Environnement,

Urban Sustainability and River Restoration: Green and Blue Infrastructure, First Edition.
Katia Perini and Paola Sabbion.
© 2017 John Wiley & Sons Ltd. Published 2017 by John Wiley & Sons Ltd.

de l'Energie et de la Mer, 2007). According to this document, the green network includes: terrestrial natural and semi-natural habitats, protected areas designed for the preservation of biodiversity, ecological corridors within natural or semi-natural areas as well as linear vegetation connecting wider natural areas. The blue network includes: rivers, streams or channels, and wetlands where the preservation or restoration to good condition is a priority (Fédération des Parcs Naturels Régionaux, n.d.).

Furthermore, the National Biodiversity Strategy 2011-2020 (Premier Ministre, 2010) states that: "The resilience and functionality of ecosystems must be maintained or even reinforced in order to preserve the evolutionary processes required for them to adapt as well as to preserve biodiversity. [...] The green and blue infrastructure, which includes both reservoirs of biodiversity and elements ensuring connectivity across the whole infrastructure, must be designed in a coherent manner on all territorial levels. [...] Ecological continuities are notably based on what is termed 'ordinary biodiversity'. They can also be found in urban environments, where green and blue infrastructures could be created or reinforced". The French law of 12 July 2010 regulating the national commitment to the environment, known as Grenelle II, confirms these provisions by adding the following goals regarding water: reduction of pollutant discharge and diffusion, restoration of habitats and ecological corridors, optimisation of water consumption, and risk management, thus improving settlement planning, moving residential areas away from flood-prone areas and reducing the share of population exposed to this hazard.

The Paillon river catchment area is included in the Basin of Rhône and Coastal Rivers. Since 2004, in this area, priorities are specified in planning documents as the territorial coherence schemes (SCOT) or the local development plans (PLU; Direction Régionale de l'Environnement, de l'Aménagement et du Logement, 2013). Water policy is planned at different levels. At the main basin level, it is regulated through the SDAGE (*SI de l'eau Rhône-Méditerranée*). At a local scale, it is coordinated through a land use planning and water management contract, known as SAGE (*Schéma d'aménagement et de gestion des eaux*). SAGE, in particular, is envisaged for smaller coherent hydrographical units (e.g., single rivers or lakes). These measures define a shared, strategic vision among representatives of the basin committee for the SDAGE and the local water commissions for SAGE (Direction Régionale de l'Environnement, de l'Aménagement et du Logement, 2013).

13.4.2   Local policies and projects

As mentioned in Chapter 9.4, Nice is situated in the PACA (*Provence Alpes Côte d'Azur*) region, an area characterised by great natural diversity for its topography, geology, and climatology. The difference between aquatic environments is remarkable. This area comprises mountain streams and lakes, Mediterranean rivers, intermittent streams, ponds, lagoons, and marshes. Water resources in this area are generally abundant but unequally distributed among regional zones and have been allocated unevenly also in the past. The water distribution patterns also vary in Nice and in the nearby Paillon River basin. In this territory, regulating the transfer of water from the alpine zone to the densely populated coastal areas is the strategy adopted to compensate hydrogeological imbalances. Moreover, in this location, the pressure on water resources and aquatic natural environments is also crucial. Flooding, in fact, is linked to the torrential regime of the Paillon river and its tributaries, especially along the coast where urbanisation is higher (PACA, 2016).

The DREAL PACA, which is the local management body in this region (*Direction Régionale de l'Environnement, de l'Aménagement et du Logement de Provence Alpes Côte d'Azur*), identifies water as an element of the living environment and also as a feature for amenity and attractiveness. It adopts an integrated approach that leads to consider water either as an essential component of the territory or as an opportunity to counter landscape fragility. The main issues in this area are the alteration of its hydrogeology and morphology and local pollution (DREAL Auvergne Rhône-Alpes - SBRMPR Délégation de Bassin Rhône-Méditerranée, 2016). The PACA region is fully included in the SDAGE applied to the Rhône Mediterranean basin, which provides for basic orientations declined in provisions (Direction Régionale de l'Environnement, de l'Aménagement et du Logement, 2013). The SAGE steps (Dupont-Kerlan, 2016) and specific environment agreements have also been applied in a number of territories within the region. Nice, in particular, has been a priority area for the implementation of joint actions determining physical restoration and flood control of Paillons and Côtiers Est.

In the last decades, the demographic and urban evolution of the Nice conurbation has caused a significant mutation of the Paillon basin, featuring the decline of agriculture, increasing urbanisation in the hills and the progressive covering of the riverbed (Figure 13.4.2). If the protection of people and property against flood risks had been the priority, in those years, also water resource management, restoration and preservation of natural habitats could have been viable goals. This kind of approach, as mentioned in Chapter 9.4, was finally undertaken by the Paillons rivers contract established among local community actors on October 25, 2010 (Figure 13.4.3). This five-year agreement, based on a contractual financial

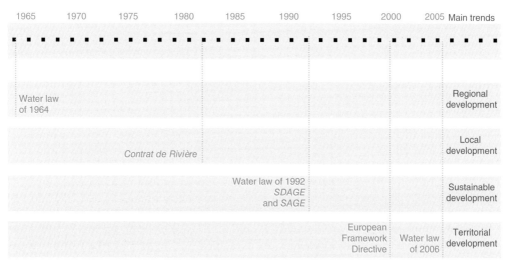

Figure 13.4.1   Water Policy in France (based on Ghiotti, 2006).

Part C

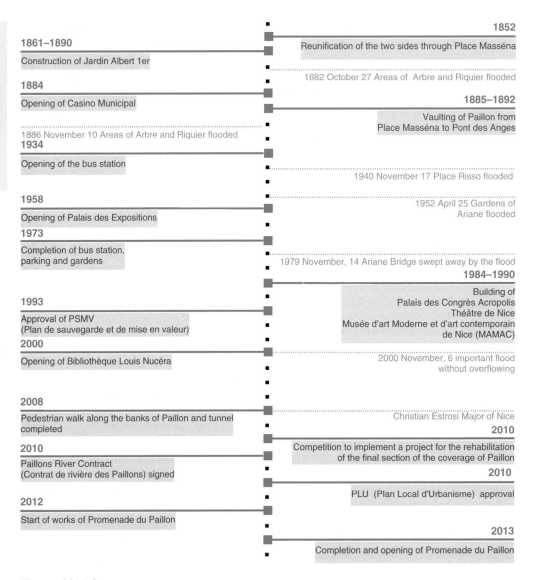

1852
Reunification of the two sides through Place Masséna

1861–1890
Construction of Jardin Albert 1er

1882 October 27 Areas of Arbre and Riquier flooded

1884
Opening of Casino Municipal

1885–1892
Vaulting of Paillon from
Place Masséna to Pont des Anges

1886 November 10 Areas of Arbre and Riquier flooded
1934
Opening of the bus station

1940 November 17 Place Risso flooded

1958
Opening of Palais des Expositions

1952 April 25 Gardens of
Ariane flooded

1973
Completion of bus station,
parking and gardens

1979 November, 14 Ariane Bridge swept away by the flood
1984–1990
Building of
Palais des Congrès Acropolis
Théâtre de Nice
Musée d'art Moderne et d'art contemporain
de Nice (MAMAC)

1993
Approval of PSMV
(Plan de sauvegarde et de mise en valeur)
2000
Opening of Bibliothèque Louis Nucéra

2000 November, 6 important flood
without overflowing

2008
Pedestrian walk along the banks of Paillon and tunnel
completed

Christian Estrosi Major of Nice
2010
Competition to implement a project for the rehabilitation
of the final section of the coverage of Paillon

2010
Paillons River Contract
(Contrat de rivière des Paillons) signed

2010
PLU (Plan Local d'Urbanisme) approval

2012
Start of works of Promenade du Paillon

2013
Completion and opening of Promenade du Paillon

Figure 13.4.2   Timeline of the Paillon River Transformations.

commitment has been signed by 45 members of the Paillons Committee including municipalities and public institutions involved in the river restoration and joint management practices. The *contrat de Rivière* is, in fact, a local contract (typically regarding a river), conceived for the first time in France in 1981. This financial and technical agreement between relevant partners addresses a concerted and sustainable scale regarding a coherent hydrographical unit. It is an important tool for the implementation of the SDAGE and its measurement programmes and it can also apply the SAGE guidelines. As explained in Chapter 9.4, the Paillons rivers contract ensures protection against floods, contributing to the management of water resources, and improves quality of habitat and water (SIP, 2016).

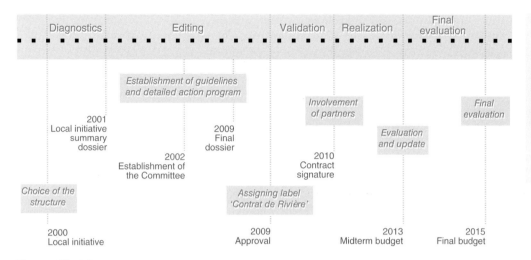

Figure 13.4.3   *Contrat de Rivière* of Paillons Process (based on SIP, 2016).

At a community level, since 2003, the Fishing Federation (*Fédération de pêchen*) and Intercommunal Union of Paillons (*Syndicat Intercommunal des Paillons*) lead an educational programme for school children, which is implemented by the Paillons rivers contract, and regards fishing and the aquatic environment. This project supports many activities conducted by local schools and institutions involved in the contract. It seeks to familiarise children with the river and its varied natural habitats. It fosters awareness on biological characteristics and it depicts the watershed as a rich and fragile entity that needs to be preserved. Thanks to the environmental laboratories devised within this programme, children experience the human impact on the ecosystem and learn to promote sustainability (SIP, 2016).

From an administrative point of view, 20 municipalities of Greater Nice compose the Paillon basin. The municipalities are gathered in four inter-municipal associations related to water management: SILCEN (Syndicat Intercommunal des Cantons de Levens, Contes, L'Escarène et Nice); SICTEU (Syndicat Intercommunal de Traitement des Eaux Usées); SIP (Syndicat Intercommunal des Paillons), SIVOM the Val de Banquière (Syndicat Intercommunal à Vocation Multiple). These public institutions coordinate actions to prevent floods and promote the restoration of the environment, the landscape and rivers, and to plan land use. Two main public institutions ensure inter-municipal cooperation: the Communauté d'Agglomération de Nice Côte d'Azur and the Communauté de Communes du Pays des Paillons. Studies and actions have been financed by the French Water Agency (Agence de l'eau Rhône Méditerranée Corse), PACA Region, General Council of Alpes Maritimes (Agence de l'eau Rhône Méditerranée Corse, 2016; Région Provence-Alpes-Côte d'Azur, 2016; Conseil-General des Alpes Maritimes, 2016; ONEMA, 2016).

The city's development is currently regulated by guidelines for territorial planning and sustainable development that include the preservation of natural areas, cultivated lands, forests and landscapes. The local PLU urban plan (*Plan Local d'Urbanisme*) determines the conditions to ensure the preservation of the quality of air, water, soil and subsoil, as well as natural resources, biodiversity, and green areas to attain ecological continuity and curb flood risk and pollution. The PLU is a tool to implement the use of green and blue infrastructure in urban planning and management. The Nice urban plan (2010), moreover, covers the entire territory of the city with the exception of the protected area Vieux-Nice, that is the subject to the PSMV (*Plan de Sauvegarde et de Mise en Valeur*) of 1993.

The guidelines of the *Projet d'Aménagement et de Développement Durable* (PADD) - which is part of the PLU - attempt to promote an innovative model of *eco-territory* in the Nice-Mediterranean area. This strategy revolves around the four key points advocated by the PLU urban project: landscape preservation and enhancement to develop a unique urban and natural environment; promotion of sustainable housing; support of sustainable transport; transforming Nice into an international metropolis. The PLU presents a vision and a political ambition for the territory. It defines the general intentions of the community and then sets the management rules, providing building guidelines, constructible and non-constructible areas, envisaged as natural and agricultural lands, as well as which zones are reserved for public facilities (Métropole Nice Cote d'Azur (a), 2016). The PLU effectively designs a sustainable city model, protecting woodlands, natural areas and urban parks and gardens, as well as the beds of the rivers and the surrounding valleys and wetlands. The protection of the watercourses, in particular, is ensured by the enhancement of the blue and green infrastructure. This policy, which is well structured within the territory, culminated in 2013 with the inauguration of the *Promenade du Paillon* linear park above the river. In 2010, this project won a competition to redesign a crucial city area, which was strongly supported and promoted by the mayor of Nice, Christian Estrosi. The linear park, designed by landscape architects Christine and Michael Péna, has devised 12 green hectares of green featuring southern Europe and Mediterranean plant species (Nice-Matin, 2010). The Promenade du Paillon has been awarded the first place in the Val'hor national landscaping competition in 2013 (*Victoires du Paysage*, organised every two years by the international horticulture and landscaping organisation *Val'hor*), as it has successfully transformed an abandoned place into a vital community area which citizens and tourists alike highly appreciate (Figure 13.4.4). This project has been realised in two phases and cost €33.4 million and has indeed permitted all residents and visitors to rediscover the river course (Le Moniteur, 2013), enhancing a green and blue infrastructure on top of the river (Figure 13.4.5).

Moreover, in 2002, prevention programmes against flooding (PAPI, *Programmes d'Actions de Prévention Contre les Inondations*) have been launched at a national level. These measures promoted integrated flood risk management in order to reduce harmful impacts on human health, property, and economic and environmental activities (Ministère de l'Environnement, de l'Energie et de la Mer, 2016). The National Flood Risk Management Strategy (SNGRI), planned in 2014, is part of the policies regarding the implementation of the Floods Directive policy. Natural risk prevention policies, as the latter, provide for knowledge of hazards and issues; surveillance, forecasting, vigilance and alert; education and preventive information; regulatory and risk prevention plans; reduced vulnerability; improved resilience and security; and climate change impact anticipation. As a result, in Nice, as explained in Chapter 9.4, the SAC flood alarm system has been set up.

Figure 13.4.4   Playground in the Promenade du Paillon (photo by Gian Luca Porcile).

Figure 13.4.5   Green and Blue Infrastructure Along the Promenade du Paillon (photo by Gian Luca Porcile).

Reducing vulnerability and increasing protection directly reduces the negative impacts of natural hazards. The Paillon River project also includes the construction of a hard-wearing concrete layer under the Nice Exhibition Centre to counter the torrential flow of the Paillon river. Moreover, in the Paillon catchment area, prevention measures comprise the construction of retention ponds and furthering wetland and mountain forests restoration where the river source is based.

As this initiative proves, the success of the Paillon River project is due to its broad scope that includes actions to reduce the intensity of flooding without neglecting the ecological, economic, social and collective aspects.

References

Agence de l'eau Rhône Méditerranée Corse. (2016). *Agence de l'eau Rhône Méditerranée Corse*. [Online]. Available at: http://www.eaurmc.fr/ [Accessed 30 January 2016].

Conseil-General des Alpes Maritimes. (2016). Conseil-General des Alpes Maritimes. *Conseil-General.com*. [Online]. Available at: http://www.conseil-general.com/en/departments/ french-general-councils/general-council-alpes-maritimes-department-06.htm [Accessed 31 January 2016].

Direction Régionale de l'Environnement, de l'Aménagement et du Logement. (2013). *Porter à connaissance DREAL PACA. SDAGE et urbanisme, des enjeux croisés, et une mise en compatibilité réglementaire*. Provence-Alpes-Cote d'Azur.

DREAL Auvergne Rhône-Alpes - SBRMPR Délégation de Bassin Rhône-Méditerranée. (2016). Les étapes d'élaboration du SDAGE 2016-2021. *rhone-mediterranee.eaufrance.fr*. [Online]. Available at: http://www.rhone-mediterranee.eaufrance.fr/gestion/sdage2016/ etapes.php [Accessed 12 February 2016].

Dupont-Kerlan, E. (2016). *Eaufrance*. [Online]. Available at: http://www.glossaire. eaufrance.fr/en/glossary/ [Accessed 12 February 2016].

European Parliament. (2000). *Directive 2000/60/EC of the European Parliament and of the Council of 23 October 2000 establishing a framework for Community action in the field of water policy*.

Fédération des Parcs Naturels Régionaux. (n.d.). *La Trame verte et bleue*. PNR. [Online]. Available at: http://www.ofme.org/documents/Accueil/Pres-TVB-Fede-des-PNR.pdf.

Ghiotti, S. (2006). Les Territoires de l'eau et la décentralisation. La gouvernance de bassin versant ou les limites d'une évidence. *Développement durable et territoires. Économie, géographie, politique, droit, sociologie*, (Dossier 6). [Online]. Available at: doi:10.4000/ developpementdurable.1742 [Accessed 14 February 2016].

Le Moniteur. (2013). *A Nice, un parc se coule dans le parcours du Paillon - Réalisations*. [Online]. Available at: http://www.lemoniteur.fr/article/a-nice-un-parc-se-coule-dans-le-parcours-du-paillon-22707119 [Accessed 14 February 2016].

Métropole Nice Cote d'Azur. (2016). *Le Plan Local d'Urbanisme*. [Online]. Available at: http://www.nicecotedazur.org/habitat-urbanisme/les-documents-d-urbanisme-en-vigueur/ nice-plu-new.

Ministère de l'Environnement, de l'Energie et de la Mer. (2007). *Le Grenelle de l'environnement de 2007 à 2012*. [Online]. Available at: http://www.developpement-durable.gouv.fr/-Le-Grenelle-de-l-environnement-de-.html.

Ministère de l'Environnement, de l'Energie et de la Mer. (2016). Les programmes d'actions de prévention contre les inondations (PAPI). http://www.developpement-durable.gouv. fr/. [Online]. Available at: http://www.developpement-durable.gouv.fr/Les-programmes-d-actions-de,24021.html.

Nice-Matin. (2010). *Une coulée verte jusqu'à la mer*. [Online]. Available at: http://archives. nicematin.com/article/nice/une-coulee-verte-jusqua-la-mer.370551.html [Accessed 30 January 2016].

ONEMA. (2016). Onema. *L'Office national de l'eau et des milieux aquatiques*. [Online]. Available at: http://www.onema.fr/ [Accessed 31 January 2016].

PACA, I. D. (2016). *DREAL PACA*. [Online]. Available at: http://www.paca.developpement-durable.gouv.fr/ [Accessed 31 January 2016].

Premier Ministre. (2010). *National Biodiversity Strategy, NBS (Stratégie nationale de la biodiversité, SNB)*. Ministère de l'Écologie, du Développement durable, des Transports et du Logement.

Région Provence-Alpes-Côte d'Azur. (2016). *Région Provence-Alpes-Côte d'Azur*. [Online]. Available at: http://www.regionpaca.fr/ [Accessed 30 January 2016].

SIP. (2016). *Rivière Paillons*. [Online]. Available at: http://www.riviere-paillons.fr/index. php [Accessed 30 January 2016].

Part C

Chapter 13.5
River Thames, England – Opportunities and Policies

Paola Sabbion

13.5.1 Water policy framework and planning strategies

The United Kingdom is tackling the anthropic impact on water, addressing especially the effects of increasing urbanisation determined by population growth (Batterbee *et al.*, 2012). In particular, a series of strategies – which started in 2008 with DEFRA official communication and will end in 2030 – have been devised at national level to achieve flood risk reduction, improve water quality, and decrease sewer loads through an integrated surface water and drainage system management (DEFRA, 2008). The Environment Agency has implemented a Directive for flood and coastal erosion risk management, *Making Space for Water*, developed in agreement with involved stakeholders and also through public consultations (DEFRA, 2005).

It is estimated that, in the Thames area, approximately 45,000 properties are at risk of flooding (100-year recurrence interval). A very large network of defences is already in place, but the protection provided could gradually diminish due to the devastating impact of climate change. The government's flood and coastal erosion risk management is attempting to prevent economic losses from natural disasters. *Thames Estuary 2100* is a long-term strategic project designed by the Environment Agency for the Estuary area, based on the prediction of sea level rise following climate change (DEFRA, 2008).

For many decades, the River Thames has been the focus of economic, historical, and environmental interest. The creation of the London Docklands Development Corporation, in 1981, has led to the regeneration of the Docklands and of the Isle of Dogs. Since the 1990s, the wider Thames Gateway area, between Canary Wharf and the North Sea, has been gaining increasing attention. In fact, it is ideal for urban regeneration due to the high availability of brownfield land. In November 2007, the Department for Communities and Local Government set out in the Delivery Plan the main goals for the revitalisation of the Thames Gateway. In 2010,

Urban Sustainability and River Restoration: Green and Blue Infrastructure, First Edition.
Katia Perini and Paola Sabbion.
© 2017 John Wiley & Sons Ltd. Published 2017 by John Wiley & Sons Ltd.

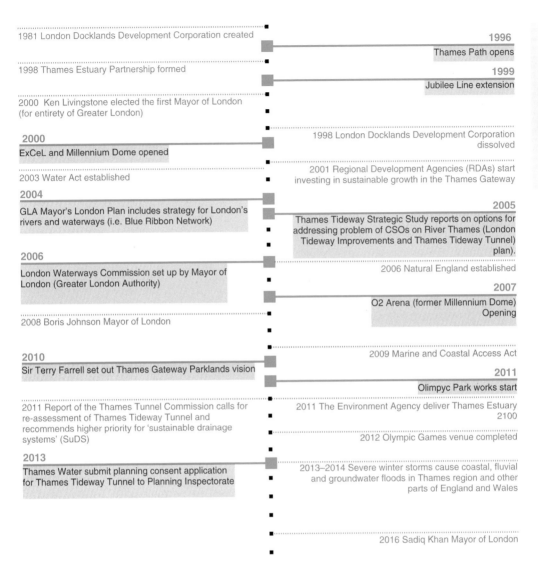

1981 London Docklands Development Corporation created

1996
Thames Path opens

1998 Thames Estuary Partnership formed

1999
Jubilee Line extension

2000 Ken Livingstone elected the first Mayor of London
(for entirety of Greater London)

2000
ExCeL and Millennium Dome opened

1998 London Docklands Development Corporation
dissolved

2003 Water Act established

2001 Regional Development Agencies (RDAs) start
investing in sustainable growth in the Thames Gateway

2004
GLA Mayor's London Plan includes strategy for London's
rivers and waterways (i.e. Blue Ribbon Network)

2005
Thames Tideway Strategic Study reports on options for
addressing problem of CSOs on River Thames (London
Tideway Improvements and Thames Tideway Tunnel)
plan).

2006
London Waterways Commission set up by Mayor of
London (Greater London Authority)

2006 Natural England established

2007
O2 Arena (former Millennium Dome)
Opening

2008 Boris Johnson Mayor of London

2010
Sir Terry Farrell set out Thames Gateway Parklands vision

2009 Marine and Coastal Access Act

2011
Olimpyc Park works start

2011 Report of the Thames Tunnel Commission calls for
re-assessment of Thames Tideway Tunnel and
recommends higher priority for 'sustainable drainage
systems' (SuDS)

2011 The Environment Agency deliver Thames Estuary
2100

2012 Olympic Games venue completed

2013
Thames Water submit planning consent application
for Thames Tideway Tunnel to Planning Inspectorate

2013–2014 Severe winter storms cause coastal, fluvial
and groundwater floods in Thames region and other
parts of England and Wales

2016 Sadiq Khan Mayor of London

Figure 13.5.1 The River Thames Timeline.

Sir Terry Farrell – a prominent British architect and urban designer – delivered his vision for the Thames Gateway Parklands (Figure 13.5.1). In 2012, the Olympic Games venue was located along the River Thames, driving the successful redevelopment of its surroundings (Figure 13.5.2).

In recent years, brownfield regeneration has become a focal point of sustainable planning. Sustainability is based on a more environmentally/ecologically-oriented framework in comparison with traditional building strategies, effectively engaging local communities during the renovation process. Brownfields occupy the greatest portion of the Thames Gateway. Usually this type of land has been previously developed and is often derelict or vacant, and sometimes contaminated by various pollutants. The presence of brownfields usually implies the lack of

Figure 13.5.2   The O2 Arena (photo by Jørgen K. H. Knudsen).

agricultural cultivations and, in the past, it has contributed to reduce urban sprawl and greenfield expansion (Dixon, 2007). Some critics comment that redevelopment can be defined sustainable only if it respects specific parameters in terms of its design, construction, participation and future uses (Williams and Dair, 2007).

In UK, government interest in brownfield redevelopment started in the late 1990s. There has since been an ongoing debate over sustainable brownfield regeneration, which is founded on social, environmental, and economic goals (Dixon, 2007). The Thames Gateway has rapidly become the symbol of a new planning policy in the United Kingdom (Miliband, 2005), representing the transition from a traditional vertical strategy (based on hierarchical structures) to new horizontal forms of governance. It has been defined as the expression of a regionalised and integrated planning practice (Raco, 2005; Allmendinger and Haughton, 2009). This desired multilevel governance is based on the development of a network of agencies working at different spatial scales. The latter involve government, local authorities, private institutions and citizens (Brownill and Carpenter, 2009).

In this context, institutions from both the public and private sectors, have set the groundwork for more adaptive interconnections and networking, focusing on the growing importance of cities and regions (Greenwood and Newman, 2010). In the case of the Thames Gateway, however, relationships between the central government and the regional and local authorities are complex and are undergoing continual change. The interactions between traditional and contemporary forms of planning appear "complex, multilayered, fluid and occasionally fuzzy" (Allmendinger and Haughton, 2009). The success of the new planning system will depend on coordination capacities and public participation implemented by public bodies, such as the Regional Assemblies and the three Regional Development Agencies (RDAs) involved in this project.

13.5.2   Local policies and projects

The Thames Gateway is an area crossing three English regions administered by 19 local authorities, including eight London boroughs. Different government ministers and officials have been involved in the development of this strategic sub-region. In 2003, the Sustainable Communities Bill has identified the Thames Gateway as one of the key growth areas for the UK (ODPM, 2005). In fact, the Thames Gateway region is intended to transform the South East region, responding to the demand for housing by regenerating existing towns and brownfields, and creating new carbon-neutral urban development (Royal Geographical Society (with IBG), 2015). In 2003, a Cabinet Committee chaired by the Prime Minister was appointed to oversee the Gateway renovation. The Department for Communities and Local Government thus established the Thames Gateway Directorate, to coordinate and develop the Thames Gateway policy (NAO, 2007). The Department for Communities and Local Government (DCLG, formerly ODPM), the Department for Transport, and the Department for Environment, Food and Rural Affairs have also been involved in this project. Moreover, a series of sub-regional agencies, including the Urban Development Corporations and the Olympic Development Authority have taken part to the Thames Gateway development (Greenwood and Newman, 2010).

Three different regions - London, East of England and South East - relying on separate assemblies and development agencies currently have a role in this project. In addition, there are numerous non-governmental organisations participating in the regeneration initiative. From 2005 to 2013, two non-departmental bodies – the Thurrock Thames Gateway Development Corporation and the London Thames Gateway Development Corporation – have been responsible for the redevelopment of land and new housing. Several partnerships have also been created in London, Kent and South Essex and are based on forms of public-private collaboration aimed at facilitating the coordination of local authorities, private companies and charitable organisations. This multifaceted context, defined as "multilevel governance", represents a shift from centralised governance to decentralised control exercised by a variety of agencies at different spatial scales (Figure 13.5.3; Brownill and Carpenter, 2009).

The Thames Gateway includes different areas with a rich heritage and identity, and features derelict industrial premises, natural terrains, agricultural lands, and historic locations. More than 8,600 ha, 11% of the Thames Gateway's land, is currently protected by national or international nature conservation designations (Farrell et al., 2010). The Thames Gateway Parklands Programme, delivered in 2010 through three local Green Greed Parterships and by Sir Terry Farrell who is in charge of the regeneration project, helps provide a strategic context. The main target is to create an accessible and coherent landscape, regenerating, developing and connecting urban and rural open spaces. The other key objective is environmental restoration. Attaining these two goals will improve the quality of life for

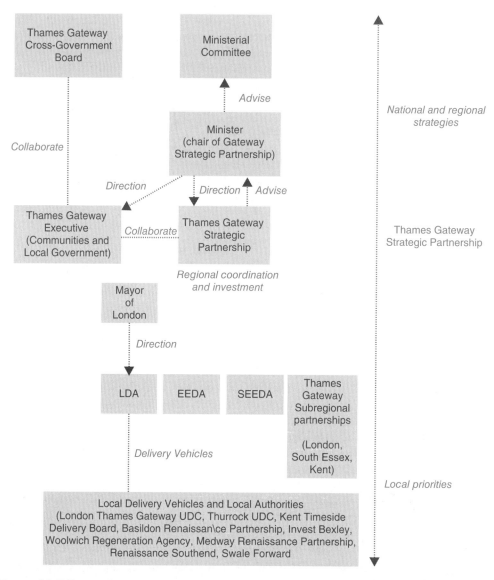

Figure 13.5.3 Conceptual Framework of Governance and Delivery Structures in the Thames Gateway, Based on (Brownill and Carpenter, 2009).

residents, create employment opportunities and attract a high number of visitors. These objectives are of key importance and have been identified in collaboration with the Government and local organisations. In particular, the Thames Gateway Parklands Programme has been delivered by East London Green Grid, South Essex Green Grid and Greening the Gateway Kent & Medway. The East London Green Grid is also part of *London's Great Outdoors*, a wider programme of public space improvement. The North Kent and South Essex Green Grid Partnerships are part of the regeneration initiative for the outer gateway area, aligned with the North Kent and South Essex Gateway Partnerships (Farrell *et al.*, 2010). Landscape renovation is also implemented according to the Thames Gateway

Figure 13.5.4   Margate to All Hallows (photo by Victor Keegan).

Figure 13.5.5   Margate (photo by Victor Keegan).

Estuary 2100 Plan (the main flood risk project in the UK based on climate change adaptation, and established by the Environment Agency in 2002), which seeks to improve the estuarine habitat and reduce tidal flood risk, encouraging flood resilience. According to this project, in fact, walls protecting the Gateway marshes should be eliminated making space for water, to prevent floods thanks to land absorption, thus restoring the natural water cycle (Figures 13.5.4, 13.5.5).

The global Gateway Parklands Programme includes 637 ha of new greenspace, 2013 ha of enhanced greenspace, 7 km of new links to the Thames Estuary Path (a 46.6km-path along the Thames through the South Essex Marshes, from Tilbury Town all the way to Leigh-on-Sea), 10 new bridges, 10.3 km of watercourses and restored canals, 110 ha of improved SSSIs (Site of Special Scientific Interest), 118 ha of new and enhanced habitats, 275 ha of remediated brownfield land, and 1,070 properties with a reduced flood-risk status. Moreover, the Thames Estuary Path will be implemented according to the Environment Agency's Thames Estuary 2100 project for the enhancement of riverine habitat (Farrell *et al.*, 2010). The Parklands can link urban settlements to environmental and recreational resources available for the resident population and visitors. The new Parklands Programme vision has set the River Thames as one of the main transport corridors in Thames Gateway, featuring nature trails, footpaths and cycle routes.

13.5.3   Project costs and benefits

Public resources have a crucial role for the Gateway's success. Partnerships, diverse funding streams and delivery mechanisms are also necessary. The Regional Development Agencies of London, East of England and South East and the Communities & Local Government have committed to support the Thames Gateway Economic Development Investment Plan. Together they have provided £200 million over the first three years with the aim of leveraging an additional £75 million from other sources. Since 2001, the three RDAs have invested around £600 million in sustainable growth in the Thames Gateway, predominantly in partnership projects resulting in a significant local outcome. According to the Plan, the Gateway development is estimated to contribute an additional £12 billion per annum to the UK economy (EEDA *et al.*, n.d.).

The All London Green Grid (ALGG) policy framework promotes the design and delivery of green infrastructure in London (GLA, 2016). The Green Grid Partnerships coordinate a network of public authorities, commercial and no-profit organisations, thanks to strategic planning based on local information and development to deliver financial investment. The three Green Grid Partnerships seek to collect necessary investments from public, charitable and commercial sources at local, national and European levels. The partnerships work to maximise the environmental value of greenspace investments through cultural projects and sporting events to encourage sustainable tourism, educational activities, and volunteer networks. Partnerships also support investments in green infrastructure, promoting sustainable drainage systems, green routes, and green roof technologies among engineers, architects, planners, and developers through the 'Grey to Green infrastructure agenda'.

The initial government investment – £31.76 million allocated by the Homes and Communities Agency – has more than doubled to £69 million thanks to match-funding and joint initiatives among public authorities, local organisations and communities. The coordination among planning authorities across North Kent and South Essex has helped to integrate Green Grid strategies in the Local Development Frameworks and Local Investment Plans. A constant cooperation among local authorities, commercial companies, and Natural England (a non-departmental public body established in 2006, sponsored by the Department for Environment, Food & Rural Affairs and promoting green infrastructure delivering) has allowed for the development of supporting projects and events. The three Green Grid Partnerships have successfully joined forces with the government and have assisted with practical implementation at the ground level (Farrell *et al.*, 2010).

Despite these efforts, the government has been criticised for seemingly moving the agenda from regeneration to housing growth (Royal Geographical Society, 2015), but traditional planning is slowly being replaced by new practices and it performs a decisive role in the complex "metagovernance" of the Thames Gateway (Allmendinger and Haughton, 2007). The decision-making process regarding large-scale projects is still managed with traditional methods; central government departments are responsible for financial support and strategic transport infrastructure (i.e. London Gateway Port; Greenwood and Newman, 2010). This can constitute a hindrance to successful sustainable development. Traditional institutional planning, in fact, is structured by market-oriented objectives that can invalidate true forms of participation (Peel and Lloyd, 2007). This type of governance can generate "conflicting goals of economic competitiveness and social and environmental sustainability, between horizontal, networked governance and [...] hierarchical direction and between a focus on delivery and participatory governance" (Brownill and Carpenter, 2009). Due to its complexity, Thames Gateway planning policy final results are still uncertain, even if the Thames Gateway revitalisation is a compelling matter due to London's population growth. It will inevitably require further planning efforts, as t represents "the work of decades not years" (Rogers, 2013).

Anyway, fifteen new major parklands projects are currently underway across the Thames Gateway. The renovation scheme will provide 267,000 m^2 of new or enhanced greenspace, 95 km of additional footpaths and cycleways, 10 km of improved watercourses, five new visitor/education centres with associated learning programmes. Many of the East London Green Grid projects are funded through London's Great Outdoors initiative. The success of the first 15 Parklands should promote confidence needed for any following investments. The project concerns several areas: Lea River, Erith, Dagenham, Rainham, Thurrock, Dartford, Medway, South Essex, Canvey Wick, and Milton Creek and connects new areas with existent parks, natural reserves, and paths (Figure 13.5.6; Farrell *et al.*, 2010).

The regeneration of lands, increased accessibility and new links between communities and open spaces will help to reinforce local identity. The Community Parklands strategy will help to enhance the Thames Gateway's value and will improve quality of life by providing access to nature, cultural activities, local festivals and sport events. Moreover, the renovation offers opportunities, such as community engagement, horticulture, local food production and the construction of educational facilities. This has already been achieved with many previous projects like the Olympic Legacy Park, Flag Riverside Country Park, Rainham Marshes, Lea Valley Park, Greenwich Peninsula, and Shorne Woods Country Park (DCLG, 2008).

Many volunteers' organisations are active in the Thames area. For example, FROG, the Foreshore Recording & Observation Group, is an active community group formed by over 400 volunteers trained in foreshore recording techniques. The FROG members work with the Thames Discovery Programme (TDP) archaeologists to

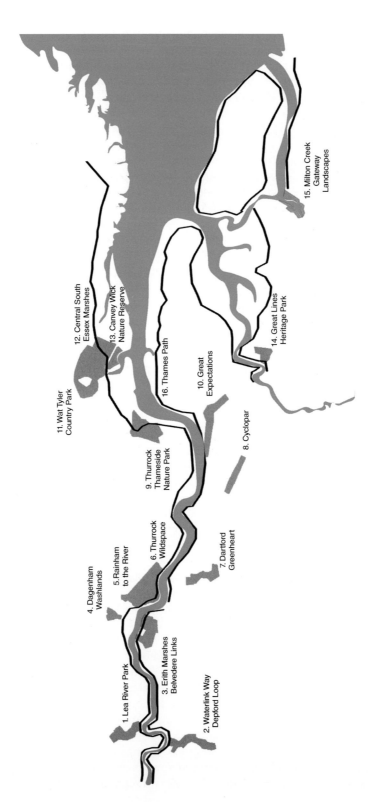

11. Wat Tyler Country Park

12. Central South Essex Marshes

13. Canvey Wick Nature Reserve

15. Milton Creek Gateway Landscapes

16. Thames Path

10. Great Expectations

14. Great Lines Heritage Park

8. Cyclopar

4. Dagenham Washlands

5. Rainham to the River

6. Thurrock Wildspace

9. Thurrock Thameside Nature Park

7. Dartford Greenheart

1. Lea River Park

3. Erith Marshes Belvedere Links

2. Waterlink Way Depford Loop

Figure 13.5.6   Projects Under Way Across the Thames Gateway, Based on Thames Gateway Parklands (Farrell *et al.*, 2010)

Figure 13.5.7 Thames Foreshore (Rotherhithe; photo by Victor Keegan).

Figure 13.5.8 Uncovering Old Wooden Structures by Thames Discovery Volunteers Near London Bridge (photo by Victor Keegan).

monitor the archaeological interest of objects found on the Thames intertidal zones (FROG, 2016). "Mudlarking" in the River Thames, which is the search of items in the mud, is a traditional activity for Londoners and there are dozens of groups and volunteers looking at the riverbanks as a great open-air archaeological site freely accessible to the public. They work to strengthen even further the connection between people and the Estuary by adapting and reinterpreting existing landscapes and improving accessibility to the waterfront (Figures 13.5.7, 13.5.8).

References

Allmendinger, P. and Haughton, G. (2007). The Fluid Scales and Scope of UK Spatial Planning. *Environment and Planning A*, 39 (6), p. 1478–1496. [Online]. Available at: doi:10.1068/a38230.

Allmendinger, P. and Haughton, G. (2009). Soft Spaces, Fuzzy Boundaries, and Metagovernance: The New Spatial Planning in the Thames Gateway. *Environment and Planning A*, 41 (3), p. 617–633. [Online]. Available at: doi:10.1068/a40208.

Batterbee, R., Heathwaite, L., Lane, S. N., McDonald, A., Newson, M., Smith, H., Staddon, C., and Wharton, G. (2012). *Water policy in the UK: The challenges*. In: 2012, Royal Geographical Society. [Online]. Available at: http://eprints.lancs.ac.uk/56158/1/RGS_IBG_Policy_Document_Water_7_32pp.pdf [Accessed 8 April 2016].

Brownill, S. and Carpenter, J. (2009). Governance and 'Integrated' Planning: The Case of Sustainable Communities in the Thames Gateway, England. *Urban Studies*, 46 (2), p. 251–274. [Online]. Available at: doi:10.1177/0042098008099354.

DCLG. (2008). *Thames Gateway Parklands vision*. London: Department for Communities and Local Government.

DEFRA. (2005). *Making Space for Water. Developing a new Government strategy for flood and coastal erosion risk management in England*. DEFRA, London.

DEFRA. (2008). *Future Water:The Government's water strategy for England*. Department for Environment Food and Rural Affairs. [Online]. Available at: https://www.gov.uk/government/uploads/system/uploads/attachment_data/file/69346/pb13562-future-water-080204.pdf [Accessed 8 April 2016].

Dixon, T. (2007). The Property Development Industry and Sustainable Urban Brownfield Regeneration in England: An Analysis of Case Studies in Thames Gateway and Greater Manchester. *Urban Studies*, 44 (12), p. 2379–2400. [Online]. Available at: doi:10.1080/00420980701540887.

EEDA, LDA and SEEDA. (n.d.). *Thames Gateway Economic Development Investment Plan*. [Online]. Available at: http://www.secouncils.gov.uk/wp-content/uploads/pdfs/_publications/TGED_InvestmentPlan.pdf [Accessed 26 April 2016].

Farrell, T., Martin, P., Johnson, B., Lynes, K., and Chambers, R. (2010). *Thames Gateway Parklands:Delivering Environmental Transformation*. London Development Agency.

FROG. (2016). *Thames Discovery Programme*. [Online]. Available at: http://www.thamesdiscovery.org/frog-blog/ [Accessed: 19 May 2016].

GLA. (2016). *All London Green Grid. London City Hall*. [Online]. Available at: https://www.london.gov.uk/what-we-do/environment/parks-green-spaces-and-biodiversity/all-london-green-grid [Accessed 19 May 2016].

Greenwood, D. and Newman, P. (2010). Markets, Large Projects and Sustainable Development: Traditional and New Planning in the Thames Gateway. *Urban Studies*, 47 (1), p. 105–119. [Online]. Available at: doi:10.1177/0042098009346864.

Miliband, D. (2005). *Thames Gateway: greenfi elds for innovation. Speech given to the Thames Gateway Forum, 23 November*.

NAO. (2007). *The Thames Gateway: Laying the Foundations*. Bourn, J. (ed.). The National Audit Office. [Online]. Available at: www.nao.org.uk.

ODPM. (2005). *Creating sustainable communities. Delivering the Thames Gateway*. [Accessed 18 April 2016].

Peel, D. and Lloyd, M. G. (2007). Neo-traditional planning. Towards a new ethos for land use planning? *Land Use Policy*, 24 (2), p. 396–403. [Online]. Available at: doi:10.1016/j.landusepol.2006.05.003.

Raco, M. (2005). A Step Change or a Step Back? The Thames Gateway and the Re-birth of the Urban Development Corporations. *Local Economy*, 20 (2), p. 141–153. [Online]. Available at: doi:10.1080/13575270500053241.

Rogers, B. (2013). Whatever happened to the Thames Gateway? *Centre for London.* [Online]. Available at: http://centreforlondon.org/whatever-happened-to-the-thames-gateway/ [Accessed 16 June 2016].

Royal Geographical Society (with IBG). (2015). The Thames Gateway. *21st Century Challenges.* [Online]. Available at: https://21stcenturychallenges.org/the-thames-gateway/ [Accessed 19 May 2016].

Williams, K. and Dair, C. (2007). A framework for assessing the sustainability of brownfield developments. *Journal of Environmental Planning and Management*, 50 (1), p. 23–40. [Online]. Available at: doi:10.1080/09640560601048275.

Part C

Chapter 13.6
Emscher River, Germany – Opportunities and Policies

Katia Perini

13.6.1   Project development

The restoration of the Emscher River concerned its entire length, covering 80 km. This is one of the largest European renovation projects with an investment totalling €4.5 billion. It was devised in the Ruhr district, the most densely populated German region (Dutch Water Sector, 2012), in the federal North Rhine Westphalia Länder. The project development and implementation lasted about 30 years and featured the creation of the Emscher Landscape Park, focused on the preservation and reuse of abandoned industrial buildings and premises (Figure 13.6.1). The renovation has led to ecological, environmental, and aesthetic improvements in a critical area during the post-industrial stage. As described in Chapter 9.6, in fact, the devastating consequences of industrial production (especially mining) have been limited thanks to accurate and long-term planning, extensive investments, technical design, and specific construction techniques. The adaptive reuse and conversion of relics and infrastructures of the industrial era is a very interesting feature. It is contributing to restore the Emscher River and the Ruhr valley, at the same time carving a unique identity for this region. This area has also been revitalised by arts, cultural and recreational events (such as concerts) and the construction of new open spaces and sport facilities, as hiking trails and climbing walls (Dac&Cities, 2014). Therefore, the Emscher conversion has renovated the river's hydrologic conditions and has increased "regional resilience by making a major contribution to improving quality of life" (Lucas, 2011).

The main actor of the Emscher River restoration has been the Emschergenossenschaft, the first German water management association. This self-managed non-profit public association was founded in 1899 to face the issues related to industrialisation and its negative consequences on the river. Its purpose is to protect the environment, promote better ecological conditions and a high quality

Urban Sustainability and River Restoration: Green and Blue Infrastructure, First Edition.
Katia Perini and Paola Sabbion.

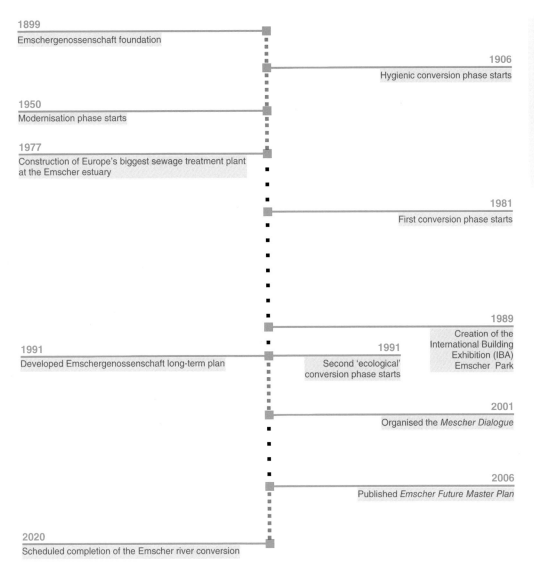

1899
Emschergenossenschaft foundation

1906
Hygienic conversion phase starts

1950
Modernisation phase starts

1977
Construction of Europe's biggest sewage treatment plant at the Emscher estuary

1981
First conversion phase starts

1989
Creation of the International Building Exhibition (IBA) Emscher Park

1991
Developed Emschergenossenschaft long-term plan

1991
Second 'ecological' conversion phase starts

2001
Organised the *Mescher Dialogue*

2006
Published *Emscher Future Master Plan*

2020
Scheduled completion of the Emscher river conversion

Figure 13.6.1   The Emscher River Timeline.

of life, achieving sustainability considering humanity' and nature's needs (Boon and Raven, 2012; WIKUE, 2013). This water board envisages measures "aimed at maintaining and further developing the beneficial effects of water for the overall ecosystem, (urban) landscape and people". Its members – local authorities and companies – deal with the issues relevant to the riverine area thanks to an integrated strategy. The decision-making process, in fact, is based on active participation (Emschergenossenschaft, 2016). Moreover, experts and specialists working in different fields can make their contribution and this allows considering all aspects related to stormwater management in a broad context, on the basis of a holistic approach (WIKUE, 2013). The Ruhrverband is another influential non-profit water management company operating in this region to increase citizens' wellbeing

Part C

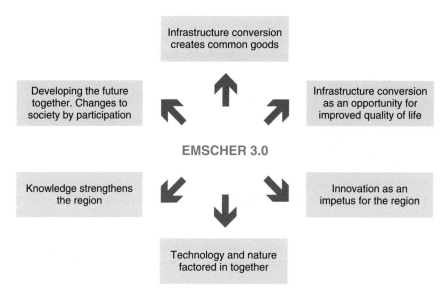

Figure 13.6.2   The Main Objective of the Emscher's Revitalisation (based on WIKUE, 2013).

and preserve the environment. It supplies drinking and non-drinking water (for companies and hydroelectric power production) and treats wastewater and water runoff to secure floodwater flow, dispose and recycle residues from sewage treatment, as well as analyse water management conditions (Ruhrverband, 2016).

The Wuppertal Institute, a German research body (WIKUE, 2013) in its report *Emscher 3.0* identifies the main conversion phases of the river from the past century to the present: the hygienic conversion phase (1906–1949); the Modernisation phase (1950–1982); the first conversion phase centred on research and testing (1981–1990); and the second 'ecological' conversion phase (1991-present, Figure 13.6.2; WIKUE, 2013). Following the foundation of the Emschergenossenschaft, during the hygienic conversion phase, cities, local communities and several companies including mining firms were involved in a common effort to sanitise industrial and domestic wastewater, preventing the discharge of contaminants into the Emscher River that created dangerous and unhealthy conditions. The Modernisation phase occurred when the industrial production was decreasing but population growth required the construction of numerous new pumping stations (Emschergenossenschaft *et al.*, 1999). In this period, the Emschergenossenschaft built Europe's biggest sewage treatment plant at the Emscher estuary in Dinslaken, which started operating in 1977 (WIKUE, 2013).

In 1989, the creation of the International Building Exhibition (*Internationale Bauausstellung*), – the IBA Emscher Park – was a turning point in the river restoration. The IBA was designed to raise awareness on the renovation process and create a positive green image for the former industrial areas. For 10 years, between 1990 and 1999, it helped to improve ecological, economic, and urban conditions along the Emscher River. It was managed by the state of North Rhine-Westphalia, the Federal Government and 17 local authorities (Dac&Cities, 2014). The restoration of this area was conceived, implementing a holistic approach and considering economic, environmental, and social aspects. As a result, a landscape park was built along the river and an administrative structure was devised for this ten-year framework (Shaw, 2002; Labelle, 2001). International competitions and seminars contributed to IBA's renewal, and, in total, 120 new river restoration projects were completed (Labelle, 2001; Landschaftspark, 2016).

According to Labelle (2001), IBA was highly innovative due to several reasons. Firstly, ecology was its central focus: industrial areas were converted into parkland, recreation areas, and cultural resources, launching the largest renaturation project in Europe (Figures 13.6.3, 13.6.4, 13.6.5, 13.6.6). Reusing industrial buildings and spaces was economically sustainable and in line with the basic ecological, social and cultural concepts of the project (Landschaftspark, 2016). The creation of "industrial monuments" played a key role in allowing residents to consider the effects and traces left by industrialisation as a valuable heritage for the new economy of the region (Labelle, 2001).

The IBA Emscher Park was also crucial to the Emscher restoration, creating green areas along the river, bike and pedestrian paths contributing to regional and urban development and planning (WIKUE, 2013). When IBA expired, "Project Ruhr" was devised to continue the clean-up of the Emscher River (Dac&Cities, 2014). In 1991, the Emschergenossenschaft decided to develop an ambitious long-term plan (expected to last two decades) to convert the river infrastructure system, channelling wastewater into underground canals (WIKUE, 2013). As described in Chapter 9.6, in the past, the subsidences deriving from the coal mining had prevented the installation of an underground sewer system. As a consequence, the river had become an "open sewer" (Deutschland, 2014). Following the construction of many pilot projects, the catchment-wide implementation

Figure 13.6.3   The IBA Emscher Park (photo by Valentina Rossotti).

Figure 13.6.4 The IBA Emscher Park (photo by Valentina Rossotti).

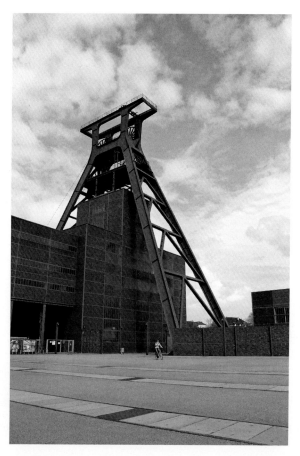

Figure 13.6.5 The IBA Emscher Park (photo by Valentina Rossotti).

Figure 13.6.6   The IBA Emscher Park (photo by Valentina Rossotti).

phase started in 2000. So far, several components of this complex infrastructure have been completed, like local sewage-treatment plants and sewage canals (more than half; Dutch Water Sector, 2012; Emschergenossenschaft, 2009; Deutschland, 2014). The completion of the 421-km underground canals is scheduled for 2017 (WIKUE, 2013). The environmental reconstruction of the river landscape is expected to be completed by 2020 (Dutch Water Sector, 2012; European Investment Bank, 2016). Infrastructure and technical strategies have a prominent role, but the restoration focuses specifically on a wide range of objectives: ecological development, safe wastewater transport and treatment, flood prevention, water balance improvement, and new recreational spaces (Figure 13.6.2; Sieker *et al.*, 2006).

Since 2001, the Emschergenossenschaft has organised the 'Mescher Dialogue' initiative which comprises a series of workshops and discussions to integrate the expertise offered by planners, environmental agencies, companies, and city departments participating in the renovation programme. As a result, in 2006, the Emschergenossenschaft published the Emscher Future Master Plan. The latter presents a comprehensive, long-term approach to coordinate water management, urban and ecological progress and design aspects. It addresses the renovation of several sections of the river, attempting to create a common network and shared pool of knowledge regarding different projects, when feasible. The Master Plan was drafted to communicate opportunities and benefits of the restoration to public authorities – that is, several different bodies are involved, as the river crosses numerous administrative borders – and local residents (WIKUE, 2013). It is managed thanks to regional planning, avoiding a top-down approach. All involved actors, in fact, "jointly develop regional planning goals in a constant dialogue and so make use of possible management frameworks" (Gerdes *et al.*, 2005). The Master Plan focuses on the following fundamental aspects (Emschergenossenschaft, 2006): flood protection, enhancing ecological restoration, designing leisure and recreational facilities, improving quality of life, unlocking economic potential, raising awareness on local history, devising strategies to attract visitors and emphasising continuity with past projects to stress the outstanding importance of this renovation initiative.

13.6.2 Policies and participation

Seventeen total local authorities are involved in the management of the Emscher River and its tributaries (Labelle, 2001). The Emscher conversion demonstrates that regional cooperation beyond the classic administrative boundaries can make a difference (WIKUE, 2013). For example, all the cities of the region cooperate with the Federal Ministry for the Environment and the Emschergenossenschaft. Public and private property owners support the project, reducing stormwater runoff to decrease rainwater and clean water inflows in the drainage system. This is a fundamental task, which has contributed to diminish runoff by 15% from 2005 to 2020 (Sieker *et al.*, 2006).

Community involvement has also been very important for the project development. In fact, during its implementation, new constructions were built in a densely inhabited area and a careful balance had to be maintained to avoid environmental alterations. Public participation was at a shallow level (information and formal consultation), but local communities were generally in favour of the Emscher conversion project (Heldt *et al.*, 2016). The Emschergenossenschaft was the major decision maker and local communities did not play an active role but supported the project (Budryte and Perini, 2016). According to Skodra (2014), involving citizens in the planning process during an urban transformation phase allows for tailor-made solutions. In this case, several initiatives were held to earn social consensus when promoting innovations and new strategies. An example is the *learning laboratory*, several workshops and discussions based on innovative design ideas drawn from the public (WIKUE, 2013).

Local communities became aware of the importance of this project also thanks to the new accessibility to their waterfront. Cycle and pedestrian paths, water adventure routes, and new open spaces were very important to raise awareness on the renovation plan and gain general agreement (WIKUE, 2013). This was crucial to its success because while the Emscher conversion is mainly based on modernising wastewater infrastructures, public perception focuses more on renaturation aspects, as these are more clearly perceivable (Stemplewski, 2012). According to the German normative framework, most of the Emscher conversion and construction projects required the involvement of all the citizens affected, who had the possibility to present objections (WIKUE, 2013). Transparent information was among the main reasons why the project won widespread approval, along with the economic and ecological development of the region (Heldt *et al.*, 2016).

13.6.3   Project costs and benefits

The Emscher river conversion is a complex project, involving important technical and financial efforts. This is a unique initiative in terms of its vast scale and level of economic investment both in a German and European perspective. In 2013, the total cost for its completion - which is scheduled in 2020 - has been estimated as €4.5 billion (WIKUE, 2013). As often happens with this type of large-scale investments, contributions have been granted by several sources. In the 1990s, the State Government of North Rhine-Westphalia supported the IBA Emscher Park with €17.9 million. Developers, private companies, non-profit groups and local town governments working on individual projects, although, provided the highest funding ratio. In the first four years, €2.5 billion had been invested: two thirds derived from public funds and the rest from private funds (Dac&Cities, 2014). The European Investment Bank was also involved in the financing aspects, as this was "one of Germany's most costly urban and regional development projects".

The EIB contributed to the sewage system improvement with €450 million, setting fixed interest rates yielding to maturity in 45 years. The EIB participated in this initiative on the grounds that "the reclaimed areas will offer growth opportunities for the region's economy" (European Commission, 2011). The Emscher river conversion, in fact, will generate economic benefits for the local communities and the Emschergenossenschaft. The high costs for sewage water and storm water management can be reduced by separating polluted water and rainwater, allowing the construction of smaller canals and treatment plants. This is can lead to water treatment levy reduction for citizens and property owners (WIKUE, 2013). In addition, as described in Chapters 5 and 8, reducing the risk of flooding can lead to very high economic gains. The complex and long construction works implemented in this area, have made the Emscher project one of the frontrunners in sustainable Urban Stormwater Management (USWM; Sieker *et al.*, 2006) and have created about 1,400 new jobs every year (European Investment Bank, 2016).

Providing access to the river and new open areas has had a positive impact on the local population. The quality of life improvement has also favoured an economic revival in the Ruhr region (WIKUE, 2013). Blue rivers and green banks attract business and tourism (European Investment Bank, 2016; Labelle, 2001).

The creation of a landscape park within the International Building Exhibition, and employing art to re-design the landscape has portrayed a new policy approach and has driven the regeneration of a degraded and fragmented region. The residents can now build on the legacy of the regions' industrial history. This project provides the exceptional opportunity to restore brownfields and polluted areas and reuse industrial buildings (Labelle, 2001).

References

Boon, P. and Raven, P. (2012). *River Conservation and Management*. John Wiley & Sons.

Budryte, P. and Perini, K. (2016). Community involvement in river restoration: American and European case studies. *In Press*.

Dac&Cities. (2014). *Emscher Park: From dereliction to scenic landscapes - Danish Architecture Centre*. [Online]. Available at: http://www.dac.dk/en/dac-cities/sustainable-cities/all-cases/green-city/emscher-park-from-dereliction-to-scenic-landscapes/ [Accessed 2 December 2015].

Deutschland. (2014). The renaturation of the Emscher. *Deutschland.de*. [Online]. Available at: https://www.deutschland.de/en/topic/culture/town-country/the-renaturation-of-the-emscher [Accessed 2 December 2015].

Dutch Water Sector. (2012). Wayss & Freytag/BAM Techniek to build 35 km underground waste water tunnel for German water board. *Dutch Water Sector*. [Online]. Available at: http://www.dutchwatersector.com/news-events/news/1967-wayss-freytag-bam-techniek-to-build-35-km-underground-waste-water-tunnel-for-german-water-board.html [Accessed 10 April 2016].

Emschergenossenschaft. (2006). *Masterplan Emscher-Zukunft. Das Neue Emschertal*. Essen.

Emschergenossenschaft. (2009). *Emscher Sewage Canal*. [Online]. Available at: http://www.abwasserkanal-emscher.de/en/emscher-sewage-canal.html [Accessed 2 December 2015].

Emschergenossenschaft. (2016). *Emschergenossenschaft. Mission statement*. [Online]. Available at: http://www.eglv.de/emschergenossenschaft/ [Accessed 22 April 2016].

Emschergenossenschaft, Peters, R., Stemplewski, J. and Arauner, H. W. (1999). *100 Jahre Wasserwirtschaft im Revier. Die Emschergenossenschaft 1899 - 1999*. Bottrop: Pomp, P.

European Commission. (2011). *European Commission - PRESS RELEASES - Press release - Rehabilitation of Emscher river: EIB finances state-of-the-art sewerage system with EUR 450 million loan*. [Online]. Available at: http://europa.eu/rapid/press-release_BEI-11-115_en.htm [Accessed 2 December 2015].

European Investment Bank. (2016). *A fresh re-start for the Emscher river ecosystem*. [Online]. Available at: http://www.eib.org/projects/regions/european-union/germany/project-a-fresh-re-start-for-the-emscher-river-ecosystem.htm [Accessed 2 December 2015].

Gerdes, F., Giese, P., Gocke, M., Hampe, J., Kuczera, S., Lemser, S., Meiering, S., Sinz, A., Theuerkauf, M., Turek, C., Wegner, J., Wessels, S. and Wilkens, M. (2005). *Neue Möglichkeiten der Regionalplanung Der Regionale Masterplan im Ruhrgebiet*. Kanafa, K. (ed.). Universität Dortmund - Fakultät Raumplanung. [Online]. Available at: https://eldorado.tu-dortmund.de/bitstream/2003/22153/1/Endbericht%20F01.pdf [Accessed 23 April 2016].

Heldt, S., Budryte, P., Ingensiep, H. W., Teichgräber, B., Schneider, U. and Denecke, M. (2016). Social Pitfalls for River Restoration – How Public Participation Uncovers Problems with Public Acceptance. *In Press*.

Labelle, J. M. (2001). *Emscher Park, Germany — expanding the definition of a 'park'*. In: Harmon, D. (ed.), 2001, The George Wright Society. [Online]. Available at: http://www.georgewright.org/37labell.pdf [Accessed 10 April 2016].

Landschaftspark. (2016). *Landschaftspark Duisburg-Nord - International Exhibition Emscher Park (IBA)*. [Online]. Available at: http://en.landschaftspark.de/the-park/evolution/iba [Accessed 23 April 2016].

Lucas, R. (2011). *Gefahrdungen von Okosystemleistungen durch den Klimawandel — Analyserahmen, onzeptentwicklung und erste Handlungsorientierungen für die regionale Wirtschaft*. Dynaklim Publikation.

Ruhrverband. (2016). *Ruhrverband: Home*. [Online]. Available at: http://www.ruhrverband.de/home/ [Accessed 22 April 2016].

Shaw, R. (2002). The International Building Exhibition (IBA) Emscher Park, Germany: A Model for Sustainable Restructuring? *European Planning Studies*, *10* (1), p. 77–97. [Online]. Available at: doi:10.1080/09654310120099272 [Accessed 23 April 2016].

Sieker, H., Bandermann, S. and Becker, B. (2006). Urban Stormwater Management Demonstration Projects in the Emscher Region. In: *First SWITCH Scientific Meeting University of Birmingham*, 9 January 2006, UK. [Online]. Available at: http://www.switchurbanwater.eu/outputs/pdfs/CEMS_PAP_Urban_stormwater_management_demo_projects_Emscher.pdf [Accessed 18 April 2016].

Skodra, J. (2014). *Emscher conversion and quality of life*. In: 23 September 2014. [Online]. Available at: http://www.eventure-online.com/eventure/publicAbstractView.do?id=247200 &congressId=8203 [Accessed 10 April 2016].

Stemplewski, J. (2012). *Medienpool: Audio*. [Online]. Available at: http://www.emscherplayer. de/playMedia.yum?mediaID=44596 [Accessed 23 April 2016].

WIKUE. (2013). *Emscher 3.0: from grey to blue - or, how the blue sky over the Ruhr region fell into the Emscher - by Wuppertal Institut für Klima, Umwelt, Energie GmbH*. Scheck H and Venjakob (eds.). [Online]. Available at: https://epub.wupperinst.org/frontdoor/ index/index/docId/5070 [Accessed 9 April 2016].

Part C

Index

Urban Sustainability and River Restoration: Green and Blue Infrastructure, First Edition.
Katia Perini and Paola Sabbion.
© 2017 John Wiley & Sons Ltd. Published 2017 by John Wiley & Sons Ltd.